The
Evaluation
Interview

About the Authors

RICHARD A. FEAR ranks among our foremost experts in the field of interviewing. A licensed industrial psychologist, he has trained thousands of interviewers in the United States and abroad. Mr. Fear currently owns and operates Interviewer Training Services, through which he provides personnel consulting services for some of the nation's largest corporations. Fear is a past vice president of The Psychological Corporation and served as a faculty member at Columbia University.

ROBERT J. CHIRON, PH.D., is president of The Chiron Group, a consulting firm specializing in career planning and executive development. His clients range from *Fortune* 100 companies to small businesses and educational institutions. Dr. Chiron earned his Ph.D. in psychology from the University of Iowa and has taught at Iowa and Columbia University. He is a registered psychologist in Illinois and a member of the American Psychological Association.

The Evaluation Interview

Richard A. Fear
Personnel Consultant, Interview Training
Services and Past Vice President of the
Psychological Corporation

Robert J. Chiron, Ph.D.
President, The Chiron Group

Fourth Edition

McGraw-Hill Publishing Company
New York St. Louis San Francisco Auckland Bogotá
Caracas Hamburg Lisbon London Madrid Mexico
Milan Montreal New Delhi Oklahoma City
Paris San Juan Sâo Paulo Singapore
Sydney Tokyo Toronto

Library of Congress Cataloging-in-Publication Data

Fear, Richard A.
  The evaluation interview/Richard A. Fear; Robert J.
  Chiron. — 4th ed.

  p. cm.
  ISBN 0-07-020220-6
  1. Employment interviewing. I. Chiron, Robert J. II.
Title.
HF5549.5.I6F4   1990
658.3' 1124—dc20   89-48122
                                                                        CIP

ISBN 0-07-020220-6

  34567890   DOC/DOC   987654321

Scannable ISBN

*The sponsoring editor for this book was James Bessent, the editing supervisor was
Jim Halston, the designer was Naomi Auerbach, and the production supervisor
was Suzanne W. Babeuf. This book was set in Baskerville by the McGraw-Hill
Publishing Company Professional & Reference Division composition unit.*

Printed and bound by R. R. Donnelley and Sons

*For more information about other McGraw-Hill materials,
call 1-800-2-MCGRAW in the United States. In other
countries, call your nearest McGraw-Hill office.*

Contents

Part 4. Additional Applications of Interview Techniques

Preface

In this fourth edition of *The Evaluation Interview*—now in its 32nd year of publication—we have turned our attention to some of the many applications of the time-tested interview techniques. Managers who have been trained in interviewing over the years increasingly draw attention to the utilization of these techniques in many of their day-to-day activities.

And now, in the wake of corporate restructuring, we find an increased emphasis on "making do" with less people in the resulting leaner organization. As a result, there is not only a greater need to hire more versatile people—people capable of handling ever-changing responsibilities—but also an equally important need to retain, retrain, and develop the best of the employees left on board. Hence, the emphasis in this fourth edition on feedback of appraisal information, team building, and "visioning," all of which draw heavily on the recommended interviewing techniques.

Dr. Robert Chiron, President of the Chicago-based firm, The Chiron Group, appears in this edition as co-author. Dr. Chiron's organization is currently serving as consultants to a number of major corporations in the areas of feedback, team building, "visioning," and interview training. His expertise in these areas comes as a welcome addition to this book.

In this fourth edition we are also featuring a new chapter on the campus interview. In spite of the importance of recruiting the most talented young people on the college campuses, this is a long-neglected subject. It is small wonder then, that most college recruiters do such an inadequate job. Our new chapter includes a new Interview Guide for the college recruiter as well as suggestions for using the 20-minute interview to best advantage, recording interview results, and selling your company.

The core of this edition, nevertheless, still focuses on the evaluation interview as a selection device. But the chapters on developing information and interpreting data include new probing questions as well as suggestions for interviewing more mature candidates, those individuals in their forties or fifties. The book is still an essentially practical work that provides readers with a "track to run on" which guides them step-by-step through a discussion of the applicant's work history, education, present social adjustment, and self evaluation.

In arriving at the philosophy and techniques here expressed, the authors have drawn upon their practical experience as their principal source. At the same time, they are deeply indebted to colleagues past and present who have contributed valuable ideas along the way. In particular, they are indebted to James F. Ross, formerly director of the Career Continuation Center, Bethlehem Steel, and now chief executive officer, American Typlex Systems, for many valuable ideas having to do with personnel procedures and EEO guidelines. They are also indebted to Valerie La Mont and Linda Chiron who provided substantial help with the manuscript.

Richard A. Fear

PART 1
Prologue

1
Sustaining the Competitive Edge

One of the important reasons why *The Evaluation Interview* has remained in print so long—now some 32 years—will be found in the fact that the techniques of the interview are so universally applicable. Managers who have been trained in interviewing subsequently find themselves utilizing the techniques not only for selection of new staff but for many other aspects of their day-to-day activities. They discover, for example, that they draw upon their interviewing skills in their discussions with subcontractors, union officials, subordinates, and even with superiors. *Wherever they are faced with situations that place a premium on drawing the other person out, finding out what is on that person's mind and analyzing the responses, they realize that they have a genuine advantage.* It is a matter of interest in this respect that one giant corporation decided to have its Washington lobbyists trained in interviewing and those individuals subsequently discovered that their meetings with Senators and Congressmen were enormously enhanced.

In this fourth edition of *The Evaluation Interview*, then, we are concerned not only with the hiring but, equally important, with the use of the time-tested interview techniques in retaining, developing, and motivating individuals. And, because of the immense changes taking place in business and industry today, we will concentrate on the relationship of the *improved individual* to an organization's ability to sustain the competitive edge.

The Nature of Change

Some 80 percent of Fortune 500 companies have experienced or are experiencing some form of restructuring—brought on in many cases by the need to compete on a global scale. Already buffeted by competition from such countries as Japan and Germany, American companies must look ahead to 1992 when the European Economic Community will remove all remaining economic boundaries between the 12 member countries. This will create a home market more populous than the U.S. or Japan and their combined economies will make them stronger in world markets. Characterized by G.E. Chairman, Jack Welsh, as "a white knuckle decade for global business...fast...exhilarating," the 1990s will be a lot tougher than the 1980s.

The world of the '90s will be recognizable but different enough to require shifts in thinking and tactics. Holding on to assumptions and methods that may have served well in the '80s will not be the key to success. While managers must be concerned with the domestic situation, they must also attend to worldwide competition for resources and markets. It will be crucial to respond with a broader vision.

Visioning, A Vehicle of Change

Companies now in the course of restructuring need to concern themselves not only with the establishment of a leaner, more efficient organization but, equally important, with a plan that spells out where they want to go and what they will have to do in order to get there.

In their desire to compete more effectively on a global scale, companies are turning increasingly to a process that has come to be known as visioning. This process—discussed in more detail in Chapter 14 of this book—involves an assessment of where the company is today, where it would like to be in the future, and what technological and organizational changes will have to be put in place in order to attain its desired status.

In a sense then, visioning provides a road map or framework for the future.

The visioning process also establishes a sequence of events which determines when each phase will be accomplished, who will be responsible for what, how much cost will be involved, and what benefits are likely to ensue. And, because the process provides a clearer definition of long-range goals, employees tend to become "caught up" in an operation that stresses creativity and initiative. If properly installed, visioning carries an emotional appeal—to inspire an organization to be all that it can be.

The Changing Organization

Rosabeth Moss Kanter, a Harvard Business School professor, talks about companies which are becoming part of the "Newstream." Such companies respond to global competition, technological innovations, and waves of mergers and restructuring by producing new ideas and strategies (*New York Times*, Apr. 2, 1989). Newstream companies have a leaner structure, a closer relationship with customers and suppliers, and a reward system for employees that is tied to performance. These adapting and adaptable companies emphasize high performance, creativity, and individual initiative. And their employees find themselves with jobs that typically are more demanding and that require new behaviors.

Elizabeth Hass of McKinsey & Co. points out that Toyota can design and introduce a new car, get feedback from the market, and then introduce this revised car in the same time that it takes General Motors to introduce a single car (*Forbes*, August 24, 1987). Obviously Toyota is an organization that can react quickly to current markets. Increasingly, being smart means being ready to take whatever form the economic environment requires.

The corporation of the future will have fewer people and a less rigid, more fluid organization. Cross-functional teams and ad hoc and permanent task forces will be used to develop speedy and creative responses to changes in the environment. Such methods of maintaining loose, flexible organizations have been dubbed the "'90s Techniques."

Team Building

In their attempts to develop more fluid organizations which can be expected to react more quickly to changes in the environment, corporations are turning increasingly to reliance on teams rather than exclusively on individual managers. And, in a team-based style of management, they often discover that the whole is greater than all of the individual efforts combined.

As discussed in detail in Chapter 15 of this book, team building involves the process of learning how to act as a coherent unit, with each individual performing optimally in his or her assigned role and supporting others in the unit in an effort to bring the joint enterprise to a successful conclusion.

Today, to a much greater extent than in the past, there is great initial emphasis placed on the development of harmonious relationships and trust building among team members. The techniques involved help members to get to know each other better, to listen to each other more closely, and to build relationships based on openness and honesty.

When properly developed, teams can help to change the basic climate of an organization by creating open and free-flowing communication, participative decision making, and increased productivity through concerned group effort. Teams can also help to create integration and improvement of human and economic objectives through enriched job commitment and greater individual freedom.

The Effect on People

The industrial upheaval resulting from the creation of "leaner" organizations has already had a pronounced effect on individual employees. Many people have lost their jobs and many others have been reassigned to new responsibilities. All of this creates confusion as to where individuals "fit" within an organization. How well individuals and organizations make this "fit" will in large part determine the extent to which these organizations sustain their competitive edge.

The Changing Workforce—Shifting Demographics

The Bureau of Labor Statistics projects that the median age of the U.S. workforce will be 37.3 by 1995. By the year 2000, 30 percent of the population will be in the 35–54 age group and the median age will be about 40. And, by 1995, the number of 18 to 24-year-olds entering the labor force will fall nearly 10 percent—about 7.5 million fewer.

It is also estimated that the number of jobs will grow faster than the labor force. To attract workers, companies will have to develop new appeals, especially to women who, by 1995, will make up a much larger portion of the labor force. More women in the workforce means more dual career families. By the end of the decade, in fact, as many as 75 percent of all families may provide dual workers, as opposed to roughly 55 percent now.

Minorities will also be increasingly prominent in the labor pool. Hence, women and minorities will account for a major percentage of labor force growth in the years to come. This means that managing people in the future will mean managing diversity.

While navigating the tides and currents of globalization in the 1990s, companies may find difficulty ensuring that they have enough hands on deck. For one thing, the aging baby boomers will leave a demographic vacuum—a scarcity of entry-level job seekers.

Productivity Through People

A company can gain competitive advantage by supplying superior products and service. But at the heart of it all are people. People, not organizations, create and innovate. People make the difference in products and service. In the final analysis, people determine whether a business succeeds or fails. To be competitive, U.S. businesses must learn to utilize the untapped creative potential of the most powerful competitive weapons they have—their employees.

All of the above discussed factors will create an ever increasing need to hire people with potential for growth and to help these people develop their latent capacities. That is what this book is all about.

Making Maximum Utilization of Human Resources

As in all previous editions of this book, the major emphasis in this edition is concerned with techniques of the interview as applied to selection. But, due to the almost universal applicability of these techniques to other aspects of management, we have decided in this edition to concentrate on feedback and development as well as appraisal.

Stimulating Individual Development

Fortunately, every organization has significant numbers of people with untapped skills and abilities—abilities of which those individuals themselves may be unaware. The task then becomes one of tapping into abilities to create and innovate wherever they exist.

The fact that most companies have so little understanding of their human resources stems from the lack of focus on objective appraisal and the feedback of appraisal information. Of paramount importance is the need to acquaint individuals with their development needs—their specific shortcomings. And this must be done in such a way that it does not destroy self-confidence but rather helps the individual face up to those traits and abilities which must be acquired in order to enhance personal development.

Development—A Shared Responsibility

We are currently experiencing a change in the psychological contract involving a shift from the understanding that employees supply loyalty, with companies supplying steady employment, to a more individualistic, protective stance on both sides. This shift places more responsibility on individuals to assess and design their own careers.

Just as companies have game plans and goals, so must individuals. The time has come for individuals to place their confidence and trust in their own skills and competences and to be aware of the need to develop and update those skills.

In the past there has not been sufficient alignment between the needs of the individual involved and the employer. Management has the responsibility to tell its people where the company is heading and what the management style will be. There have been instances, for example, where management has outlined a career path for a given individual without ever telling the individual what that path was. As indicated earlier, in today's environment individuals are encouraged to assess and design their own careers, and the first step involves the one of assessing one's skills against the firm's needs now and in the future. If certain people, for example, find that their skills support strong individual functional excellence at the expense of team collaboration, those people might not represent an appropriate "fit" in a certain organization. There would then be a need to adapt or "develop" in terms of the company's needs or to seek a job elsewhere. As a part of the restructuring process, some people have been *surprised* to learn that they were no longer needed in the future organization. Had such people, as a result of objective assessment and feedback, been helped to clarify their own position in the company, this situation might not have occurred.

The importance of individual performance in creating and maintaining long-term performance is being increasingly recognized. The payoff for organizations which recognize that they must help people develop their abilities comes in increased loyalty and commitment, improved quality and innovation. "The line worker committed to constant improvement and instantly retrained must become the chief agent for adding value and achieving continuous innovation" (Tom Peters, *Economist*, March 4, 1989).

Motivation

Studies have shown that when the needs of the individual are in concert with the needs of the organization the motivation to perform with excellence is more soundly based. And now is an especially appropriate time to reexamine ways to motivate people to achieve at their highest levels and to identify impediments to individual performance.

In order to become more productive, people need a sense of "ownership." Ownership can mean an equity share, a sense that the employee counts, a feeling of responsibility for one's job and ultimately for the success of one's organization.

An increase in commitment occurs when people are given responsibility for producing and are held accountable for results. The most effective and enduring way to motivate people is to encourage them to participate in the pursuit of a common goal. Highly motivated people want and expect to receive opportunities to achieve and to demonstrate their full abilities. They also expect to receive appropriate rewards for performing well. The relationship between performance and rewards should be strong.

Feedback—The All-Important Development Tool

Feedback is a powerful organizational tool for improving motivation, improving employee relations, and setting the stage for new learning. And it is as valuable a resource to individuals as it is to organizations. When managers take the time to discuss objective and well-documented information concerning employees' shortcomings or development needs, they help employees to identify those traits and abilities that must be modified or improved in order to make progress in their career path.

Most managers are not at all adept when it comes to giving feedback because they have not been properly trained in using this as a developmental tool. As a matter of fact, when managers are asked to identify the function in which they feel most uncomfortable they invariably place feedback close to the top of the list. Why is it that feedback should be seen in this context? One important reason may be found in the fact that the process is not understood or communicated in a way that helps to create value—value in terms of enhancing performance, confronting lack of performance, and shaping behavior. In the final chapter of this book we will spell out specific techniques for achieving these results and we will show how the evaluation interview plays a major part in the completion of the entire process.

Tying in evaluation and feedback represents an enormously important factor in the changing organization due primarily to the increased pace of change and the uncertainties that accompany it. In order to remain competitive, companies will have to find improved ways to attract the best from a shrinking pool of applicants, will have to hustle to hang on to the employees they have, and will have to become committed to the continuous development of their people. (See Chapter 16 for a detailed discussion of feedback.)

The Campus Interview

For many companies the recruitment of better qualified employees begins on the college campus. Yet, even in the larger, more sophisticated corporations this all-important function is, in most cases, poorly handled and ineffectually carried out.

College recruiters typically interview some 12 to 15 seniors in a given day—at one-half hour intervals. They usually devote about 20 minutes to the interview, 5 minutes to recording their reactions, and the remaining 5 minutes to preparation for the next student. Anyone who has ever done this will agree that this represents an exhausting day, particularly when no more than two or three students seem worthy of further consideration!

There are two principal reasons why campus recruiting is so ineffectual: (1) the recruiters have not been carefully trained as interviewers, and (2) the recruiters approach their task with the thought of *selling* the student on the company rather than *evaluating* the individual's conceivable worth to the organization. Because recruiters are frequently untrained as interviewers, they feel awkward in this situation and spend more than half of their precious 20 minutes talking about the company rather than zeroing in on the student's qualifications. In all too many cases, then, they make their final judgment on grades alone—a totally inadequate criterion. This means that they miss some truly outstanding people and recommend some individuals who may not be very mature or reasonably motivated. Equally serious, students brought in by the recruiters are introduced to managers who are themselves untrained in interviewing and hence make their hiring decisions largely on the basis of "chemistry," a few technically oriented questions, and how well they think the candidate will "fit in."

Some companies today are making an all-out effort to improve their college recruiting because they realize at long last that the campus interview represents an indispensably vital link in the selection process.

In Chapter 13, therefore, we are adding appreciable material on the campus interview—how to utilize the 20 minutes to best advantage, how to record the information, and how to sell the company, all in 30 minutes. This material will include a new interview guide as well as a report which demonstrates how much evaluative information can be obtained in 20 minutes by a trained interviewer.

2
Job Description and Behavior Specifications

It shouldn't come as a surprise to find that many organizations do not have adequate job descriptions, and very few have anything in the way of behavior specifications—those aptitudes, abilities, and personality traits essential for successful job performance. Some companies, in fact, have no job descriptions at all, and others like to keep their job descriptions rather vague for the purpose of greater flexibility.

Yet accurate job descriptions and behavior specifications are absolutely fundamental to the development of any selection program. Information contained in these two forms should provide the basis for the development of the application form, the preliminary interview, the employment tests, and the employment interview itself. How can an interviewer evaluate the qualifications of an applicant without knowing what to look for?

In this chapter, therefore, we will give brief attention to the development of job descriptions and then follow up with a detailed consideration of behavior specifications.

Job Description

Job descriptions are normally prepared by a company's personnel department or the industrial engineering department in close collaboration with the manager of the job to be described. They should include the following:

Job Duties

There should be a paragraph on job duties detailing day-to-day activities and responsibilities for that job. This can include such factors as the extent of independent judgment required, access to confidential information, the extent of supervision and direction received, the degree of internal and external contacts, equipment or machinery used (such as facility with computers and computer languages required), physical environment (office, shop), amount of travel involved, and responsibility for the "bottom line."

Education

The section on education should include a minimum level of required education (college degree, graduate study), any preferred college major, and important requisite courses (accounting courses, for example). Some job descriptions may substitute related job experience, for example, Master's degree or four years related work experience. Educational requirements must be directly related to specific job tasks, and there should be no one in the job who does not satisfy the minimum requirements.

Experience

This is simply the number of years of previous experience required for successful job performance. Figure 2-1 details a sample job description for the position of auditor.

It should also be noted here that some candidates for high-level positions negotiate the specifics of the job description in order that the job for which they are applying be more in line with their experience and the activities that give them most satisfaction. And some companies are quite willing to make such changes if it means being able to attract highly qualified individuals.

Behavior Specifications

Since most companies do not have behavior specifications—and since such specifications are so fundamental to the development of a sound

---

Sample Job Description for an Auditor

Examines and analyzes accounting records of establishment and prepares reports concerning its financial status and operating procedures. Reviews data regarding material assets, net worth, liabilities, capital stock, surplus, income and expenditures. Inspects items in books of original entry to determine if proper procedures in recording transactions were followed. Counts cash on hand, inspects notes receivable and payable, negotiable securities, and cancelled checks. Verifies journal and ledger entries of cash and check payments, purchases, expenses and trial balances by examining and authenticating inventory. Reports to management concerning scope of audit, financial condition found, and sources and application of funds. May make recommendations regarding improvement of operations and financial condition of company. Works independently and usually travels to various divisions of the corporation. May supervise two to four assistants, but does not have "hire and fire" responsibility. Travel away from home base can average 40 to 60 percent. Long work days (10 to 12 hours) toward the end of the fiscal year can be very enervating.

Requires college degree in finance or accounting with at least six courses in accounting as well as special training in auditing.

This job requires at least two to three years' experience in a variety of accounting positions.

Figure 2-1.

selection program—interviewers are urged to develop their own set of specifications.

The first step in building behavior specifications involves the interviewer studying the job description. As a second step, interviewers should study applicant data and other background information of incumbents on that job in an effort to determine unique experience, training, and specific skills. They will then be ready to visit the plant or office in order to observe the job in question and talk with the supervisor and individual workers. The behavior specification questionnaire shown in Figure 2-2 is a useful guide for organizing the desired material.

Again, using the auditor position as an example, Figure 2-3 shows what a properly and thoroughly assembled set of behavior specifications would look like.

A word of caution is in order. Items appearing on behavior specifications should be regarded as *factors favorable to success* and nothing more. These specifications represent a synthesized list of subjective

Behavior Specification Questionnaire

Position title _____

Interviewee _____

Location _____ Date _____

1. What kind of *aptitudes* are required for this job?
   Verbal _____

   Numerical _____

   Mechanical _____

   Clerical speed and accuracy _____

   Other _____

2. MENTAL ABILITY. What interpretation, selection, and analysis is required for the job? To what extent do mental skills involve judgment and ingenuity? How complex are the problems to be solved?

   _____

   _____

   _____

3. EMPLOYMENT TRAINING. *Once the employee is hired,* what training and experience are necessary for the average employee to become proficient in performing the job? How long does it take the average employee to absorb the training and experience? _____

   _____

   _____

4. RESPONSIBILITY FOR PERFORMANCE AND MATERIALS. How closely is the employee supervised? What materials or machinery are involved?

   _____

   _____

   _____

5. RESPONSIBILITY FOR CONTACTS. To what degree are poise, cooperation, and tact required in maintaining good working relationships? Is the employee required to communicate with co-workers only or with the general public as well, directly or by telephone?

   _____

   _____

   _____

Figure 2-2.

6. RESPONSIBILITY FOR THE DIRECTION OF OTHERS. How many people does an incumbent in this job supervise? Does this person have disciplinary responsibility? _____

_____

_____

7. WORKING CONDITIONS. To what degree are there any disagreeable environmental factors? What about travel and long hours? _____

_____

_____

8. CRITICAL PERSONALITY TRAITS NEEDED. What about important traits of leadership, sales, sense of urgency in getting the job done, degree of maturity required? _____

_____

_____

9. OTHER REQUIRED CHARACTERISTICS. _____

_____

_____

(Continued)

opinions. And, valuable as these are, they cannot be quantified. For example, because everyone involved has said that a given job requires superior mathematical ability, interviewers cannot insist that every successful applicant for that job obtain a score that ranks him or her in the top 10 percent on a test of numerical ability. Finally, no candidate is expected to possess every single one of the favorable factors. But the more of these factors applicants have, the better qualified they are.

In developing behavior specifications, interviewers should concentrate first on those jobs for which the most people from outside the company are selected. As time permits, they can then develop specifications on those jobs which they are less frequently called upon to fill.

Before embarking upon the task of developing behavior specifications, interviewers should have in mind the *general idea* of the qualifications normally found in successful employees on a wide variety of jobs. This permits them to ask about the relevance of a given trait, should the supervisor or subordinate fail to include it. If interviewers

---

Sample of Behavior Specifications for Auditor's Position

1. *Required aptitudes*
   a. High degree of numerical aptitude.
   b. High degree of clerical speed and accuracy.
   c. Above average verbal ability.

2. *Mental ability.* High level mental ability is required. This job involves a great amount of mathematical reasoning. Statistical data must be *interpreted* in the light of the facts and the company's needs. The auditor must be able to plan and organize and be able to see the broad picture. Financial statements and other reports have to be prepared for management—hence, the need for good verbal ability.

3. *Employment training, once hired.* The employee normally takes a six-month to a year company-sponsored course in auditing practices. And that person spends at least one year as an assistant to an auditor in the field before being "turned loose" on his own.

4. *Responsibility for performance and materials.* Employee works independently on his or her own without a great amount of supervision. Must have excellent computer facility.

5. *Responsibility for contacts.* Auditors are often viewed as "investigators" by management whose books they are auditing. Hence, they are not always popular in a particular organization. For this reason, they should have an abundance of poise, tact, and an ability to establish rapport.

6. *Responsibility for the direction of others.* The auditor usually supervises two to four assistants but does not have disciplinary responsibility. But this individual must have infectious enthusiasm for the work—enthusiasm that rubs off on the assistants and thus makes the long hours less burdensome.

7. *Working conditions.* This job requires 40 to 60 percent travel and long hours toward the end of the fiscal year. Therefore, the employee needs a lot of energy and physical stamina as well as the ability to adjust to the living away from home.

8. *Critical personality traits needed.* Because of the judgment factor involved and the access to confidential information, the incumbent must have a high degree of maturity and integrity. And, because the auditors have to face up to management and be willing to make confrontations when needed, they should be tough-minded.

9. *Other characteristics.* Because of the confinement of this work and the attention to detail needed, the better auditors tend to be slightly introverted and reflective.

Figure 2-3.

are able to give the impression of having some understanding of certain jobs, they will gain quicker rapport with supervisors and subordinates alike.

With these objectives in mind, we have prepared a series of general behavior specifications for a number of key higher-level jobs, based upon knowledge gained from evaluating candidates for these jobs over a period of many years. It should be emphasized that the specifications that follow are *general* rather than *specific*. Hence, they cannot be expected to represent the requirements for any one job in any given organization. On the contrary, they are designed to give the interviewer a general overview and to be used primarily as background information. Specific job demands vary widely from company to company, depending upon job content, organizational setup, and company atmosphere. In developing the following specifications, we have omitted certain common denominator traits that are important in practically all jobs, traits such as honesty, loyalty, willingness to work hard, and the ability to get along with others.

Management

Qualifications for executive positions vary with respect to level of responsibility and the kind of people to be supervised. The chief accountant, for example, need not have the same degree of dynamic, tough-minded leadership normally required in the plant superintendent. In general, however, the qualifications for the executive may be broken down in two categories: leadership and administrative ability.

Leadership	*Administrative Ability*
Assertiveness	High-level mental ability
Production-mindedness	Good verbal ability
Tough-mindedness	Good numerical ability
Self-confidence	Ability to think analytically and critically
Courage of convictions	
Ability to take charge	Good judgment
Ability to organize	Long-range planning ability
Decisiveness	Good cultural background
Ability to inspire others	
Depth and perspective	
Tact and social sensitivity	

The ideal executive is a happy blend of a leader and the administrator. As a leader, executives must be able to influence their subordinates so that they will willingly carry out their wishes. On the one hand, they must be forceful, dynamic, and willing to take charge. Since they are dealing with the human element, they must at the same time use tact and social sensitivity in their general approach. Social sensitivity, or awareness of the reactions of others, plays a big part in the development of good human relations. Leaders who understand their subordinates and sense their reactions know which ones need forceful direction and which ones need a pat on the back in order to obtain optimal job performance.

True leaders must have decisiveness, born of self-confidence and courage of convictions. They must believe implicitly in their own abilities and, once they have set their course, they must follow through without any waivering of purpose. In this connection, too, they should be tough-minded, in the sense that they must be willing to make difficult decisions that may tread on the toes of a few but work for the good of the many.

In the final analysis, industry rewards those who are able to get things accomplished. Thus, leaders must be able to organize and inspire their subordinates so that they accomplish their purpose in the shortest period of time. This ability is often referred to as "production-mindedness."

As a behind-the-scenes administrator, executives are faced with day-to-day as well as long-range planning. Since this is an intellectual function, it requires a rather high degree of mental ability. Executives are called upon to think in the abstract and to integrate a large number of complex factors. To do a top job as a manager, then, the individual's mental level should be appreciably above that of the average college graduate. This also holds for verbal and numerical abilities. The former plays a big part in one's ability to communicate, to express oneself orally and on paper. Executives who cannot establish good lines of communications are handicapped indeed. Although numerical ability may not be quite as important as verbal ability in many executive positions, it nevertheless plays an important role in such functions as setting up budgets, analyzing statistical reports, and the like. And, with the increasing role of automation in the plant and office, managers without a fair amount of sophistication in quantitative analysis will be lost in the shuffle. The administrator is constantly faced with the task of analyzing various problems and breaking them down into their component parts. In working out solutions to these problems they cannot afford to take things at face value. They must examine each factor critically, looking beneath the surface to explore any hidden meaning.

If they are to exercise good judgment, it logically follows that managers must have depth and perspective. They must see every item in relation to the whole picture. Otherwise, they will find themselves in the position of not being able to see the forest for the trees. Experience has shown that a good cultural background adds appreciably to one's ability to see the overall picture. Some knowledge of the arts and some understanding of the cultures of other people normally produce a body of knowledge that contributes to intellectual maturity and judgment. This is a factor to which many industrial leaders refer when they characterize someone as "broad-gauged."

The executive qualifications discussed above are, of course, not all inclusive; there are obviously many other traits and abilities that make a contribution. We would like to emphasize again that no single executive is likely to possess all of the above qualifications. None of us is perfect; we all have some shortcomings. For the most part, we carry out our jobs as well as we do because certain of our assets are strong enough to compensate for our shortcomings. So it is with executives; they may possess certain traits in such abundance that they largely make up for what they lack in other areas.

Research and Development

Jobs in this category spread over a wide scale as far as job content is concerned. At one end of the scale we have the "blue sky" research worker who is searching for truth for truth's sake. At the other end of the scale, we find the practical pilot-plant operator who is principally concerned with getting the "bugs" out of some process that others have conceived and developed. The vast majority of research and development people, however, fall somewhere between the two extremes of the scale. Their general qualifications can be summarized as follows:

Superior mental capacity	Creativity
Superior numerical ability	Carefulness
Good verbal ability	Methodicalness
Good mechanical comprehension	Ability to handle details
Ability to think analytically and critically	Patience
Tendency to be reflective	Good academic training
Intellectual curiosity	

There can be no substitute for top-level mental and mathematical abilities if one is to operate with a high degree of productiveness in a research and development job. In fact, this type of a position probably places more demands on intellect than any other industrial assignment. Much of the work involves thinking in the abstract and using current knowledge as a springboard to new and uncharted fields. In many technical jobs, moreover, mathematics and physics are requisite to obtaining the desired objectives. Thus, the best people invariably possess numerical facility as well as an understanding of mechanical principles. As a group, they are also remarkably analytical and critical in their thinking.

The ability to conceive new ideas is, of course, an important requirement in a research and development person. Here again intellect plays an important part. Although all brilliant people are not necessarily creative, one seldom finds really creative people who do not have a relatively high degree of intelligence. Such persons are usually reflective, in the sense that they have a strong theoretical drive. They are the kind of people who have so much intellectual curiosity that they are motivated to dig to the bottom of a problem and find out what makes things tick. Their curiosity leads them to forsake the status quo in quest of new and better ways of doing things.

Because the job requires reflective individuals and those who can adjust to a somewhat confined work situation, research and development people usually display some degree of introversion. For the most part, they are not the kind of people who require contact with large numbers of people in order to find satisfaction on the job. On the contrary, they are usually content to work by themselves or as a member of a small group.

Technical experiments are of such a precise nature that one minor slip may completely invalidate the results. Consequently, research and development people learn as a result of sad experience that their approach to problems must be carried out methodically, systematically, and with painfully accurate attention to detail. Nor can they afford to be impatient if their first hypothesis proves to be inadequate. The majority of new developments come only as a result of attacking a problem over and over again.

In view of the high technical demands and the unusual complexity of the work, extensive academic training is naturally an important prerequisite. Whether the individuals work as chemists, chemical engineers, or mechanical engineers, they must have taken full advantage of their educational opportunities and acquired a tremendous body of knowledge and skills before they arrive on the industrial scene. Ordinarily, then, our top research and development people will have obtained high academic grades in college and in graduate school. And many of them will have earned a Ph.D. in their chosen field.

Production Supervision

The people who oversee the manufacture of the final product include supervisors, general supervisors, and plant superintendents. Hence, job requirements will vary with respect to the level of responsibility. The differences between supervisors on the one hand and plant superintendents on the other are those of degree rather than kind, however. We expect plant superintendents to have a higher degree of the essential qualifications than those possessed by general supervisors. Presumably, this was the reason they were promoted to their jobs. In turn, general supervisors rose from the supervisors rank because they had a little more of what it takes. Experience has shown that the following qualifications are generally basic for production supervision:

Good mental ability	Production-mindedness
Good verbal ability	Ability to improvise
Good numerical ability	Assertive
Good mechanical comprehension	Tough-mindedness
Ability to see the overall picture	Self-confidence
Ability to plan and organize	Tact
Strong practical interests	Social sensitivity

Production supervisors are a special breed. They are the people who devote most of their attention to putting out day-to-day fires, eliminating production bottlenecks. It is their prime function to get the final product "out the door." Consequently, they must have exceedingly strong practical interests and must be unusually production-minded. Supervisors, general supervisors, or plant superintendents who are not highly motivated to get things done in a hurry are not worth their salt. Since production bottlenecks may occur in the most unexpected places, production people must be good improvisors, individuals who can solve problems for which there has been little time to prepare. On the basis of their ingenuity and past experience, they must somehow make the thing work, even though a better solution to the problem may subsequently be found.

Anyone who is called upon to solve problems must, of course, have a fair amount of mental ability. Because the production supervisor's job is so much concerned with ability to communicate to others, verbal ability represents an important requisite. Numerical ability perhaps plays just as important a role as verbal ability in this type of work. A certain degree of number facility is involved in such job functions as scheduling, preparing time sheets, and analyzing statistical reports. Here, too, the ever-increasing introduction of robots into the manufacturing process places a premium on quantitative analysis. More often than not, the manufacturing process has to do with making "hardware," objects such as appliances, airplanes, automobiles, and furnishings. Such an activity, therefore, requires mechanical know-how and understanding.

Although production supervisors are first and foremost leaders, they must also have some traits of the administrator in their makeup. They are faced with the problem of planning and organizing their work, and must be able to see the broad picture. If they give an inordinate amount of attention to one specific aspect of the work, the manufacturing process as a whole will suffer.

This type of work places unusually heavy demands on the leadership function. Production supervisors must have those qualities that enable them to inspire their people, motivating them to get out the production in the shortest period of time. Confronted with the task of supervising some employees who may be hard to handle, the supervisors must be particularly tough-minded, assertive, and self-confident. At the same time, they cannot afford to ride roughshod over their subordinates. A certain amount of tact and social sensitivity is important here not only in dealing with subordinates but in dealing with the union as well.

Sales

There is perhaps more variation in sales jobs than in any other single business function. They range all the way from high-pressure, foot-in-the-door selling to low-pressure, technical sales service. Hence, some of the traits listed below will loom more important in some sales jobs than in others. But all salespeople have two important functions in common: they are required to contact people, and they are called upon to persuade others to their point of view. These functions inevitably demand the following qualifications:

Good verbal ability	Strong desire to make money
Good self-expression	Assertive
Extroversion	Tough-mindedness
Color	Self-confidence
Infectious enthusiasm	Tact
Sense of humor	Social sensitivity
Persuasiveness	Self-discipline
Practical interests	Perseverance

The best salespeople are normally those who need the stimulation that comes from dealing with people in order to find job satisfaction. Quite the opposite of the reflective individual, they tend to be extroverted, assertive, colorful, and infectiously enthusiastic. They call upon these traits in their efforts to persuade others to buy their product. Competition being what it is, the sales job is not an easy one. The better people are highly articulate, possess good basic verbal ability, and know how to handle themselves adroitly in face-to-face situations. The latter ability, of course, involves tact and social sensitivity. Salespeople must know when to talk and when to keep still, and must be continually alert to the customer's reactions. This permits them to take a different tack if they note that their first approach is not getting across. A good sense of humor is indispensable in many types of sales jobs.

Salespeople's lot can be quite an arduous one. They often live out of suitcases and spend days at a time on the road away from their families. There must be some motivation, then, that attracts them to this field, in addition to the one of having a chance to deal with people. That motivation is usually compensation. Most salespeople are extremely practical and have a strong desire to make money. Because many salespeople are paid on a commission basis, the better ones find that they can make more money in sales than in any other type of work for which they might qualify. It is true that sales jobs as a whole pay better than many other types of work.

The task of getting a hearing demands certain traits of personality. Busy executives often feel that they do not have time to see the salesperson and instruct their secretaries accordingly. In order to gain a hearing, then, salespeople must be unobtrusively assertive and self-confident. Too, they must be sufficiently tough-minded to take rebuffs in stride.

Many salespeople work largely on their own, with very little supervision from their immediate superiors. This calls for a good bit of self-discipline. The ones who go to the movies in the afternoon just because they have made a big sale during the morning seldom turn out to be top producers. They must be constantly aware of the law of averages, that the more calls they make the more sales they are likely to get. In going after big accounts, moreover, they cannot become discouraged. They must persevere, calling on that account again and again until they finally make the sale.

Finance

This category includes a series of jobs ranging from the accounting clerk to the company comptroller. Again, although there is a marked similarity in the traits required in all of these jobs, the degree of each trait required will vary in accordance with level of responsibility. The lower-level jobs, of course, do not make as much demand on the intellectual and administrative factors. In practically all financial jobs, however, the following traits and abilities play an important role:

High-level mental ability	Good judgment
High-level numerical ability	Ability to see the overall picture
Good verbal ability	Carefulness
Good clerical aptitude	Methodicalness
Ability to think analytically and critically	Orderliness
Ability to plan and organize	Introversion
Attention to detail	

Although employees in the financial field, of course, deal with people, they are principally concerned with figures and with things. Their work is likely to be rather confining, and the people who adjust most easily to this type of work are, therefore, inclined to be somewhat introverted. Since even the smallest error must be found before reports are submitted, financial people place great stress on accuracy and close attention to detail. As a group, they are very careful, methodical, and systematic.

High-level intelligence, combined with superior numerical facility, are prime requisites in financial jobs. Arithmetical computation is not in itself sufficient. Practically all of these jobs require a high degree of mathematical reasoning. Statistical data must be *interpreted* in the light of the facts and in the light of the company's needs. Clerical detail must be handled quickly and accurately. This is why the better people tend to have high clerical aptitude. At some point, financial statements and other reports have to be prepared for top management. Hence, a degree of verbal ability is necessary.

At the upper levels, finance people are required to supervise relatively large groups of workers. Since the majority of their subordinates are likely to be somewhat introverted, however, they are normally not required to exert dynamic, tough-minded leadership. Rather, their leadership is of an administrative character. Principal emphasis here is placed upon good judgment, ability to plan and organize, and ability to see the broad picture. Comptrollers must be able to watch all the company operations and must be able to assimilate and integrate their findings so that they can keep their fingers on the financial pulse of theentire enterprise. Above all, they must be analytical and critical. Comptrollers take nothing for granted; they are accountable to top management and therefore must not only be in possession of the facts but must be aware of the underlying reasons.

Modern industry is showing an increasing tendency to diversify and to develop multiple products. Multiplant operations make the financial job all the more complex. To qualify for top-level positions in this field, then, individuals should have sound academic training. Today, many of the better young candidates have a master's degree in business administration, with a major in finance.

Employee Relations

There was a time when little thought was given to the demands of employee relations work. For this reason, the personnel staff in many companies were not carefully selected or trained in their specialty. Nor were these people given the chance to develop the skills with which to do their job—at least to the same degree as personnel in other jobs.

It is good to be able to report, however, that the situation is gradually changing and that employee relations is finally emerging as a profession. This happy development is due primarily to two factors: the labor unions and management's final awakening to the need for stimulating the growth and development of all personnel. Because their tactics have been so effective, labor unions have literally forced management to staff its employee relations department with more competent people, men and women who can meet with labor leaders on an equal footing. After many years of neglecting the human element in an industry, management has at long last discovered that its work force represents its greatest single asset. Today, many progressive organizations sponsor comprehensive programs designed to help each individual realize his or her greatest potential. These programs include more effective selection and placement procedures, better-designed merit-rating procedures, and a wide variety of employee-training procedures. Such activities obviously require able people at the helm.

The employee relations function, as it now exists in the more progressive organization, may be divided into two categories: personnel services and labor relations. The former includes recruiting, selection, placement, wage and salary evaluation, employee benefits, and training. As might be expected in view of the differences between these two functions, the qualifications necessary for success in the personnel services end of the business vary somewhat from those required in labor relations work. There are many individuals capable of doing a bang-up job in personnel services who are completely incapable of bargaining with unions. The best qualified employee relations person, of course, will possess qualifications for both types of jobs. These are the people who have the best chance eventually of heading up the employee relations department. In order to clarify the difference between the two major employee relations functions, requisite traits are listed separately below:

Personnel Services	*Labor Relations*
Good mental ability	Good mental ability
Good verbal ability	Good verbal ability
Good self-expression	Good self-expression
Ability to think analytically and critically	Ability to think analytically and critically
Good judgment	Judgment
Ability to plan and organize	Shrewdness
Social drive (desire to help others)	Assertive
Genuine liking for people	Tough-mindedness
Extroversion	Courage of one's convictions
Friendliness	Self-confidence
Warmth	Fortitude
Tact	Perseverance
Social sensitivity	Fair-mindedness
	Ability to improvise

Many people are initially attracted to personnel services because they have a genuine liking for people and are strongly motivated to help others. This is all to the good because these qualities play an important part in such activities as placement, training, and employee benefits. Individuals who carry out these duties are usually extroverted, friendly, and the kind of people to whom others like to take their problems. To help others with their problems, a personnel employee must be able to approach individuals and win their confidence. This obviously takes an abundance of tact and social sensitivity.

But people in personnel must not be so highly motivated to help others that they permit their hearts to run away with their heads. Many of their duties—particularly that of employment interviewing—call for mature, objective decisions. Because these decisions involve people rather than things or ideas, they should be nonetheless objective and impartial. Practically every personnel function involves the evaluation of people in one way or another. Hence, the job requires intelligence, judgment, and good powers of analysis. Personnel people work largely through the verbal medium, moreover, and should be able to communicate effectively.

Although people in the labor relations field need many of the traits and abilities required by people in personnel services, their job demands an additional constellation of personality characteristics. They have to deal with representatives of labor, many of whom are aggressive, hard-boiled, and able strategists. Thus, labor negotiators have to be exceedingly tough-minded, so that they will be able to take it when the going gets rough. They must be self-confident, assertive, and have the courage of their convictions. Good labor negotiators are also shrewd individuals, people who have a little of the "Yankee horse-trader" in their makeup. At the same time, they must develop a reputation for being completely fair; otherwise they will never be able to win the confidence of labor representatives or develop a working relationship with them.

Bargaining sessions consume long, weary hours during which each side jockeys for position. Company representatives at the bargaining table must learn to meet fire with fire, match persistence with persistence, and maintain their position without getting discouraged. They also have to be good improvisers, in the sense that they can cope with unanticipated developments. All of this takes its toll of many individuals. As pointed out above, there are numerous people in personnel services who simply do not have the resilience and mental toughness to stand the gaff in labor relations.

Matching the Applicant with the Job

We have discussed at length the need for acquiring a complete understanding of the jobs for which applicants are to be selected. Remember, though, that the behavior specifications outlined above, while not all-inclusive, nevertheless represent the *ideal* worker. In the appraisal of candidates, it is unlikely to find any one individual who possesses all the favorable factors for any given job. All of us have our shortcomings, and it has already been pointed out that the interview that brings to light no unfavorable information is a poor interview. Almost every candidate will therefore lack some of the desirable factors. But the best of these people will have assets in such abundance that they compensate for their liabilities. The interviewer's job, then, is to find the applicant who has the most desirable qualifications for a specific job.

At this point, it is only fair to ask the question, "How do we go about determining whether or not an applicant actually possesses the appropriate qualifications?" Well, a few of these qualifications can be determined by means of aptitude tests. But tests are primarily useful in measuring *abilities alone*. It is necessary therefore to rely upon the interview as a means of appraising *personality, motivation, interests, character,* and the *nature of intellectual functioning*. Subsequent chapters of this book show how the various selection steps may be used to accomplish this task.

3
Preliminary Selection Steps

No matter how well trained their interviewers are, companies should not select new employees on the basis of the interview alone. This is far too time-consuming as well as extremely inefficient. In this chapter, then, we will discuss the techniques that can be used to screen out the less qualified applicants.

Since the final interview is a time-consuming and hence relatively expensive procedure, it should be used only with those candidates who satisfy the minimum job requirements. The more progressive companies, therefore, utilize a series of screening techniques designed to eliminate rather quickly those applicants whose qualifications are inappropriate. Such devices, when properly used, are of value to the candidate as well as to the company. The overall hiring procedure normally consumes several hours, and candidates should not be asked to waste their time being processed for jobs which they have little chance of obtaining. An employment setup that does not allow for reasonably quick screening is not only inefficient but also unfair to the individual.

The selection of higher-level people in many companies is often ineffective. This usually consists of a series of interviews with department heads and other key people. Since most such people have not been trained in the techniques of developing information and interpreting it correctly, the results are often far from what they should be. In any panel of five individuals, there may be one or two keen observers of human nature, persons who *can* make a good employment decision. But their votes are frequently overridden by others in the panel who base their decisions on hunch alone. Panel interviewing represents a decided ordeal for higher-level applicants. They are subjected to a day-long experience during which they are usually asked the same questions over and over again. This is not only hard on the applicant but bad for the company image.

In companies where interviewers have been trained, there is only one evaluation interview. If the decision in that interview is negative, no further interviews are scheduled. Rather, the unsuccessful applicant is assigned to a person of lower rank who provides a tour of the company for public relations purposes. This is a great time saver for important people who would normally participate in a panel interview and can actually save thousands of dollars over a period of a year.

Some years ago, the author was asked to review selection procedures for hiring college graduates in a very large company. At the outset, he was told that this technically oriented company placed such high value in hiring the best qualified new people that each of five top managers spent at least 1 hour interviewing every single candidate. In that year, they had each interviewed 196 candidates and selected 27. By placing a dollar figure on the value of 1 hour's time for managers at the top level, multiplying that by 5 and again by 196, it was determined that the company was spending well over $100,000 per year on a selection program that produced less than thirty people—and not doing a very good job of it at that! This is a classic example of the extent to which an inefficient selection program can waste the valuable time of highly placed people. By training interviewers to do a much better job of preliminary selection on the college campuses, installing aptitude tests, and training personnel people to conduct the evaluation interview, only a fraction of the initial population of candidates were subsequently referred to the five top managers—all of whom expressed astonishment at the greatly improved calibre of the people they were now seeing.

As implied above, when the evaluation interviewer's decision is positive, applicants are then scheduled with other people in the organization whose purpose may be that of checking technical qualifications and selling the applicant on the company. Certainly, applicants have the right to meet and talk with the person for whom they will be working as well as other important individuals in the organization. This should help them make up their mind as to whether or not they wish to accept the employment offer.

Companies with well-organized personnel departments utilize a number of screening devices such as a preliminary interview, an application form, aptitude tests, and the reference check. As important as these steps are, however, at some point the all important hiring decision must be made and that normally occurs at the end of the final interview. Hence, the final interview represents the solid core of any good selection program.

The early selection steps, then, have two functions: (1) to eliminate those applicants whose qualifications can be determined as inappropriate at that stage, and (2) to provide information that will be helpful to the interviewer at the time of the final decision. In effect, these selection steps represent a series of screens through which the successful applicant must pass, each screen being constructed of finer mesh than the previous one so that only the most appropriately qualified candidates will survive. This means that the final interviewer sees only a fraction of the number of people who apply for jobs and is thus able to spend as much time as needed with each surviving candidate.

Despite the fact that this book is primarily concerned with interviewing techniques, some discussion of preliminary selection devices helps to place the interview in proper perspective.

Recruiting

It is axiomatic that no hiring program can be effective unless the number of applicants for a given type of work is substantially greater than the number of jobs to be filled. The very word "selection" implies the choice, for any given task, of the one best qualified individual from among a number of available candidates. Wherever careful selection is applied, it is of paramount importance that there be a relatively large reservoir of candidates from which the final selectees are chosen. This is what is known as the *selection ratio*. Ordinarily this ratio should be at least five or six candidates for each person finally selected.

The law of supply and demand always operates in so far as the labor population is concerned, and the available pool of candidates for jobs requiring highly developed skills and long years of training is always limited. At the same time, it is important to choose the best people obtainable. In times of great industrial activity, many companies take a defeated attitude toward the recruiting problem. They give up too easily, without having tapped all possible sources of supply. Too often, they settle for a "warm body." More alert organizations, on the other hand, maintain an aggressive recruiting policy. This is especially important today in order to find and hire qualified minorities. Some companies pay a premium to any current employee who personally recruits people who are eventually hired. Other companies contact minority clubs and other organizations as a part of their recruiting program. And many organizations hire students for summer jobs at the end of their junior year. This not only provides a firsthand impression of the student's worth but also weighs heavily in that student's eventual employment decision once college has been completed.

Most recruiting for higher-level jobs is of course done on the college campuses. There the recruiter has approximately one-half hour to evaluate each interested student and prepare for the next one. Thus, the recruiter may see as many as fifteen or sixteen students in a given day and this turns out to be a very grueling day indeed. Suggestions for carrying out this interview are discussed in Part 4 of this book.

Application Form

The application form represents such an important initial screening device that most companies would do well to examine critically their own application forms. Are they up-to-date in the sense that they do not ask for information which is currently illegal, such as an applicant's specific age, marital status, or number of dependents? Do they provide space for coded information concerning sex and age, as a means of monitoring the applicant flow and insuring the selection of a sufficient number of minorities and females? Do they provide space for an applicant's likes and dislikes on various jobs and best and least liked subjects in school?

Since as many as 50 percent of all applicants for lower-level jobs—and a high percentage of applicants for higher-level jobs as well—can be eliminated on the basis of application data alone, the application form should obviously contain as much information as possible. As noted earlier in this chapter, the elimination of a sizeable number of applicants at this first stage of selection means that final interviewers will be required to see fewer people and hence will be able to spend more time with the people that they do see. Obviously, too, the elimination of large numbers of applicants at the very beginning of the selection process saves the company a great deal of time and money.

Job descriptions and behavior specifications represent the key to the proper elimination of applicants on the basis of the application form. Thus, if the specifications indicate a minimum number of years of specific experience or education, application forms can be quickly scanned to determine those individuals who satisfy those requirements as well as those who do not. The latter can of course be screened out at this time.

If, in the interest of hiring people with good job stability, a company has the requirement in writing that it will not hire individuals with more than two jobs during the past 5 years, additional candidates can be eliminated on that basis. Gaps in dates of employment—except in the case of full-time homemakers—raise further questions. If such gaps cannot be satisfactorily accounted for in the subsequent preliminary interview, some persons may be eliminated on that basis. Failure to move ahead or to achieve reasonable raises in pay over a period of time raise still further questions—questions that must be discussed in the preliminary interview.

When specifications prescribe a fair degree of mathematical facility, persons who least liked "number crunching" on previous jobs and least liked mathematics in high school or college would not seem to represent a good "fit" for the job in question. If all other aspects of a person's history seem suitable, though, such an individual might be passed on to the employment test stage for the purpose of determining just how much mathematical aptitude he or she possesses. Finally, if a job requires shift work and if an applicant indicates distaste for shift work or flat refusal to do it, elimination becomes automatic.

The Preliminary Interview

The preliminary interview has three primary functions: (1) to make certain that the applicant has answered all questions on the application form, (2) to *screen out* candidates who are obviously unqualified for the job or jobs in question, and (3) to provide information for the final interviewer on those applicants who have been *screened in*. Because important decisions must be made within a short period of time—usually 5 to 10 minutes—the preliminary interviewer should be well-trained and exceedingly perceptive.

Preliminary interviewers usually use the completed application as the basis for their brief discussion with applicants. If some previous job appears to have some relevance to the job for which the candidate is applying, the interviewer may ask for a more complete description of that experience. If an individual's education or background appears limited, the interviewer may ask about any additional schooling, such as evening courses, correspondent courses, or on-the-job training.

It is a matter of common sense that only those candidates who are obviously unqualified should be screened out by means of the application and preliminary interview. Doubtful cases should be screened in, thus giving the individual an opportunity to take the employment test and perhaps to participate in the final interview. This is particularly true in the case of minorities and females, where affirmative action goals must be kept in mind. It is conceivable that final interviewers—with more time to explore an individual's history, may be able to discover some compensating asset for what appears to be a somewhat serious shortcoming. This is not to say that employment standards should vary with respect to sex or race. In the final analysis, employment standards should be the same for men and women and for minorities and nonminorities alike.

Perceptive preliminary interviewers can frequently uncover information that should be followed up in the final interview. Such information should, of course, be written down and passed along to whoever makes the final decision. For example, the preliminary interviewer may discover that a given individual left a certain job before obtaining the next position. Although this normally reflects poor judgment and some degree of immaturity, it would normally be insufficient to eliminate that person from further consideration. At the same time, it could represent valuable input for the final interviewer. Or, the preliminary interviewer may get the feeling that an applicant is not telling the truth, but because of lack of sufficient time may not be able to document this sufficiently, and, accordingly, passes on these impressions for further investigation by the final interviewer.

Obtaining Candidates' Permission for Reference Checks

One important function of the preliminary interview is that of obtaining an applicant's permission to carry out reference checks on previous places of employment, *whether or not the company plans to make a check on every applicant.* It is now rather common knowledge that information provided on application forms frequently differs from information provided by previous employers. Some applicants tend to exaggerate and some others are guilty of failure to tell the truth. But if applicants have signed a statement authorizing a prospective employer to verify application information, they are more likely to tell the truth, particularly since such statements usually include a clause that any misrepresentation will be cause for elimination from employment consideration or for immediate discharge. When individuals sign such a statement, moreover, they are also more likely to provide a truthful account of their vocational and educational history in their final interview.

Preliminary interviewers should carefully observe applicants' behavior at the time they sign the authorization for release of information. If they seem at all reluctant or tentative, this observation should be recorded and passed along to the person who carries out the final interview.

Applicants who are screened *in* on the basis of their application forms and preliminary interviews should be told about the next step in the selection program. In companies with a more sophisticated personnel department, this step would normally be that of taking aptitude or dexterity tests. Under current EEO guidelines, however, employment tests can be included in the selection program only if they have been adequately validated, in the sense that they have been found to provide a positive indication of ability to perform on a given job. In those companies where tests are not a part of the selection program—and that includes most companies today—applicants who survive the preliminary interview will proceed directly to the final interviewer.

Aptitude Tests

As noted earlier, aptitude tests as an important preliminary selection step have largely disappeared from the industrial scene over the past few years. So many charges of discrimination have been leveled at these tests since the enactment of the Civil Rights Act that most companies now believe that it is illegal to use any kind of employment test. But this is not the case at all. A careful reading of the EEO Guidelines reveals that aptitude and dexterity tests may still be used *providing they have been statistically validated, in the sense that a positive relationship can be shown between the test scores and success on the jobs for which the tests are being used as a predictor.* The Civil Rights Act, then, does not state that tests cannot be used, the act simply requires that any test utilized in the selection program must have been appropriately *validated.* Since far too many companies were using aptitude tests without any knowledge as to whether or not such tests were making any positive contribution, the Civil Rights Act has had a positive effect. It is only unfortunate that so many companies have eliminated the use of tests entirely rather than to undertake validation studies. Actually, aptitude tests have a long history of reliability in measuring such factors as mental ability, verbal ability, numerical ability, mechanical aptitude, clerical aptitude, as well as manual and finger dexterity. Such tests can provide far more valid results than can be obtained by means of the interview, no matter how well-trained the interviewer may be. Every effort should therefore be made to restore tests to their rightful place in the selection program.

Unfortunately, most companies do not have the expertise to develop and validate their own tests. But there are many reputable consulting organizations who specialize in this function. Companies desiring to restore aptitude tests to their selection programs should retain the services of a knowledgeable consultant to help them with this phase of their program.

Validity Generalization

Validity generalization, or transportability, represents a relatively new concept that enables a much wider utilization of aptitude tests than is generally realized. The term simply means that if a test can be shown to be valid for a given job in one plant situation, that same test can be assumed to be valid *for that specific job* in other plant locations. In a class action suit (*Pagues v. Mississippi State Employment Service*) in the U.S. District Court for the Northern District of Mississippi, the court stated: "Allegation that validity is specific to a particular location, a particular set of tasks, and to a specific application population is not true." In support of this opinion it has further been stated (*Friend and Fuller, et al. v. Leidinger, Fulton, Thorton, and Fionegan*), in the U.S. Court of Appeals for the Fourth District: "To require local validation in every city, village, and hamlet would be ludicrous." The impact of these rulings is far reaching indeed. For one thing, they enable an organization to use tests *that have already been validated elsewhere* for certain specific jobs. And, if a corporation has developed and validated a test for a given job for one plant or office setup, the rulings enable it to use this same test in the selection of applicants for the same job in other plants and offices. Thus, if a test publisher in its manual for a given test can show positive validation and reliability for a test of clerical aptitude, for example, any organization can assume that this test will be valid in its own setting, providing it is used for the same job and for a similar population to the job and population upon which the test was originally standardized.

The State Employment Service

Many personnel people are not aware of the fact that the state employment service can be of tremendous assistance to their organizations. This agency will screen applicants to company specifications and even administer a variety of employment tests that have already been validated for a large assortment of jobs. We know of one large corporation, for example, that utilizes the state employment service to screen and test applicants for employment in sixteen different states. The utilization of this service represents tremendous assistance to any company, since it eliminates the necessity of conducting preliminary interviews and giving employment tests. Moreover, companies using the state employment service do not have to be concerned with the validity of the tests that this agency utilizes since they only give tests that have been developed and validated by the United States Employment Service (USES). Over a period of many years, the USES has developed and validated tests for an astonishingly large number of jobs, ranging from automobile assembler to arc welder. Most of these tests are designed for entry-level plant and office jobs.

It is important to note, however, that the state employment service is available only to those companies that have appropriately developed affirmative action goals in writing and to companies who request a sufficient number of minorities and women to meet these goals. When state employment services are requested, this request must be put in writing. And it must be agreed in the request that actions taken by the state on behalf of an employer are the liability of the employer, not of the state. This means that the employer must know exactly what the state is doing so that it can, if necessary, defend this procedure. Any relatively large corporation would do well to take its request for assistance directly to the office of the state director.

Reference Check

Ideally, it would be preferable to check references prior to the final interview so that discrepancies between application data and reference check could be discussed at the time. In most cases, however, this is impractical because the return of reference information usually takes several days or even weeks. As a consequence, it is more practical to complete the final interview and then run reference checks on only those who have survived that final stage of the selection process.

Personnel people know that reference checks have their limitations. Some previous employers fail to respond and those who do respond are often reluctant to report any negative information. Therefore, it is best to request only factual information such as dates of employment, positions held, reasons for leaving, and attendance record. Reference checks are usually run on only the last 5 years of employment; attendance records are usually limited to the past 2 years.

Reference checks should be made only by mail. In large corporations, it may not be possible to run a check on every single person to be hired. In that case, the company will check perhaps one out of three or one out of five, making certain that on a percentage basis it processes an equal percentage of white males, females, and minority applicants.

Discrepancies

In cases where there is a substantial discrepancy between application information and the reference check—or where information of a derogatory nature is returned to the company by a previous employer—applicants must be given an opportunity to present their side of the story. If the discrepancy is sufficiently serious and if the applicant fails to convince the interviewer of his or her honesty, the applicant is normally turned down for employment. If that person has already been employed, he or she will usually be terminated. In all fairness, though, such an applicant must be given a hearing.

Physical Examination

Physical examinations are expensive—ranging anywhere from $50 to $100 per person. Hence, only those applicants who survive the final interview should be referred to the medical department. The principal purpose of the physical examination is to determine if applicants can physically perform the work for which they are being hired (critically important in the case of the handicapped). This decision can only be made by a qualified physician and hence should never be made by anyone in the personnel department.

Documentation

As in the case of all the other selection steps, a record must be compiled as to why an individual was medically rejected or limited for employment. The notation may be brief, but it must be specific and to the point. All comments should be dated and signed for future verification.

Preliminary Selection Steps Provide Valuable Leads for the Final Interview

As pointed out several times in this chapter, there should be open lines of communication between those who carry out the preliminary selection steps and the final interviewer. The preliminary interviewer frequently develops information which is inconclusive and should be passed on to the final interviewer. The person who administers the company's aptitude test can also make valuable observations. That person may notice that an applicant "jumps the gun," beginning the test before the starting signal has actually been given and continuing to work after the stopping signal has been indicated. Such behavior might represent a possible clue to dishonesty in certain situations or might indicate that the applicant has a strong need to be competitive. Forewarned, the final interviewer is therefore in a position to follow up in an area that might have otherwise escaped attention.

Having discussed the preliminary steps of the selection program, we are now ready to take up the final step—the final interview. This is discussed in two parts: Developing Relevant Information and Interpreting Information Developed.

PART 2
Developing Relevant Information

4

Inherent Character of the Evaluation Interview

In the final analysis, interviewers are faced with only two broad objectives. They must be able to develop relevant information, and they must be able to interpret the information they bring to light. These objectives are sufficiently complex, however, that all of the chapters in Part 2 and Part 3 of this book are directed to their accomplishment. The next three chapters are concerned with helping interviewers obtain the necessary information and the subsequent five are devoted to interpretation.

In earlier chapters we have referred to the final, or evaluation, interview as the most important selection procedure. This is the most critical aspect of the selection program since it is here that all information obtained from the preliminary interview, the application form, the aptitude tests, and the reference check is integrated with other factors of the individual's background and the final decision is made. Applicants who have survived to this point obviously have something to offer. They have passed the employment tests, they have demonstrated some stability in their employment history, and their previous work history and educational background reflect some degree of relevance in terms of the jobs for which they are being considered. But there are still very important questions about these individuals that have not yet been answered.

Up to this point, we do not know how diligently they will be willing to work, whether they are likely to get along well with people, whether they can adapt to the environment of the plant or office, whether they can solve complex problems, or whether they have potential for leadership. It is to these important areas that we address ourselves in the final interview.

Essential Aspects of the Final Interview

We have commented earlier that a vast majority of interviewers are "turned loose" in their jobs without any formal training at all. As a consequence, many interviewers do not interview in accordance with any plan and, hence, do not use their time effectively, many do far too much of the talking themselves, and many, perhaps unconsciously, base their final decision on surface impressions because they do not know how to probe for relevant, hard data.

In the kind of interview described here, we *do* operate according to plan (see the Interview Guide in the Appendix). We take applicants back to their earlier work experience and proceed chronologically through all their jobs up to their present position or last job. From there we discuss educational background, starting with high school and proceeding to college and graduate school. During all this discussion, we probe for clues to behavior in an effort to get a clear picture of strengths and shortcomings.

This is the type of interview, moreover, where the applicant has center stage and is encouraged to do most of the talking. Using techniques which are discussed in a subsequent chapter, interviewers develop such a high degree of rapport that applicants talk spontaneously and, hence, usually provide a clear picture of who they are and what they are like deep down inside. In such an interview, interviewers usually find it necessary to talk only about 15 percent of the time. This gives them a first-rate opportunity to sit back and analyze clues to behavior as they are reflected in the applicant's spontaneous remarks.

Unlike interviewers who base their hiring decision on a hunch or surface impressions, we make every effort to *document* our findings with concrete data drawn from the applicant's history. Thus, a finding such as *willingness to work* should be based upon such evidence as early conditioning to work as a young person, long hours spent on certain jobs, "moonlighting" (working on two or more jobs at the same time), or carrying out a substantial (20 hours a week or more) part-time job while carrying a full academic load in school.

Philosophy of the Interview

Experience has shown that the best way to predict what a person will do in the future is based on what he or she has done in the past. Although it is possible for individuals to grow and develop, and in that way to *modify* their behavior, few people are likely to overcome completely the effect that long years of behaving in a certain manner has produced in them. Hence, if a man has worked hard all his life from the time he was a teenager, he is very likely to work hard for his new employer. And if a woman has shown the ability to adapt to new and changing situations in her previous job experiences, she is more likely to be able to make whatever adjustments may be required in the new job for which she is being considered. Moreover, if she has been able to stay with most of her previous jobs for a reasonable period of time—3 to 5 years—she is quite likely to remain with her new employer for a like period. Finally, if candidates have demonstrated the *ability to get along with people* on previous jobs, in extracurricular activities in school, or in activities outside of work or school, they are very likely to get along well with people in their new plant or office situation.

Functions of the Interview

In addition to the integration of all information obtained from previous selection steps, it becomes the function of the interviewer to (1) determine the relevance of an applicant's experience and training in terms of the demands of a specific job, (2) appraise his or her personality, motivation, and character, and (3), in the absence of aptitude tests, evaluate mental ability.

The third factor—mental ability—is of particular importance in selecting people for higher-level jobs. Most companies prefer to hire individuals with potential for advancement, and here intelligence plays an important part. Other factors being reasonably equal, the extent to which an individual is capable of promotion to more complex and demanding jobs is frequently determined by the amount of mental ability he or she possesses. Suggestions for making these determinations appear in later chapters of this book.

Once all these factors have been assessed, the interviewer is in a position to make the final hiring decision. This is of necessity a subjective decision, a decision based upon the interviewer's experience, judgment, and training. But, in this type of interview, the decision should be based on factual evidence rather than the unsupported hunch. In the final analysis, interviewers not only evaluate a candidate's assets and liabilities in terms of the demands of a given job, they must also judge the extent to which the assets *outweigh* the liabilities, or vice versa. Only in this way can they rate applicants as excellent, above average, average, below average, or poor.

Since most applicants approach the interview with the objective of putting their best foot forward, the interviewer must be motivated from the very beginning to search for unfavorable information. Otherwise, the interviewer is likely to be taken in by surface appearances and behavior. Interviewers are human and thus, despite their efforts to maintain objectivity, they react more favorably to some persons than they do to others. When the initial reaction is favorable, the interviewer has a natural tendency to look only for those clues that will confirm the original impression. It must be remembered, though, that no one of us is perfect; we all have shortcomings. *The interview that results in no unfavorable information is inescapably a poor interview.*

Actually, this interview is an exercise in indirection. By means of adroit suggestions, comments, and questions, we try to elicit spontaneous information without having to ask direct or pointed questions. Obviously, if we are unable to get the desired information by means of indirection, our questions must become gradually more direct. Even so, we try to soften such questions by the use of appropriately worded introductory phrases and qualifying adjectives. Specific techniques for accomplishing this objective will be found in a later chapter.

5

Developing Rapport and Helping the Applicant to Talk Spontaneously

In an effort to help applicants "open up" and tell their entire story, we introduce a number of techniques here which have been clinically tested over the years. If these techniques are used successfully, applicants gradually develop confidence in the interviewer, and realize that it is to their advantage to disclose not only assets but also those areas which need further improvement. They thus become partners in the interview, assume center stage, and spontaneously discuss their life story.

In far too many interviews, the so-called *question and answer technique* prevails. In such an interview, the interviewer asks the questions; the applicant answers the questions and waits for the next one. This type of interview is not only stilted and mechanical but, more seriously, gives applicants an opportunity to *screen their replies*. Thus, they're inclined to provide responses which they think will put them in the best light, rather than tell the story as it actually is. Moreover, interviewers do almost half the talking, leaving applicants with that much less of an opportunity to discuss all the relevant aspects of their background.

The question and answer approach to interviewing also tends to take on the aspects of an inquisition. Applicants feel that they are being *grilled* and hence are uncomfortable. As a consequence, they often provide as little information about themselves as possible *and almost never discuss any of their shortcomings*.

In this chapter we will discuss a completely different kind of interview. Instead of putting applicants on the spot, the interviewer should try to develop a harmonious relationship, one in which applicants not only feel comfortable but also develop so much confidence in the interviewer that they begin to talk *spontaneously*. Instead of waiting for the next question, therefore, they tend to discuss their background with appropriate elaboration, to the extent that their discourse becomes natural and unconstrained. When people talk spontaneously, information seems to well up and bubble out in such a way that there is no need or, indeed, opportunity to screen their replies. Hence, spontaneous information is much more likely to reflect an individual's true feelings, needs, or anxieties, and more often than not, spontaneous information contains clues to shortcomings. Remember, interviewers must search for applicants' shortcomings as well as their assets. Otherwise, it is not only impossible to make appropriate job placements but individuals may be hired for job situations in which they would be incompetent and conceivably quite miserable.

Techniques for developing rapport discussed in this chapter work so well that some applicants tend to talk too much—to the point that the problem becomes one of *controlling* their discourse rather than getting them to open up. Interviewers who take the time to acquire proficiency with these techniques will discover that they have a completely new tool at their disposal, a tool that will not only help them in the interview but also come to their assistance in many other aspects of their lives. People who have learned how to develop rapport become better supervisors, do a better job of feeding back appraisal information, and even become more popular at social gatherings.

Small Talk

In any conversation between two people, it is only natural to begin with some pleasantry rather than to delve directly into the purpose of the meeting. As far as the interviewer is concerned, in fact, this becomes an important aspect of establishing initial rapport. This is the interviewer's first opportunity to get applicants to assume a major portion of the conversational load. If they can be helped to do most of the talking during this early phase of the interview, they naturally assume this to be their role throughout and often fall into this role without any difficulty at all. However, if the small talk revolves around a series of short, direct questions, such as "How was your trip?" it usually leads to a question and answer approach where the interviewer does as much as half the talking. In that case, applicants have the right to assume that their role is one of simply answering any question that may be addressed to them rather than talking spontaneously.

The Importance of Beginning Small Talk with a General Question

Rather than pose questions that invite short yes or no responses, it is more desirable to use a general "pump-priming" question—one that cannot be answered without a fair amount of discussion. Such questions require preparation, however, and cannot be expected to be phrased on the spur of the moment. Prior to the interview, therefore, the interviewer should study the completed application, in an effort to come up with a topic on which the applicant might be expected to talk freely and perhaps enthusiastically. Such a topic might be concerned with a particular interest, some indicated achievement such as a scholarship, or perhaps differences encountered living in two different parts of the country. The interviewer should be armed with one or two such topics prior to the interview. Whatever the topic, the initial question should be broad enough in nature, so that the applicant will be required to talk 2 or 3 minutes in order to answer it. Several examples of such pump-priming questions are listed below.

1. "I notice from your application that you apparently like to ski. Tell me how you got involved in skiing and where you most enjoy it. What kind of satisfaction do you get out of it?"

2. "In looking over your application, I noticed that you were given an award at the Ford Motor Company for making a valuable suggestion concerning your work. Tell me what the award involved and what the suggestion accomplished."

3. "I notice from your application that you have worked in California as well as here in the midwest. How do the two areas of the country compare with respect to things like climate, cost of living, recreational opportunities, attitude of the people, that sort of thing?"

Questions such as those listed above are sufficiently complex that it usually requires at least 2 or 3 minutes to answer them. If the applicant stops after a sentence or two, simply wait, drawing upon the technique to be discussed later—the calculated pause. In posing any incidental question designed to promote small talk, interviewers should make an effort to be as pleasant as possible, treating the subject as what it actually is, an "ice breaker," rather than a more serious part of the interview.

As long as the applicant keeps talking, interviewers should not take any part in the discussion at all. They should simply smile, nod their heads, and engage in other nonverbal, supportive behavior discussed later on in this chapter. They should never break in with questions of their own, no matter how interested they may be in the topic under discussion. At this stage of the interview, it does not matter at all what applicants say, so long as they take over the conversation. Should their conversation come to a halt, interviewers can perhaps keep it going a little longer by repeating a part of the original broad question which has so far been unanswered. Small talk ranging from 2 to 3 minutes is usually sufficient to ease whatever nervousness an applicant may have initially experienced. The sound of one's own voice in a strange situation usually helps to develop confidence, ease initial tension, and build rapport. When applicants are not immediately put on the spot by being asked to tell about some more serious aspect of their background, they do not feel the need to sell themselves, and, thus, they have the chance to relax and to chat informally about matters which are of no great concern.

The Calculated Pause

We have mentioned that interviewers should wait out applicants who stop talking without having answered all parts of a multifaceted question. This is called the *calculated pause*, and is used as a *conscious technique*. Interviewers without much experience tend to become uncomfortable whenever a slight pause in the conversation occurs and are therefore likely to break in prematurely with unnecessary comments or questions. But experienced interviewers purposely permit a pause to occur from time to time because they know that applicants will frequently elaborate on a previous point rather than allow the discussion to come to a standstill. The applicant often senses that the interviewer's silence calls for a fuller treatment of the topic under consideration.

In the conscious use of the pause, interviewers *must not break eye contact*. If they look down at their guide, applicants naturally assume that they are formulating another question and, hence, wait for that question to be articulated. However, if interviewers do not break eye contact and *look expectant* as the pause elongates, applicants feel a certain degree of pressure and usually search quickly for something else to say. Obviously, if applicants fail to respond within a few seconds, interviewers should relieve the pressure by asking another question. To do otherwise might risk a loss of rapport.

Under normal circumstances, the calculated pause is remarkably effective in drawing out spontaneous information. Equally important, interviewers have to do less talking when they use an occasional pause and, therefore, perfect the art of becoming a good listener.

Once perfected, the calculated pause is a powerful technique, particularly when not used too frequently. It also has wide application outside the interview situation. It is a useful tool for salespeople in determining a customer's needs, it is widely used in the legal profession, and it is a valuable technique for use in labor negotiations in determining what is on the other person's mind.

Facial Expressions

We have just mentioned that interviewers should *look expectant* as a means of making the calculated pause effective, but looking expectant and being *facially responsive* are conscious techniques that should be utilized throughout the interview. Anyone can manage an expectant look by lifting the eyebrows a little and smiling slightly. This expression gives the interviewer the appearance of being *receptive* and serves as a powerful tool in getting the subject to open up. People who are facially responsive react facially as well as verbally to another individual's comment. When that individual smiles, the interviewer should smile; when the applicant talks about an unfortunate experience, the interviewer's face should show concern.

Facial expressions play a particularly important role when asking questions that border on the personal. The edge is taken off a delicate or personal question when it is posed with a half smile with the eyebrows raised. And, as we shall see later on, facial expressions are of paramount importance in probing for an individual's shortcomings. Finally, facial expressions help to give one the appearance of being understanding, sympathetic, and receptive. There are some individuals, in fact, who are so adroit with facial expressions that they are able to keep the subject talking almost by that means alone. It is a matter of fact that some people's countenances are naturally more animated than others. Thus, some people find it necessary to work at being facially responsive, while others find it very natural.

People being trained as interviewers sometimes raise the question, "Isn't it possible that I will look like a phony if I try too hard to become facially responsive?" The answer to this, of course, is a qualified "yes." Facial expressions, as in the case of all other conscious techniques, can be overdone and can give interviewers the appearance of being artificial and insincere. Experience has shown, however, that *most people do not use enough facial expression*. It is the rare person indeed who tends to overplay this aspect of interviewing technique.

When we stop to realize that there are only two means at our disposal in getting through to people in social situations—facial expressions and voice—it certainly behooves all of us to make maximum utilization of whatever talents we have in these two important areas. One has only to look at television programs to note how effective people can be who have had specific training in vocal and facial expression. Although most of us cannot approach this professional level, we can do a lot more with our faces and with our voices than we are currently doing. Conscious effort along these lines can pay big dividends in improved interpersonal relationships.

Voice

It has often been said that a series of lessons with an elocutionist will enhance anyone's career. This is because people judge us not only by what we say but also by how we say it. In fact, others may not hear what we say if we have not learned how to speak effectively. This is particularly true in the interview situation where we consciously use the voice as a rapport-building technique.

The art of persuasion obviously relies heavily upon the voice. In the interview, we use every means at our disposal to persuade applicants to reveal all their qualifications and characteristics—shortcomings as well as assets. In their attempts to improve vocal effectiveness, interviewers must keep two things in mind: (1) they must not talk too loudly, and (2) they should try to use all *ranges of the voice*. When interviewers talk too loudly, they tend to threaten applicants to some extent and to push them off center stage. Since applicants should do some 85 percent of the talking, they must be "front and center" during the entire interview. When interviewers talk too loudly, they tend to relegate the candidate to a minor role. Since interviewers do not want that to happen, they should try to keep their voices at a rather low conversational level, in that way encouraging the applicant to take over.

It is much easier to teach people to speak more softly than it is to teach them to use all ranges of their voices. In particular, interviewers should concentrate on greater utilization of the upper range of the voice. When applicants are asked questions or given compliments, for example, interviewers should try to use the upper range of the voice. This has the effect of sounding more interested in what the other person may have to say, and, in turn, that person becomes more highly motivated to give the answer sought after and does a more complete job of revealing innermost thoughts.

As in the case of facial expressions, vocal intonations should mirror the applicant's moods. When applicants discuss unfortunate or unhappy aspects of their background, the interviewer's voice should take on a sympathetic tone, and when applicants divulge something of a highly personal nature, the interviewer's voice should reflect an understanding quality. Complete responsiveness on the part of the interviewer has an unusually powerful effect upon the other person, making that individual not only willing but often actually anxious to talk about things that are uppermost in her or his mind.

Of course, vocal inflection can be overdone. This should be avoided at all costs because it gives the impression of insincerity and may have the effect of alienating individuals rather than attracting them. Again, though, it is the rare individual who falls into this trap. Most of us do not use sufficient vocal intonation and hence could profit from training in this area. For many years, the General Electric Company has sponsored a course called "Effective Presentation." This course has become one of the most popular courses in the GE training program, with some people finding it so helpful that they have taken it a second time. Interviewers would be well-advised to take courses of this nature if such courses exist in their organization.

Lubrication, or Reinforcement

There is perhaps no more powerful tool in the interviewer's arsenal than that of commenting positively on an applicant's achievements. Some people in the field refer to this as "stroking," some call it "reinforcement," and others just refer to it as "giving an applicant a pat on the back." We like to think of it as "lubrication." Just as a drop of oil from time to time keeps a piece of machinery running, so do positive comments interspersed throughout the interview help to maintain rapport and keep applicants talking.

In the interview situation, lubrication, or reinforcement, can be both verbal and nonverbal. Comments such as "Very impressive!" or "You deserve a lot of credit for that!" or "Excellent!" give applicants the feeling that their achievements are being appropriately recognized, and they respond accordingly. Such achievements as (1) high grades in school, (2) promotion on the job, (3) unusually long hours spent on a given job, (4) election to class office, or (5) being invited back for a second summer of part-time work merit favorable recognition on the part of the interviewer. When achievements of this kind are recognized by interviewers in the form of a compliment, applicants often visibly warm to the discussion and become increasingly expansive and spontaneous in their ensuing remarks. To be appreciated is a human need, and the job applicant is no exception in this respect.

Few people realize, however, that lubricating responses can be *nonverbal* as well as verbal. Frequent nodding of the head and sounds of affirmation such as "Uh huh" and "Hmmm" help applicants feel that interviewers are paying attention and appreciate what they are saying. Actually, one-word interjections such as "Fine!", "Terrific!", or "Impressive!" can be worked into the discussion without interrupting the applicant at all. The frequency with which forms of lubrication are utilized during the interview depends largely on the applicant's makeup. If the person is a relatively sophisticated, secure individual, a considerable amount of lubrication would not be appropriate. In such a case, nonverbal reinforcement and a few verbalized comments would normally be sufficient. If an applicant is insecure and relatively unsophisticated, a great deal more lubrication would be in order.

As noted earlier, intonation plays an important part in supportive comments. When the voice is consciously placed in the upper register, rather than mumbled or "swallowed," the comment takes on greater significance. It has the effect of making the interviewer sound more impressed with the applicant's achievement. This has the long-range effect of building so much rapport that applicants become subsequently more willing to discuss some of their shortcomings. People do not mind talking about some of their problems if they are absolutely certain that the listener is completely aware of their successes.

Playing Down Unfavorable Information

Just as we compliment applicants on their achievements, so should we *play down* their problems or difficulties. This is done to make it easier for individuals to talk about negative aspects of their backgrounds, and since we are searching for shortcomings as well as assets, this becomes an important part of the interview technique. Playing down takes the form of some casual, understanding remark. If, for example, a woman talks about the "terrible time she had with mathematics in school," this can be played down by such a sympathetic remark as, "All of us have different aptitudes; the chances are that you may have been a lot stronger in the verbal area." Or, if a young man admits to lack of self-confidence, the interviewer might say, "Self-confidence is a trait that most people develop as a result of living a little longer and acquiring more experience."

When applicants discuss unfavorable information of a more serious nature, such as poor attendance on a previous job or a fiery temper, a casual, sympathetic remark on the part of the interviewer would *not* be appropriate. In such a case, it is better to compliment the individual for being able to recognize the problem and face up to it. An appropriate comment might be, "The fact that you are aware of this situation and have been able to face up to it means that you have already taken the first step toward doing something about it." Such a statement by no means makes light of the individual's problem but does acknowledge being able to face up to it, and this is usually enough to make a person feel better about having revealed the difficulty.

There is one further thing to keep in mind. Interviewers should *never tell applicants anything that is untrue*. If a person should admit to a lack of initiative, for example, one would never say, "Oh, that is something you should be able to overcome very easily." Since traits of this kind tend to become quite deeply imbedded in the personality structure, they are *not* easily overcome. Most applicants would be aware of this and hence would detect the ring of insincerity in an interviewer's comment. Techniques for stimulating behavioral change and development will be found in Part 4 of this book in the chapter on feedback of appraisal information.

We would like to emphasize once again, though, the importance of playing down unfavorable information. The interviewer who gives the slightest indication that judgment is being adversely influenced by unfavorable information will get no further information of this kind. Once interviewers react negatively—either verbally or facially—they disqualify themselves as sympathetic listeners. No one willingly and spontaneously talks about difficulties and failures in a climate where the listener does not give the appearance of being understanding. On the other hand, when such information is not only accepted without surprise or disapproval but also played down, the applicant is permitted to *save face* and hence usually finds it easy to discuss additional negative data if this should be part of his or her history.

Comprehensive Introductory Questions

Although the first comprehensive introductory question is asked immediately after small talk, we are discussing this technique at the very end of this chapter in order to give it emphasis. The comprehensive introductory question represents *the single most important technique for getting applicants to do most of the talking.* This type of question is so comprehensive, in fact, that many applicants can talk several minutes and still not answer all aspects of the question.

Once the small talk has come to an end, interviewers bridge the gap between the small talk and the first introductory question with a comment such as, "Let me tell you a little bit about our discussion today." They then direct the conversation to the real purpose of the session by making an appropriate *opening remark.* This general opening remark should include a statement of the company's interest in placing new employees in jobs that make the best use of their ability. It should present an *overview* of the interview by pointing out that the discussion will include as much relevant information as possible about work history, education, and interests. A question such as the following will usually suffice: *"In this company, we believe that the more information we can obtain about people applying for work the better able we will be to place them in a job that makes best use of their abilities. I would therefore like to have you tell everything you can about your work experience, education and training, and present interests."*

Having provided the applicant with the discussion of the purpose of the interview and having given an overview of the general topics to be considered, the interviewer launches immediately into a discussion of previous work experience, the first topic that appears on the Interview Guide (see Appendix). This is accomplished with a comprehensive introductory question, for example, *"Suppose you begin by telling me about your previous jobs, starting with the first job and working up to the present. I would be interested in how you got each job, your duties and responsibilities, the level of earnings, your job likes and dislikes, and any special achievements along the way."* The very comprehensiveness of this question provides applicants with a basis for a considerable amount of discussion and, as indicated above, represents the single most important factor in getting them to talk for as much as 85 percent of the interview time.

After the work experience has been completed, interviewers should launch into the second topic for discussion—education. A question such as the following will do the job here: *"Suppose you tell me now about your education, starting with high school and working up through college. I would be interested in the subjects you liked best, those you did not care so much for, the level of your grades, your extracurricular activities, and any special achievements. What subjects did you like best in high school?"*

Applicants are not expected to remember every single item in the introductory question. They will often have to be reminded, for example, to discuss subject preferences or asked to talk at greater length about extracurricular activities. Such follow-up questions, though, are simply *reminders* of some of the things applicants have been initially asked to talk about. As such, they do not represent new questions and hence do not require quite so much concentration on the applicant's part.

The Importance of Memorization

Interviewers are advised to *memorize verbatim* the questions presented above. This will make their interviews a lot smoother, and because they do not have to concern themselves with formulating such questions, they are much more free to *listen* to what applicants have to say.

Assume Consent

In verbalizing introductory questions, interviewers should use every means at their disposal to *sell* candidates on the desirability of providing the necessary information. In particular, they should consciously use appropriate facial expressions and vocal intonations. And their very manner should *assume consent.* Just as an effective salesperson assumes that the customer wants to buy, so the expert interviewer assumes that applicants will be happy to respond to all of his or her questions. Questions are best phrased *positively*, in such a way that there is no alternative but to answer them. The phrase "suppose you tell me" is always more effective than the phrase "I wonder if you would be willing to tell me." The latter choice of words provides the alternative of not answering and thus fails to assume consent. Also, it gives the impression that the interviewer is not confident and thus may not be certain whether or not he or she should ask the question.

The techniques discussed in this chapter are almost foolproof in terms of getting spontaneous information and getting the applicant to do the major share of the talking. Interviewers, in fact, who study these techniques carefully and use them as described here will often be quite amazed how productive they can be.

EEO Considerations

1. Do not overdo rapport-getting techniques with minorities or women. This is not necessary, and they will be quick to discern the special treatment.

2. Do not assume a "holier than thou" attitude or "talk down" to the

applicant. Interviewer and interviewee must be on the same wavelength.

3. Be careful about informal chitchat before beginning the interview proper. Interviewers have been known to make such statements as, "I have a daughter about your age, and I can't imagine her wanting to work in this industry."

4. Informal talk at the end of the interview can also create problems. There have been instances where interviewers began talking about sports but, without being aware of the impression they were making, ended up by taking a stand on racial issues. As soon as the interview has been completed, thank the applicant, say you will be in touch with him or her, and stand up as an indication that the discussion has been concluded.

5. Minorities and females who anticipate a negative hiring decision monitor the interviewer's facial expression very closely. In such cases, therefore, interviewers should try all the harder to mask their true reactions. Facial expressions that reflect a negative reaction have been known to lead to charges of discrimination. In these cases applicants charge that the interviewer was biased—that they "never had a chance."

6. Never patronize members of a protected group (minorities, females, or the handicapped) by indicating in any way that they are being hired because the company has an EEO program. Such a statement may lead applicants to believe that they are not being hired on the basis of their qualifications, and people do not like to think that they have been accepted only because standards have been lowered or rules have been bent.

6

Probing More Deeply for Clues to Behavior

Most interviews, in the hands of untrained interviewers, are little more than *surface* discussions—discussions that seldom reveal what a person is like deep down inside. This is why attempts to validate the interview as a selection device have seldom shown positive results. Most interviewers do not get a truly clear picture of such important factors as an applicant's motivation, level of maturity, or basic intelligence. The untrained interviewer simply does not possess the *tools* to probe for important factors of this kind.

In this chapter, therefore, we will make every attempt to supply these tools—in the form of probing questions that have been developed over a lifetime of interviewing. Some of these questions appear on the Interview Guide and should be used verbatim. It is suggested that interviewers make a lap for themselves by crossing their legs and placing the interview guide on the knee. This position makes it easy for them to refer to the guide constantly and read the questions off of the guide verbatim.

In the previous chapter we presented comprehensive introductory questions designed to launch the discussion in each area of the interview, but those questions, of course, will by no means do the entire job. Interviewers must use so-called *follow-up questions*—questions that follow the comprehensive introductory question—to keep applicants talking and to probe more deeply for clues to behavior. Actually, follow-up questions represent an extension of the comprehensive introductory question. They are used to prod applicants from time to time, in this way helping them to reveal their life story to the fullest extent and to become more *definitive* concerning its important aspects. Actually, interviewers' remarks should be interjected so artfully that the interviewers seldom, if ever, assume center stage. Rather, they dart in and out with such facility that applicants seldom become aware of the fact that their discourse is being directed.

Interviewing as Conversation

Since interviewing also represents *conversation* between two people, comments are usually more natural than questions. Whenever a comment can be substituted for a question, in fact, conversation flows more smoothly and interviewers lessen the impression of being *investigative* in their approach. If they want more information on a given subject, they can frequently get such information by the simple comment, "That sounds very interesting." So encouraged, the applicant is quite likely to provide further elaboration without having been specifically asked to do so. We do not want to give the impression here that there is anything wrong with asking questions. Comments interspersed with questions, however, provide more variety and help the interview to seem more natural.

Keep Questions and Comments Open-Ended

There is a great tendency for interviewers to put words in the applicant's mouth by asking leading questions or making leading comments. By so doing, they unintentionally structure their remarks so that a favorable response is strongly suggested. A comment such as, "I suppose you found that job very boring," pushes the applicant to answer in the affirmative even though that may not have been the case at all.

A leading question such as, "Did you rank pretty high in your high school class?" makes it difficult for the applicant to give a negative response. Since the interviewer has asked a leading question, the applicant is greatly tempted to say "Yes." The applicant whose grades were poor, and who honestly admits it, may realize at once that this could create a negative impression and may become uncomfortable in the interview situation and unwilling to offer any more potentially negative information.

In order to avoid such leading comments or questions, the interviewer should keep remarks *open-ended*. An open-ended question is one that does not telegraph an anticipated response, leaving the applicant free to discuss favorable or unfavorable information. A question such as, "What about grades in high school," gives no clue at all as to the weight which the interviewer may place on grades. In such a question, applicants are free to structure the reply themselves, pointing out that their grades may have been average, above average, or even below average.

There is a wonderful phrase—"To what extent"—that makes any question open-ended. Instead of using a leading question such as, "Were you successful on that job?" the question can be open-ended by saying, "*To what extent* were you successful on that job?" Or, instead of saying, "Did you *enjoy* that experience?" one might say, "*To what extent* did you find that experience satisfying?" in that way converting the question to an open-ended situation.

There is another remarkably effective way to ensure an open-ended response—the use of the question, "How did you *feel about* that situation?" When you say, "Did you *like* the people there?" you push the person to say "Yes." But, when you say, "How did you *feel about* the people there?" you can anticipate an objective response.

Talk the Applicant's Language

There is no quicker way to lose rapport than to use words which are outside the applicant's vocabulary. The applicant becomes quickly confused and is made to feel inferior. Interviewers who are good listeners can determine an applicant's range of vocabulary in a relatively short period of time and subsequently make every effort to use words which the applicant readily understands.

Questions and Comments Must be Work-Related

To stay within EEO guidelines, questions must be primarily concerned with the relevance of an applicant's work history and education to the job under consideration. The primary concern should be the extent to which applicants can handle a job and will make mature, stable employees. Questions should no longer be asked about specific age, marital status, number of dependents or personal finances.

At the same time, interviewers do still have the right to determine *how well* applicants have performed on their previous jobs or in school. This is obviously work-related because it provides strong clues concerning an individual's ability to handle a job for which he or she is being considered. If there is a consistency of good performance on previous jobs, it can be assumed that good performance may be expected on a new job.

Function of Follow-Up Questions

As we have already seen, the function of follow-up remarks is essentially that of helping the applicants present a clear picture of their qualifications. By means of adroit questioning, interviewers must be able to draw out applicants so that they can present their real assets. Equally important, interviewers must be able to structure the discussion in such a way that they get a clear picture of candidates' shortcomings. Within this broad framework of objectives, however, follow-up remarks serve a number of specific functions.

Reminding Applicant of Omitted Parts of Comprehensive Introductory Questions

The questions that are used to introduce the discussion in each of the major interviewing areas are so comprehensive that candidates will often forget to discuss some of the items in response to the comprehensive introductory question alone. Usually they will have to be *reminded* to discuss such job factors as likes, dislikes, earnings, and accomplishments. And they may have to be reminded to discuss such things as subject preferences, grades, and extracurricular activities. Then, there are other items listed under each interviewing area on the Interview Guide that may have to be brought to the applicant's attention in follow-up questions. For example, if an applicant fails to tell why he or she left a certain job, the interviewer will have to bring this up in the form of a casual follow-up question.

Getting Further Work and Education Information Relevant to the Job

We have already noted that the interviewer must have a clear mental picture of job description and behavior specifications at the time an applicant's qualifications for a given job are discussed. As the interview progresses, the extent to which the applicant's work history and education measure up to these job and worker specifications should be mentally checked by the interviewer. The applicant will not know which aspects of his or her background to emphasize, in terms of establishing the relevance of past performance to future work responsibilities, since the applicant has not been acquainted with these specifications. The interviewer must therefore be helpful in this regard.

To use an example, let us assume that technically trained people are being interviewed for a job that involves a considerable amount of report writing. In this case, the interviewer would use follow-up questions in an effort to determine the amount of report writing a given candidate has done in previous jobs and the degree of writing facility acquired. The interviewer would, of course, try to mask the intent of the questions with appropriate phrasing and casual, offhand presentation. It could be phrased, "In connection with your research and development work with that company, was there more emphasis placed on the actual technical experimentation or on the writing of results?" After the discussion the interviewer might add, "How did you *feel about* your accomplishments there? Did you feel that you were relatively more effective in the actual experimentation or in the report writing?" Even though the applicant may feel that he or she made the greatest contribution in laboratory experimental work, information concerning report-writing ability will usually be volunteered in response to such a question. And he or she will often place a relatively objective value judgment on writing ability, particularly since it will not be clear how important this may be for the job in question.

Clarify True Meaning of Applicant's Casual Remarks

Clues to the applicant's behavior will not always be clear-cut. In response to a question concerning job dislikes, for example a candidate may say that detail work was less satisfying. Now, the interviewer cannot assume from such a remark that the applicant cannot do detail work. The interviewer must try to pin down this clue by fixing the *degree* of dislike. In this case, a response to the original remark could be, "Many people find detail work much less interesting than other aspects of their job." This kind of a sympathetic response often encourages the applicant to elaborate. In so doing, an *intense dislike* of detail may be revealed in the form of an open acknowledgement that he or she is not very proficient in the type of work that requires close attention to detail. Or the applicant may indicate that, while not enjoying detail, he or she nevertheless finds it relatively easy to carry out when it is an important part of the job. Obviously, the interpretation of these two responses would be quite different. The first response, if supported by other clues pointing in the same direction, would lead the interviewer to the possible conclusion that the applicant was not a good detail person. The second response, on the other hand, would lead to no such conclusion.

Searching for Support of Early Established Hypotheses

Highly skilled interviewers often pick up little clues to the applicant's possible behavior relatively early in the discussion, and these clues help them to establish a *hypothesis* with respect to the possible existence of certain assets or liabilities. They know, however, that such hypotheses must be supported by more tangible evidence; otherwise they must be rejected entirely. Interviewers therefore use exploratory questions to probe for clues that might support their hypothesis. If none is found, they must, of course, discard that hypothesis and search for new ones.

For purposes of illustration, we will assume that the interviewer has obtained some initial impressions of the applicant that point in the direction of superficiality, lack of depth, and limited powers of analysis. As he leads the applicant from area to area, he will, of course, be on the lookout for supporting evidence or for the lack of it. From time to time, he will interject so-called "depth questions"—questions that require a fair amount of analysis. For example, he may ask the applicant what a job has to have in order to give her satisfaction. Or he may ask what gains in terms of personality development accrued as a result of military experience. If the candidate's responses to a series of such questions reveal little ability to dig beneath the surface, the interviewer may rightly conclude that the individual is indeed superficial and without much ability to analyze.

Let us take another example. In this next case, we will assume that an interviewer has formed an early hypothesis that an applicant may be somewhat lazy. Let us say that she has arrived at this tentative judgment because of a man's professed unwillingness to work overtime hours. In order to check and support this initial hypothesis, the interviewer will use follow-up questions to probe specifically for such factors as (1) how much effort the applicant may have expended on other jobs, (2) how hard he studied in school, and (3) any demonstrated willingness to carry out constructive tasks either at home or in the community after putting in a regular work day. If she finds that the candidate (1) took the easy way out to avoid tackling difficult problems, (2) studied just hard enough to get by, or (3) decided against graduate work because it would have meant going to school at night—if she is able to get consistent information of this kind—she is able to *document* her views concerning the candidate's lack of motivation. The point to remember here, though, is that this kind of information probably would not have been brought to light had it not been for the fact that the interviewer probed for the appropriate clues by means of follow-up questions.

Quantifying Information

In the effort to *document* the findings with respect to the applicant's behavior, it is important to get as *definitive* responses as possible. When successes, failures, or even reactions are spoken about in general terms therefore, the interviewer must get more specific answers. For example, if he simply indicates that his grades in college were "above average," a good follow-up question would be: "Does that mean that your grades ranked you in the top ten percent of your class, the upper quarter, the upper third, or perhaps the upper half?" Or, if a candidate merely indicates that she was given a raise in salary after her first six months on the job, the interviewer must follow through with: "What did that amount to in terms of dollars?" Again, if a candidate indicates being "out of work for a while," it is important to establish how long the unemployment actually lasted.

Wherever possible, try to get numbers—the number of hours worked on a part-time job while attending school, specific SAT scores, class standing and number of students in the graduating class, and in the case of a student with a part-time job requiring many hours per week, the number of credit hours taken simultaneously.

Kinds of Probing Questions

We mentioned previously that many interviewers fail to probe beneath the surface because they do not have the tools to do the job. The material that follows provides such tools in the form of three kinds of extremely important questions.

The Laundry List Question

Applicants almost invariably find some areas more difficult to discuss than others. Confronted with a question that requires considerable analysis, they frequently "block" and find it somewhat difficult to come up with an immediate response. In such a situation, the interviewer comes to the applicant's assistance with a *laundry list* question. As the name implies, this kind of question suggests a variety of possible responses and permits subjects to take their choice. If candidates block on the question, "What are some of the things that a job has to have to give you satisfaction?" the interviewer may stimulate thinking by such a laundry-list comment as, "Well, you know some people are more interested in money, some want security, some look for the satisfaction of working with their hands, others enjoy working as a member of a team, and others like a job that takes them out of doors a good bit of the time. What's important to you?" Given a variety of possible responses, applicants are normally able to get their thoughts together and supply a considerable amount of information.

The laundry-list question can also be used as a means of confirming clues to behavior that the interviewer has obtained from some previous aspects of the discussion. Let us assume, for example, that an applicant has dropped some hints that seem to indicate a dislike for detail. The interviewer can often follow up on such clues by including a reference to detail in the laundry-list question at the end of the discussion of work history. For example, the interviewer may say, "What are some of the things that a job has to have in order to give you satisfaction? Some people want to manage whereas others are more interested in an opportunity to come up with new ideas; some like to work regular hours whereas others do not mind spending additional hours on a job—hours that might interfere with family life; some like to work with details while others do not; some are quite happy working at a desk while others prefer to move around a good bit—what's important to you?"

If, in response to the above question, the candidate said, "Well, I certainly do not want anything that involves a lot of detail; actually, I'm not at all good at that type of work," the interviewer would certainly have obtained further confirmation of the subject's reaction to detail. The very fact that the individual selected this item for discussion reflects the importance she attaches to it. If the applicant were being considered for a job where attention to detail figured importantly in the specifications, her response could be interpreted as revealing a relatively serious shortcoming.

Besides taking a candidate "off the hook" alleviating the tendency to "block," the laundry-list question has the further function of spelling out to the applicant what the interviewer specifically has in mind. By the very nature of the items used in the series of possible responses, the interviewer encourages the applicant to respond specifically rather than generally, and makes certain that the responses will be helpful in the evaluation of the individual. Toward the end of the candidate's discussion of work history, for example, the interviewer asks him what he has learned about his *strengths* as a result of working on various jobs. In order to tell the applicant what the interviewer specifically has in mind, he uses such a laundry list as: "Did you find that you worked a little harder than the average individual, got along better with people, organized things better, gave better attention to detail—just what?" Such a laundry-list question helps to "tie down" individuals' responses, so that they talk in terms of *traits of personality, motivation, or character.*

Two Step Probing for the "Why"

This question represents our best tool for developing evidence of analytical and critical thinking. With the first step, we proceed from the general to the specific. "What subject, from among all of the majors offered in your college, did you decide to major in?" In the second step, we probe more deeply for the "why." "What was there about biology that attracted you?"

One person might reply, "Oh, I guess I liked my original professor, and I found the subject easy." (Not at all analytical.) Another person might say, "Well, biology is a very orderly and systematic science, and I guess I am like that too. I was also fascinated by how much I learned about how my own body functions. And, finally, in this era of burgeoning biogenetics, any undergraduate degree in biology represents a great springboard to interesting graduate study." (A far more analytical and mature response.)

Experienced interviewers know that *why* an individual took some course of action is frequently more revealing than *what* he or she did. This is true because why people do things tells us a great deal about their judgment, their motivation, and other factors of their personality structure. Probing for why an applicant left a given job, for example, may provide clues to such factors as inability to relate to authority (problems with the boss), inability to do the work, dissatisfaction with close supervision, or the kind of restlessness that motivates a person to move on to something new. When applicants leave a job before obtaining another one, a why question may reveal a tendency to rationalize, to try to explain away one's failure. A reply such as, "I couldn't very well look for a new job while working 8 hours a day on the present job," taken even at face value indicates poor judgment and immaturity. But it also may be a cover for precipitative action based on a quick temper or even for having been fired.

It is not only important to find out what applicants liked or disliked about their job but perhaps more important still to learn the why of their likes or dislikes. This is what is meant by probing more deeply. If a woman indicates that she liked working with computers, a why question such as, "What is there about working with computers that appeals to you?" would be in order. Such a question may reveal that she has a flair for mathematics, that she enjoys problem solving, that she appreciates the accuracy and thoroughness that are a part of such detailed work, or that she enjoys an opportunity to work on her own without close supervision. When a man indicates a dislike of mathematics in school, a question such as, "What was there about math that turned you off?" would be in order. A reply such as, "I never could understand what I was supposed to do," could conceivably provide a clue to mental ability.

When a woman, for example, indicates that she has an *ability to get along with people*, the interviewer should dig deeper by saying, "What traits do you have that make it possible for you to get along with people as well as you do?" The reply to that question may reveal such valuable traits as tact, empathy, or sensitivity to the needs of others.

It is suggested that *why* questions be used sparingly throughout the interview. For one thing, there is not sufficient time to probe for the why of everything the applicant says. Also, too frequent use of this technique puts too much pressure on the applicant and results in the feeling that he or she is being grilled. Hence, the technique must be reserved for probing in the most fruitful areas. These areas obviously differ from person to person, but with practice and experience interviewers will learn how to recognize fruitful areas for further probing when they occur.

Double-Edged Questions

Double-edged questioning is used to make it easy for applicants to admit their shortcomings and to help them achieve greater self-insight. The questions are double-edged in the sense that they make it possible for the subject to choose between two possible responses. Moreover, the first alternative is usually phrased in such a way that the subject would not choose that alternative without feeling possessed of the ability or personality trait in question to a fairly high degree. The second alternative is phrased so that it is easy for the applicant to choose that alternative, even though it is the more undesirable of the two possible responses. Hence, *this type of question is used only to probe for shortcomings.*

Having asked applicants to reveal their strengths, one can logically follow up with a question about shortcomings. A question about shortcomings can be presented as a laundry-list question, with the double-edged question used as a follow-up. Thus, an interviewer might say, "What are some of the things about yourself that you would like to improve? Would you like to develop more self-confidence, acquire more tact, learn to control your temper better, improve your attendance record—just what?" If the applicant finds it difficult to answer this question, the interviewer may probe more specifically with a *double-edged* question such as, *"What about tact; do you have as much of that as you would like to have, or is this something you could improve a little bit?"* Given something specific to talk about, most applicants tend to respond quite spontaneously and often reveal a good bit about their shortcomings.

In interviewing people for office jobs, interviewers often find a double-edged question such as, "What about your ability to spell; do you have that ability to the extent that you would like, or is that something you could improve a little bit?" quite revealing. How confident the individual may be in her or his ability to spell is often revealed in tone of voice or facial expressions. If there is any hesitancy in the reply or if the person frowns, this may be indicative of a problem area. The point here, though, is that the double-edged question was used to launch this discussion. Most people find it much easier to discuss things that they could *improve* rather than qualities that they *lack*. Thus phrased, the double-edged question represents an adroit way to introduce the subject of shortcomings.

How to Soften Direct Questions

In their efforts to probe more deeply for clues to behavior, some interviewers tend to be too blunt and direct in their questioning. Since this risks a possible loss of rapport, many such questions can be softened by the use of appropriate *introductory phrases* and *qualifying words*. Such introductory phrases as the following will help to soften almost any direct question:

Is it possible that...?

How did you happen to...?

Has there been any opportunity to...?

To what do you attribute...?

Qualifying words and phrases such as "might," "perhaps," "to some extent," "somewhat," and "a little bit" are also effective in softening direct questions.

A study of the two types of questions listed below will reveal the extent to which the direct question has been softened by means of introductory phrases and qualifying words. The questions on the left are obviously too direct; those on the right are more appropriate.

Too Direct	*More Appropriate*
1. Why did you leave that job?	1. *How did you happen to* leave that job?
2. Why do you think you had trouble with your boss?	2. *To what do you attribute the minor* difficulties you experienced with your supervisor?
3. How much money did you save that summer?	3. *Was there any opportunity* to save *any* money that summer?
4. Why did you decide to take a cut in pay in order to get transferred to that other job?	4. *What prompted your decision* to take a cut in pay in order to get transferred to that other job?
5. Do you lack self-confidence?	5. Is self-confidence *perhaps* a trait that you might improve *to some extent?*
6. Are you overly sensitive?	6. *Is it possible* that you *may* be *somewhat* over sensitive to criticism?

Note-Taking

Discussion of the techniques of the interview would not be complete without some reference to the taking of notes. This subject, incidentally, has stirred a considerable amount of controversy over the years, some authorities claiming that note-taking results in a loss of rapport and others indicating that the interviewer should feel free to take as many notes as he or she desires.

We take the view that there is no reason at all why trained interviewers should not be able to take as many notes as they deem necessary. One who has achieved genuine skill in the use of such techniques as facial and vocal expression, pats on the back, playing down of unfavorable information, and adroit questioning should be able to take notes in such a way that the applicant becomes almost unaware of this activity. The candidates usually become so absorbed in the discussion that they take little notice of the skilled interviewer's note-taking.

However, any writing done by interviewers should be carried out as unobtrusively as possible. Thus, they should keep a pad of paper on their knee throughout the discussion and should keep a pencil in their hands at all times. The simple movement of placing the pencil on the desk and picking it up at frequent intervals can often be distracting.

Notes should only be made when candidates relate objective data concerning their background or when they tell about their past achievements. Whenever they impart information of a highly personal or derogatory nature, interviewers should obviously refrain from any writing. Rather, interviewers should wait until applicants volunteer the next bit of favorable information and, at that time, record both the favorable information and the unfavorable data previously obtained.

Finally, skilled interviewers learn to record their findings without diverting their attention from the candidate *or breaking eye contact for more than a few seconds at a time*. This places the note-taking function in its proper perspective, as a seemingly minor aspect of the interview.

EEO Considerations

1. Keep questions job-related.

2. Do not ask questions of minorities or females that you would not ask of nonminorities or males.

3. Never ask questions out of curiosity alone. All questions should have a valid purpose.

4. Never ask a single female about her plans for marriage.

5. Never ask a female if she has someone to care for her children while she works or what her plans are for having children.

6. Do not ask an older worker how many more years he or she plans to work. This could be construed as age discrimination.

7. If the job involves travel, working long hours, or potential transfer, attitudes toward such conditions cannot be asked of females alone. If this question is to be used, it must be used with *all* applicants—males and females alike.

7
Techniques of Control

In the two previous chapters devoted to the techniques of the interview, emphasis has been placed primarily on ways and means of getting the applicant to talk freely. This of course represents a first objective. The interviewer can learn little unless the applicant talks spontaneously.

Spontaneous discourse in itself, however, is not sufficient. Discussion must be guided and channeled in such a way that applicants tell what the interviewer needs to learn rather than simply what they themselves want to relate. Indeed, it is quite possible for an applicant to talk as long as 3 hours in an uncontrolled situation without giving as much salient and evaluative information as could have been provided in 1½ hours of guided conversation.

Teaching interviewers how to exercise optimum control represents one of the most difficult tasks in the entire training procedure. During the early stages of their training, interviewers invariably exercise too little control. In their desire to get spontaneous information, they are inclined to let applicants go on and on, just as long as they talk freely. As a consequence, the interview suffers from lack of intensive coverage in the important areas and from lack of balance—too much emphasis on one area of the applicant's background and too little on other areas. In addition, such an interview takes far too much time.

With proper training, though, interviewers gradually learn to use just the right amount of guidance and control, and they learn to do this tactfully and unobtrusively. In the very early stages of the interview, they permit applicants to talk quite freely, even though some of the resulting information may not be particularly relevant. They do this in order to *set the pattern* of letting candidates do most of the talking. Once this pattern has been established, though, they do not hesitate to interject comments and questions at critical points, in order to ensure intensive coverage and sufficient penetration in each area of the applicant's background.

Why Control is Necessary

As noted above, measures of control are designed to (1) ensure adequate coverage of each area of the applicant's background, (2) secure appropriate penetration into the truly salient aspects of the candidate's previous experiences, and (3) utilize the interviewer's time efficiently and economically.

Appropriate Coverage

Some applicants build up such a head of steam that they tend to *take over the interview* and run away with it. In so doing, they may skip over some important areas too quickly and leave out other factors entirely. They tend to discuss only what they want to tell rather than what the interviewer needs to know.

When applicants begin to take charge and to race over their history too rapidly, the interviewer should step in and control the situation, tactfully reminding such a person to discuss likes and dislikes on each job, reason for leaving, and the like. Otherwise the individual could conceivably cover an entire area such as work experience in as few as 10 minutes, without providing any real clues to behavior or any substantial information about accumulated skills.

Balance

During the early stages of their training, interviewers frequently fail to apportion interviewing time appropriately. They permit the candidates to spend far too much time on one area of their background and far too little on some of the other areas. Such interviews lack balance.

Problems concerned with balance usually occur as a result of allowing the applicant to provide too much irrelevant detail about previous work experience. In an insufficiently controlled interview, some applicants find it quite easy to spend as much as 1½ hours discussing their previous jobs. In so doing, they naturally include a lot of unnecessary and irrelevant information. When this occurs, the interviewers suddenly realize that too much time has been spent on the work area. Then, in order to complete the discussion within a reasonable period of time, they push the applicant through the other background areas too rapidly. The ensuing lack of interview balance precludes comprehensive evaluation of the individual's overall qualifications.

Now, it is not reasonable to expect all information supplied by applicants to be relevant. Of necessity, much of the discussion provides little more than a framework that is used by interviewers as a basis for probing into more fruitful areas. At the same time, interviewers must continually guard against excessive and irrelevant detail. They must continually ask themselves, "Am I learning anything about the applicant's behavior or anything about the extent to which he or she meets the job specifications, as a result of this particular segment of the discussion?" If the answer is "No," the candidate must be tactfully pushed along to another topic.

In order to achieve proper balance, interviewers should place a clock on the table. And they should casually refer to the clock at rather frequent intervals. Time spent in the various interview areas with applicants for higher-level jobs should be apportioned roughly as indicated below. (These time limits can be appreciably shortened in interviews with candidates for lower-level positions—usually 40 to 45 minutes.)

Work history—55 to 65 minutes

Education—15 to 20 minutes

Present social adjustment—5 to 10 minutes

The above timetable permits a minimum of 1 hour and 15 minutes and a maximum of 1 hour and 35 minutes. It must be emphasized, though, that these time allowances are to be used only as a rough *guide*. Since there are marked differences between individuals, it will obviously take longer to interview one person than another. Factors that influence interviewing time requirements are primarily those of *age* and *psychological complexity of the individual*. Older applicants normally require more time because they have more experiences to be discussed and evaluated. Regardless of age, the individual who is complex psychologically requires greater time because there are more facets of the personality to be considered.

There are cases, too, where the suggested timetable may have to be modified with respect to the amount of time required for a given interview area. If the applicant is fresh out of college, for example, and has had few summer or other part-time jobs, it will obviously be unnecessary to spend as much as 55 minutes on the work history area. In evaluating such an individual, proportionately more time should be spent on education and on the other areas of the background.

Penetration

In general, applicants supply two types of information: *descriptive* information and *evaluative* information. If the interview is not sufficiently controlled, almost all of the information may be of a descriptive nature. Applicants may describe the companies for which they have previously worked, go into elaborate details concerning job duties, and talk a lot about the fun they had in college. Now, some of this descriptive information serves a purpose, but it does not tell us much about the individual makeup.

Hence, interviewers must control the discussion to get *evaluative* information—information that can be used as a basis for determining the applicant's personality, character, and motivation. By artful and tactful questioning, they must *penetrate* to the candidate's basic reactions to key situations, with a view to determining the possible effects of those situations on the individual's growth and development. For example, to learn that a man spent 5 years in the army, attended a variety of schools, fought in the tank corps overseas, and was awarded a Bronze Star is not sufficient. We want to know, in addition, how he got along with his superior officers, how well he adjusted to military life, and how much he developed and matured as a result of the overall experience. Normally, the average applicant will not supply answers to these questions unless his or her discussion is *channeled*. In other words, the interviewer must find a way to cut off descriptive information and probe more deeply for evaluative data.

Economy of the Interviewer's Time

Good interviewers are always jealous of their time. Although they must not in any way convey this fact to the applicant, they nevertheless use control in order to complete interviews in the shortest possible time and still get the best possible picture of the candidate's qualifications. The interview that runs for 2½ to 3 hours is ordinarily an inefficient one. Such an interview not only consumes more time than is necessary but results in so much irrelevant detail that interpretation becomes more difficult. In other words, the interviewer has difficulty separating the wheat from the chaff primarily because there is so much chaff.

If interviewers are to assume a normal case load of two to three comprehensive interviews per day, they cannot afford to spend much more than 1½ hours per interview and still have time to write their reports. Moreover, interviewing is a very fatiguing experience because of the attention factor. If interviewers spend too much time on one interview, they will not have sufficient energy to give other applicants the attention they deserve.

The indicated case load of two to three evaluation interviews per day may strike some as a surprisingly low number. It is true, of course, that employment interviewers can conduct a relatively large number of *preliminary interviews* in a single day. And they can carry out as many as six or seven final interviews on applicants for lower-level plant or office assignments. But it is unreasonable to expect them to do more than three comprehensive interviews per day in the case of persons being considered for higher-level positions. Since the evaluating of key applicants represents such a critical function, it is much better to hire and train additional interviewers than to overload the interviewing staff.

Techniques of Control

It is one thing to talk about the needs for control and quite another to discuss how it can be accomplished. Fortunately, though, we have two effective techniques to draw upon for this purpose: (1) the Interview Guide and (2) interruption.

Interview Guide

Many inexperienced interviewers approach the interview with no plan at all. They simply pick out some item of the application and go on from there. Such interviews usually suffer from inefficiency and ineffectiveness. Applicants tend to ramble in their discussion and fail to cover some of the more important aspects of their backgrounds.

The Interview Guide, found in the Appendix of this book, provides a "track to run on" and hence represents a very important aspect of control. This guide can bring order, system, and intensive coverage to a discussion that might otherwise have been inconclusive. The Interview Guide not only specifies the sequence of the discussion but also includes important factors to be taken up in each major area. The guide is so important that interviewers are advised to keep this form on their laps and refer to it every 2 or 3 minutes throughout the interview. This permits the interviewer to use questions on the form verbatim and ensures against omission of important items.

Some interviewers also feel self-conscious about reading questions off the form and hence try to paraphrase these questions, using their own words. This is a mistake in two respects. In the first place, experience has shown that reading questions from the Interview Guide does not disturb applicants in the least. In the second place, most interviewers find it very difficult to formulate questions on the spur of the moment that are as effective as the questions printed on the guide.

Interruption

When an applicant begins to talk too much—particularly in terms of irrelevant detail and descriptive information—the interview must be controlled by means of *interruption.* Interruption represents a very effective means of control, but this technique must be employed so subtly that applicants do not realize that they are being interrupted. In order to accomplish this, two additional techniques are utilized: *timing* and *lubrication.* It is of course impolite to interrupt people in the middle of a sentence, and, yet, if we wait until the end of a sentence, they will already have launched into the next sentence by the time we get around to interrupting them. Hence, the interruption must be *timed* to occur before they have actually completed the sentence. Interviewers therefore learn to interrupt as soon as applicants have completed a thought but *before they have had a chance to complete the sentence.* Moreover, an interruption is always accompanied by a lubricating comment such as, "That's very interesting," or "That must have been very satisfying." The lubricating comment represents the introduction to the comment that will redirect the discussion and move applicants along to another topic. If, for example, an applicant tells too much about his or her likes on a given job, the interviewer may say, "You must have found that very satisfying. Tell me about some of the things you did not like quite so well."

As will be noted from the above, timing means *anticipating the end of a thought* and lubrication in this sense means *making a positive or favorable comment* Utilization of these two techniques tends to soften the interruption in such a way that applicants may not even realize that they are being interrupted. Because interviewers have commented favorably on a given topic under discussion, applicants are willing to relinquish that topic and permit themselves to be redirected to a new subject.

Interviewers should not be too hasty in interrupting applicants when they wander off the track or go into a bit too much detail, because hasty interruption risks the loss of rapport. Give individuals a minute or two to get the uninteresting or irrelevant topic "off their chests" before shutting them off and redirecting their conversation.

Let us assume that a male applicant, for example, races lightly over his first two or three jobs, apparently thinking that they are not ger-

mane to the discussion. Since this would normally occur at the very beginning of the interview and since a pattern should be established of
having an applicant carry the conversational ball, he would be allowed
to talk for 3 or 4 minutes, then, just as he was about to put a period at
the end of a sentence, the interviewer would inject a positive comment
and redirect him to a more thorough treatment of his first job. The interviewer might say in this instance, "You have certainly had some interesting early experiences—so interesting in fact that I would like to
know more about them. Suppose you tell me more about your likes, dislikes, and earnings on that first job."

Let us take another example, where an applicant, a woman, perhaps,
conceivably wanders off the track and launches prematurely into another interview area. In response to the question, "What did you like
best on that job," she might reply, "I enjoyed the calculations. You
know, I am very good in math. I won the math prize in high school and
did exceptionally well in calculus. Our high school had two very fine
math teachers, and I learned a lot in their classes." If this woman was
not interrupted, she might very easily go on to further discussion of her
high school experience and forget all about the discussion of her various jobs. After she has been given a minute or two to discuss her mathematical proficiencies, therefore, the interviewer interrupts by anticipating the end of one of her thoughts with a comment such as, "I think
it's great that you have such an interest and aptitude in math—particularly since you want to become a systems analyst. Tell me about some of
the other things you liked on that job with Carter Steel." Because this
woman has not been interrupted in the *middle* of a thought and because she has received a favorable comment about her mathematical
proficiency, she would normally be quite willing to be redirected back to
her work experience.

The Importance of Interviewing Manner

Despite the fact that interviewers only do about 15 percent of the talking, they nevertheless guide the discussion by their very manner and by
the way they carry out their role. Although they are friendly, disarming,
and permissive, there is a point beyond which they cannot be pushed.
By means of vocal and facial expressions, they *assume consent*. This
means that they ask their questions and make their comments in such a
way that the applicant is expected to answer. This inner firmness creates an atmosphere of "remote control." Thus, interviewers take active
control only when they have to, but they are always ready to step in
when the occasion demands. Since interviewers are already in the power

position—it is the applicant who is seeking the job—they can usually maintain control in a very unobtrusive fashion.

Upon occasion, one meets an applicant who is inclined to be facetious. Such a person may make light of some of the interviewer's questions or may even challenge their relevancy. Such a situation obviously requires firmer control. When a question is challenged or treated facetiously, interviewers should simply restate the question, giving their reasons for asking it. By their general manner rather than by anything they say, interviewers underscore their seriousness of purpose. This approach almost invariably prevails, the applicant becoming very cooperative thereafter. Some applicants like to test the interviewer, just to see how far they can go. Once they determine the point beyond which they cannot go, they usually become very cooperative.

Other Factors of Control

Applicants obviously vary widely with respect to their interview behavior. It is therefore impossible to discuss all situations where control may be necessary, but there are some general rules that may be applied in almost every case.

Develop Information
Chronologically and Systematically

Applicants, of course, are given considerable freedom in their choice of subject matter, but they should nevertheless be encouraged to supply information chronologically and systematically. In discussing their work experience, for example, they should be asked to start with the very first job and work up to their most recent experience. This not only gives a sense of order to this segment of the interview but also makes it easier for the interviewer to ascertain the applicant's vocational achievements over the years. In the educational area, it is always best to start with the first years of high school and go on to the subsequent years or even to college if that level of education has been attained. This gives interviewers an opportunity to see how applicants fare as they progress to more difficult academic subject matter and have to compete with more able individuals. (Many of the less gifted people drop out of high school after a year or two.) The interview guide, of course, spells out the indicated chronology.

Exhaust Each Interview Area Before
Going on to the Next One

Constant reference to the Interview Guide helps interviewers to get all important information in one area before going on to the next. One might find, for example, after completing the work history that he or she has neglected to determine an applicant's earnings. The interviewer should go back and get this information before launching into education.

When an applicant is permitted to crisscross between areas, it becomes very difficult for interviewers to evaluate total achievement in one area. Moreover, after the applicant has left the room, they invariably find that they have forgotten to get some important bit of information.

When omissions do occur and when interviewers do not become aware of this until they are midway in the next area, they should complete the discussion in the current area before going back to get the desired information. To interrupt in the middle of a discussion of education in order to get job earnings breaks the applicant's train of thought and makes it more difficult later for him or her to resume the discussion of education at the point at which it was interrupted.

With Recent College Graduates,
Explore Summer Jobs Thoroughly

Many young applicants tend to skip over summer jobs too quickly, feeling that they are not relevant to the job for which they are applying. Summer jobs may not be entirely relevant, but they do tell us a great deal about applicants—the *initiative* they may have demonstrated in getting these jobs, the capacity to *adapt to and stay with boring or routine assignments, the ability to get along with people* from diverse backgrounds. Hence, when applicants tend to race over summer experiences, interviewers must use control with a comment such as, "I would like to know a lot more about that first summer job—how you got it, what you did, your likes, dislikes, and so forth."

Effective Control Requires
Judicious Pacing

Here we return to a subject discussed at the beginning of this chapter. If spontaneity of response is to be maintained, control must be exercised tactfully, unobtrusively, and *at appropriate intervals*. This means that the interviewer must never ask a series of questions one after the other. This gives the appearance of grilling applicants and puts them on the spot. Thus, after asking a penetrating question, the interviewer must find other ways to encourage discussion before asking a second penetrating question. These other ways consist of facial expressions, verbal pats on the back, vocal intonations, and consciously designed pauses.

Although interviewers encourage applicants to talk spontaneously, every once in a while they stop them to keep them on the track or to probe more deeply for salient information. Then they immediately give them their head, encouraging them to carry on. In short, they consciously *pace* the interview in such a way that they get all the necessary information without *pressing* the applicant and without losing rapport.

EEO Considerations

1. With those minorities or women where rapport seems more difficult to establish—and with such nonminorities as well—do not control quite as strictly. Permit such candidates to talk freely, even if the discourse tends to ramble and to be descriptive in nature. Although this will result in "more chaff along with the wheat" and will take more time, it will nevertheless provide more clues to behavior than would have come to light in an interview that was more strictly controlled.

2. With applicants who are particularly sensitive about the possibility that they may not be hired, interviewers should be especially adroit in the manner in which they interrupt such applicants for purposes of control. The timing and lubrication that are a part of interruption must be handled with great care. A sensitive person who feels that he or she has been cut off may interpret the cause of the interruption as a function of race, sex, or a handicap rather than as a function of completing the interview on time.

PART 3

Interpreting Information Developed

8
Interpretation, An Introduction

Since securing information has such a direct bearing on the evaluation of the applicant's overall qualifications, discussion in previous chapters has already touched upon certain factors of interpretation. When, as in the case of securing and interpreting interview information, activities are performed simultaneously, it is somewhat difficult to discuss one activity without considering the other. In the next several chapters of this book, emphasis swings from securing information to interpretation of findings. Because of the interdependence of the two, however, no effort will be made to confine the discussion to interpretation alone. In fact, subsequent chapters will be concerned with the *specifics* of exploring and interpreting each major area of the interview. Chapter 9, devoted to interpretation of work-history information, will also include further suggestions for carrying out the work-history discussion. In like manner, succeeding chapters will deal with education, and present social adjustment.

Prior to any discussion of information obtained from the various interview areas, some consideration must be given to the interpretation process itself. In this present chapter we shall therefore discuss some general factors of interpretation. This material represents background information concerning the process of evaluation as a whole. These general factors must be kept in mind in evaluating all interview findings, regardless of the interview area from which such findings emerge.

Complexities of Interpretation

Evaluation of interview data represents an involved mental process. In the first place, interview data are not made up of hard, cold facts that can be reduced to any precise mathematical formula. For the most part, they are composed of clues that alert the interviewer to the possible existence of certain traits of personality and motivation. In the second place, the interview produces a large mass of information *only part of which is relevant in terms of interpretation*. As the discussion progresses, the interviewer must constantly separate the wheat from the chaff. In the third place, a given applicant's qualifications comprise a relatively large number of individual traits and abilities. Interview data must therefore be obtained and organized in such a way that there is sufficient supporting information for evaluating each of the requisite characteristics. It is not enough to know that the applicant has had sufficient technical training and experience; the interviewer must also decide the extent to which that applicant possesses such characteristics as honesty, willingness to work, ability to get along with others, emotional stability, self-confidence, and ability to plan and organize.

Despite the complexities of evaluation, experience has nevertheless shown that, within a few days, appropriately qualified individuals *can* be trained to interpret interview findings with a relatively high degree of accuracy.

First Considerations

Since there is no point in interpreting information which we do not believe or cannot take at face value, we must first try to determine whether or not an applicant is telling the truth and whether or not the individual's standards are unrealistically high or low. Although answers to these two questions may not be obtained until the interview is perhaps half over, it seems logical to treat these two factors here before getting involved with interpretation per se.

How to Determine if an Applicant Is Telling the Truth

There are at least three valid means of determining the extent to which an applicant may be telling the truth: *(1) internal consistency, (2) the amount of unfavorable information an applicant provides,* and *(3) an obvious tendency to exaggerate accomplishments.*

By "internal consistency," we mean consistency of information between the two major areas of the interview, work history and education. Hence, if an individual is immature, evidence of this should appear in *both* of these major areas. It would be most unlikely, for example, that an applicant would reflect a high degree of maturity as a part of her or his work history but a low degree of maturity with respect to education. If such a situation should occur, the interviewer should immediately suspect that the person might not be telling the truth. To be more specific, a male applicant, for example, might reflect immaturity by mentioning unsound reasons for leaving jobs, poorly thought-out vocational goals, or aspirations way out of line with his abilities. In order for the discussion of education to be internally consistent, this same applicant might be expected to reveal such clues to immaturity as (1) studying hard on only those courses which he liked, (2) rationalizing failures by blaming teachers or the school system, or (3) selecting a major course of study with no thought at all as to how that major might be used after getting out of school. It is when the data become *inconsistent* that the interviewer should begin to question the applicant's story. Thus, if the applicant cited above claimed that he (1) did his homework every single evening, (2) studied a lot harder on the courses that he did not like in order to get good grades, or (3) never cut any classes, the interviewer might begin to feel that he was telling us what he thought we wanted to hear rather than what actually happened.

When applicants appear to be on the level and provide a fair amount of unfavorable information along with the more favorable data, this can be regarded as firm evidence that they are telling the truth. If, for example, a female applicant admits that she was fired from a given job, that her attendance was not all that good, or that her typing speed is only 30 words a minute, the interviewer gets the feeling that she is telling us her life story just as it actually occurred. With such an applicant, therefore, considerable credence can be placed on statements about achievements.

Some applicants have a rather strong tendency to exaggerate their achievements, and this is quite easily picked up. In discussing outside interests, for example, a woman might claim that she reads four or five books a week. If that same woman had indicated a dislike of verbal subjects such as English, foreign languages, and history, her claim of reading four or five books a week would be internally inconsistent and probably an exaggeration. Likewise, a man who claims never to have spoken a word in anger strikes us as too good to be true and is probably exaggerating.

As we shall see later on in this chapter, however, applicants' characteristics should not be judged on single clues. Rather, the interviewer should try to develop a *series of clues* before making a judgment on a characteristic as important as honesty. How to develop this kind of documentation is the subject of the three chapters on interpretation.

It may seem to some that no applicant would be likely to provide some of the negative information indicated above, but that is simply not true. When interviewers are successful in developing rapport and getting spontaneous information, they find themselves regularly obtaining information of a negative character that is even surprising to them.

Unrealistic Personal Standards

·Even when the interviewer believes that applicants are telling the truth, not all their comments are taken at face value when it has been determined that their personal standards are unrealistically high or low. When asked to tell about his shortcomings, a male applicant, for example, might indicate that he "probably should work a little harder." This might seem completely inconsistent if the interviewer has already developed a considerable amount of hard data supporting a willingness to work very hard. The interviewer may then suspect that the applicant's professed shortcoming stems from his tendency to be a perfectionist and hence to feel that he never does anything as well as he should. In such cases, interviewers rely upon accumulated hard data (clues to willingness to work hard picked up through the discussion of work history and education) rather than upon applicants' statements regarding their shortcomings. Personal standards may also indicate seeming inconsistencies at the other end of the spectrum. When asked to indicate her strengths, a woman, for example, may claim to be a hard worker when all the hard data indicate that just the opposite may be the case. But the inconsistency here may be based upon *low personal standards* rather than upon dishonesty. Some people's standards are so low that it does not take much to satisfy them. Hence, they may think of themselves as hard workers when this is actually not the case at all.

Fortunately, the hard data (clues to behavior) usually turn out to be consistent with an applicant's own assessment of his or her abilities. Inconsistencies that are due to unrealistically high or low personal standards will not be frequent, but they should be identified as such when they do occur.

Process of Interpretation

As one might expect, it is easier to train interviewers to secure the necessary information than it is to train them to interpret the findings.

Since interpretation obviously involves a mental process, it requires a fair amount of analytical ability—ability not only to recognize clues to behavior but to catalog such clues in terms of assets and shortcomings. As the discussion progresses, the interviewer must constantly separate the wheat from the chaff, searching for clues to such characteristics as willingness to work, ability to get along with others, emotional maturity, and leadership potential.

Interpretation as an Ongoing Process

Interviewers who wait until the end of the interview to decide what they think of an applicant are hopelessly lost. The interpretation process, in fact, begins as soon as applicants enter the room and continues until they leave. Clues to behavior build throughout the interview so that an applicant's overall qualifications normally become quite evident by the time the interview has been concluded. Interviewers who do a good *ongoing* job of interpretation should know whether or not they want to hire the individual by the time that person leaves the room. In interviewing more and more people, interviewers build up a *frame of reference* which enables them to compare the qualifications of a given applicant with those of all the other people they have recently seen.

Interviewers Learn to Mask Their Reactions

As the applicant's story unfolds, interviewers mentally scrutinize each bit of information for possible clues to behavior. Yet they carry out this evaluation process in such a way that they completely mask their true reaction and hence do not give the applicant the slightest inkling of how they are interpreting a remark. To do otherwise might risk loss of rapport. An interviewer who registers surprise or disapproval as a result of uncovering unfavorable information frequently turns applicants off to the point where the interviewer never succeeds in getting them to open up again.

Cataloging Clues

As soon as an applicant enters the room, interviewers should begin to get impressions of that individual in terms of possible effectiveness in the job for which he or she is being considered. It may be noted, for example, that a candidate presents a nice appearance and has an appreciable amount of poise and presence—clues that may be cataloged mentally as factors in the person's possible effectiveness with people. As the interview progresses, the interviewer may become impressed with the complete candor with which the applicant discusses strengths and shortcomings and may catalog that as an indication of sincerity and maturity. (Individuals who know themselves in terms of their strengths and limitations are often more mature than their chronological age group.) Later on, the candidate may indicate that he or she often stays on after quitting time in order to get a job done or even comes in on a Saturday. The interviewer catalogs this, naturally, as a clue to conscientiousness and willingness to work. And so it goes throughout the interview. Each statement the applicant makes is carefully examined in terms of its implied as well as its obvious meaning. Resulting clues to behavior are then mentally cataloged as possible indications of such traits as initiative, perseverance, emotional adjustment, adaptability, and leadership potential.

Relevance of Applicant's Work History and Education

Interviewers look not only for clues to behavior but also for the extent to which an applicant's previous experience and training have provided adequate preparation for the position in question. If the job in question, for example, involves excessive detail, interviewers would be quick to note any previous detail-oriented experience and how the individual reacted to this. They know full well that individuals who have already experienced this kind of work know what they are getting into and adapt to it much more readily than someone without such experience.

Mentally Organize a List of Assets and Liabilities

As the discussion progresses, interviewers mentally compile a list of the applicant's strengths and shortcomings with respect to the job under consideration. Although their outward manner is permissive and disarming, they nevertheless evaluate analytically and critically everything an applicant has to say. As the interview progresses from work history to education and finally to outside interests, a general pattern of behavior normally begins to make itself evident. Thus, interviewers may get clue after clue attesting to a candidate's forcefulness, willingness to accept responsibility, and strong drive to get things done quickly. At the same time, since a high degree of strength in certain areas may be accompanied by concomitant shortcomings in other areas, interviewers may also pick up a series of clues indicating lack of tact, inflexibility, or even ruthlessness. As they catalog such clues, they find it increasingly possible to build a list of assets and liabilities. In fact, such a list of assets and liabilities should be so well documented by the end of the discussion that interviewers can write them down immediately after the applicant leaves the room. At that point, interviewers make the hiring decision on the basis of the extent to which the assets outweigh the liabilities or vice versa.

Searching for Clues to Mental Capacity

In addition to the search for personality traits and relevance of previous experience and training, interviewers also look for the *level of the applicant's basic abilities*. As noted in Chapter 3, aptitude tests can be of tremendous help in establishing the level of a candidate's mental, verbal, and numerical ability, clerical aptitude, and mechanical comprehension. However, such test results are not often available, and in such cases interviewers must do the best they can to establish ability levels on the basis of interviewer findings. Specific suggestions for accomplishing this task will be found in subsequent chapters. Suffice it to say here, though, that some of the best clues to mental ability will be found in such factors as (1) level of grades in terms of effort required to get those grades, (2) college board scores, and (3) an applicant's ability to respond to the more difficult depth questions.

What to Interpret

As indicated earlier, every interview results in *relevant* and *irrelevant* information. Actually, much of what the applicant may have to say is likely to be *descriptive*, providing little in the way of clues to behavior. Interviewers, of course, try to keep such information to a minimum, controlling the discussion so that applicants concentrate on *evaluative* data. Even so, a certain amount of descriptive information is certain to ensue. Interviewers naturally pay as little attention as possible to such irrelevant data, constantly identifying the important information and making their interpretations accordingly.

In general, the more relevant information is likely to be found in applicants' *attitudes* and *reactions*. Thus, interviewers learn much more about people as a result of their attitudes and reactions toward a given job than from a description of the job duties. Such attitudes and reactions often provide specific clues to such important factors as initiative, empathy, ability to organize, and self-confidence.

Since interviewers are also looking for the relevance of applicants' work experience and education in terms of the job for which they are being considered, interviewers must carry a mental picture of the job specifications into the discussion with them. When listening to the description of previous jobs, for example, the interviewer must be quick to notice any similarity between those jobs and the job for which the applicant is being considered. It must also be decided whether candidates are capable of performing the job in question with minimum orientation or whether a protracted training period will be necessary to bring them to a productive level. In like manner, the interviewer must evaluate candidates' education, deciding whether or not they have the kind and quality of technical training that will enable them to perform effectively.

How to Interpret

We have talked above about the importance of determining the *relevance* of an applicant's work history and education. This is a relatively simple task since one has only to compare what candidates have done in the past with what they may be expected to do on the job for which they are being considered. All that is required is an ability to get information and a clear picture of the demands of the job in question. Understanding and utilizing the process described below—the concept of *contrast*—will help immeasurably in carrying out this interpretative function.

Concept of Contrast

This process involves the continual contrasting of each aspect of an applicant's job and school history with the specifications of the job under consideration. In those areas where little or no contrast is involved—or where the difference is in a positive direction—no real adjustment problem exists. This of course represents a favorable finding. On the other hand, where the contrast is appreciable, candidates might be expected to experience a very real adjustment problem in acclimating to the new job situation. Although the difference may be insufficient to exclude applicants from further consideration, such a difference nevertheless represents an unfavorable factor.

Let us assume, for example, that a given job calls for work of a highly confining nature. Applicants who have done confining work as a part of their previous experience—and who have apparently been able to accept it quite readily as part of the job—might be expected to be able to adjust to the new job much more easily than applicants without such experience. With the former group the contrast would not appear to be very great, while with the latter group the contrast would in all likelihood be significant.

Another such unfavorable contrast would be found in applicants who are already earning more money on their present job than what they would be paid as a starting salary on the new job. They might express a willingness to take the new job at a lower salary because it may offer greater long-range opportunity. Once they have been on the job for a while, however, a certain amount of dissatisfaction is likely to develop. This dissatisfaction may be stimulated further by a spouse who finds it necessary to make ends meet on a smaller budget. Many such individuals decide that they can't wait for future salary increases and begin looking for another job. If, on the other hand, applicants are to be paid a starting salary in excess of their present earnings, they can be expected to be more satisfied with their new lot, other things being equal. This of course represents a difference, or contrast, in the positive direction and is evaluated by the interviewer as a *favorable factor*.

The kind of close supervision involved in previous jobs and in a proposed new assignment may also provide an unfavorable contrast. A secretary who has had previous experience running an office and taking care of much of the correspondence might become quickly dissatisfied in a new job where every single piece of correspondence was dictated and where everything was very closely supervised. When such individuals take new positions involving much closer supervision and much less opportunity to exercise their own initiative, they normally find adjustment somewhat difficult. The alert interviewer recognizes the potentially unfavorable contrast and adds this to the list of negative factors.

Interpretation by Direct Observation

One can make *some* valid judgments about people simply by observing them directly. Thus, interviewers find it quite easy to evaluate such obvious characteristics as appearance, poise, presence, grooming, and self-expression. They simply observe an applicant's outward behavior during the discussion and make their judgments on these characteristics accordingly.

It is even possible to learn something about personal forcefulness and tact by means of direct observation. For example, the interviewer might note that a given candidate's personality has considerable impact and that the individual is exceedingly forceful and dynamic in conversation.

Since personal forcefulness represents an element of leadership, the interviewer would be quick to note that as a favorable factor. However, that same individual may frequently interrupt an interviewer in the middle of a sentence or may talk disparagingly about certain minority groups. This kind of behavior obviously represents a lack of tact and social sensitivity.

It must be pointed out again, though, that interpretation by direct observation is limited to the more obvious or easy-to-evaluate characteristics. It is of very little use in determining the more important factors such as honesty, judgment, intelligence, and perseverance. Yet, interpretation by direct observations is the only means available to most untrained interviewers. This is why the interview has often fared so poorly when subjected to validation studies.

Interpretation by Inference

Since interpretation by direct observation represents a relatively limited device, what method do we use to evaluate the more important characteristics? We use a time-tested method called *interpretation by inference*. By definition, this means that we *infer* from a *series of clues* the extent to which an individual possesses a given trait or ability. The phrase "series of clues" in this definition is extremely important since it would be most unfair and inaccurate to base an evaluation on a single unfavorable situation. Even if a person admits to having been fired from a given job, that, in itself, would not represent an adequate basis for assuming the person was a troublemaker or a poor worker. It is conceivable, in fact, that the supervisor may have been at fault. But, if there are problems on other jobs, if the person talks disparagingly about coworkers, and if there were disciplinary problems in school, we can determine with some assurance that this individual is not able to get along with people very well. This assurance stems from the fact that we have developed a *series* of clues rather than based our evaluation on a single happenstance. And, because these clues have spanned two areas of the interview—work history and education—we have established a pattern of internal consistency. When an individual has any given trait in some abundance, clues to such a trait will not be limited to a single area of the interview. Rather, such clues will surface in both the work history and education.

In the effort to document a trait such as lack of mental toughness, clues to this shortcoming might surface in the work history as unwillingness to discuss a below-average performance appraisal even when the person felt that the rating was unfair or when that same individual admitted a reluctance to ask questions of an older, more experienced employee. Clues to lack of mental toughness might conceivably come to light in the educational area in the form of a confessed aversion to arguing the person's point of view with any of his or her teachers.

In evaluating older individuals, persons in their early forties for example, the interviewer must be very careful not to evaluate them in terms of *what they were like 15 or 20 years ago.* A young man, for example, in his early twenties may have been quite footloose and fancy-free, hopping from one job to another without any sense of direction at all, but that same individual may have settled down to the point that his history over the past 10 years or so may have been very stable. Hence, the evaluation is based on clues to behavior grounded in the person's more recent history.

We have indicated earlier that clues must be interpreted as soon as they become evident. This provides interviewers with a beginning or starting point on which they can build later on. Using such a clue as a *temporary* supposition, they mentally catalog it as a possible indication of a given trait. With this supposition as a foundation, they subsequently probe at appropriate intervals throughout the discussion for additional specific clues to support the supposition. An interviewer, for example, might obtain an early clue to immaturity, thus providing a temporary supposition; however, if no clues to immaturity become evident in a man's history over the 10 most recent years, the interviewer would have had to throw out the initial hypothesis. On the other hand, some people never seem to grow up. Evidence may show that job-hopping, chronic dissatisfaction with practically every job, and poor judgment are still deeply rooted in an individual's behavior. In such a case, there is ample evidence—in the form of many clues pointing in the same direction—to eliminate the candidate from further consideration.

For purposes of further illustration, let us assume that an applicant has expressed a strong dislike for detail in connection with a prior clerical job. The interviewer catalogs this appropriately and wisely decides to wait, listen, and not *prejudge*, at the same time, actively probing for further evidence, particularly in those areas which would be most likely to provide clues to a dislike of detail. Thus, when the applicant discusses a subsequent job as a computer programmer, the interviewer, knowing that this type of work involves a great amount of detail, will try to get further evidence of this trait by stimulating in the applicant a spontaneous recital of likes and dislikes in that job. If the individual does not mention attention to detail as either a like or a dislike, the interviewer may ask a question specifically about the applicant's feelings concerning the detail involved: "How did you feel about the detail involved in that job?" Later on, the interviewer may probe in like manner for the candidate's reaction to a detail-oriented subject in school such as mechanical drawing and toward the end of the discussion may try to get further confirmation of a possible dislike of and inability to carry out detailed work by bringing this up under self-evaluation as a possible shortcoming. Utilizing the *double-edged question,* the interviewer might say, "What about attention to detail? Do you have as much of this as you would like to have, or is this something that you could improve a little bit?" If, at that point, the applicant candidly admits to not handling detail well, the interviewer will have brought to light a serious shortcoming, *providing that the worker specifications indicate attention to detail as an important requisite.*

We therefore see that interpretation by inference goes on throughout the interview, the interviewer making tentative hypotheses and probing specifically for confirming evidence.

Hypotheses Based on Leads from Previous Selection Steps

Since the final interview is preceded by such employment steps as the application form, the preliminary interview, and the aptitude tests, it represents an ideal opportunity to follow up on some of the *leads* which may have emerged from some of those early steps. Such leads often give the interviewer a tremendous head start as far as the interpretive process is concerned. Even before the interview begins, for example, the interviewer may have a lead to possible lack of motivation. Let us assume that the tests of mental ability reflect a high level of intelligence. The interviewer will expect to see this reflected in above-average grades in school. If such does not turn out to be the case, the interviewer will immediately probe for reasons why, suspecting low-level application or disorganized study habits. Or, in another example, the preliminary interviewer may have noted a slight tendency to be evasive. With that lead in mind, the final interviewer will be immediately alerted for any signs of dishonesty. Thus, by studying information available to them before the interview, interviewers can frequently develop usable hypotheses which they carry into the discussion and seek to support or reject on the basis of the evidence presented. It should be emphasized, though, that a lead is just that and nothing more. If it cannot be supported by hard data, it must be discarded.

Trait Description

If we are to rate a given applicant on a series of traits, our understanding of the meaning of these traits must be as clear as possible. Unfortunately, psychologists themselves find it difficult to agree specifically on the definition of many traits of personality, motivation, and character. Hence, it is expected that many people will quarrel with the definitions listed below. At the same time, these definitions do provide a functional description of the trait and should therefore be of assistance to the employment interviewer.

Emotional maturity: the ability to behave as an adult, to take the bitter with the sweet, to face up to failure without rationalizing or passing the buck, to acquire self-insight, to establish reasonable vocational goals, and to exercise self-control.

Assertiveness: aggressiveness in social situations; impact of one's personality upon other people—not to be confused with drive to get a job done.

Tough-mindedness: willingness to make difficult decisions involving people for the good of the organization, to stand up for what one thinks is right and not to shrink from confrontations with others when necessary.

Social sensitivity: awareness of the reactions of others; judgment in social situations.

Conscientiousness: willingness to put in additional time and effort on a given task in order to complete it in accordance with one's personal standards.

Self-discipline: ability to carry out the less pleasant tasks without undue procrastination.

Initiative: self-starter; willingness to try new methods, provide one's own motivation without undue prompting from superiors.

Analytical capacity: ability to break down a given problem into its component parts in a logical, systematic manner.

Ability to plan and organize: ability to lay out a given task in logical sequence, approaching first things first in a systematic manner, planning future steps in such a way as to accomplish the whole task efficiently and thoroughly.

Critical thinking: ability to dig down deeply in order to get to the bottom of problems, to probe beneath the surface in order to test the findings in terms of one's own experience, hence not to take things at face value.

Self-confidence: willingness to take action based upon a realistic assessment of one's own abilities.

Emotional adjustment: ability to stand up under pressure, to take a reasonably cheerful outlook on life, to be at peace with oneself.

Team worker: willingness to do one's share of the work, ability to get along with other members of the team, willingness to subordinate one's ego to the extent that one does not try to become the "star" of the team or to claim too much credit for the joint accomplishment.

9
Interpreting Work History

In the previous chapter, we talked about general factors of interpretation—what the process involves and how to go about putting it into operation. In this chapter, we get down to *specifics*; we consider what the discussion of work history may reveal about an applicant's personality, motivation, and abilities. In addition to establishing the relevance of applicants' previous work experience in terms of the job for which they are being considered, we need to look specifically for clues to such factors as mental capacity (if tests are not available), honesty, adaptability, and other work-related personality traits.

We have mentioned earlier that this kind of interview differs from most interviews in the sense that an attempt should be made to *document* the findings with hard data. Instead of coming away from an interview with a hunch that a given individual may be a hard worker, data to support such a finding should be sought, in the form of such factors as long hours spent on a given job without complaint, substantial numbers of hours a week working on a part-time job while carrying a full academic load, or perseverance on a summer job involving hard manual work for the entire summer. In the attempts to get hard data, moreover, every effort should be made to *quantify* information—to get numbers. When a person works on a part-time job while attending school, for example, the number of hours worked per week should be established. It might be as few as 6 or 8 or as many as 25 to 30. By the same token, it is not enough for people to say that their attendance record was "good." Employees' ideas of good attendance can vary greatly. Quantification should be established by asking the number of days absent during the year.

Applicants' work history ordinarily represents a major portion of their life's experience and, as such, not only provides an indication of their ability to do a certain job in question but also supplies many clues as to *how* they will do it. The manner in which a person works is often the best single source of information concerning personality strengths and weaknesses. It is fitting, then, that applicants be encouraged to give a rather exhaustive account of their work background, particularly as it pertains to items listed under work experience on the Interview Guide.

In this chapter, we will offer suggestions for structuring discussion of the work history. This will be followed by an item-by-item discussion of factors listed under work experience on the Interview Guide (see Appendix 1).

How to Structure Discussion of Work History

The reader will recall that, in the effort to get applicants talking spontaneously, the discussion of all major areas of the interview begins with a comprehensive lead question. In launching the work history discussion, interviewers may use such a comprehensive question as, "*Suppose you start by telling me about your work experience, beginning with the first job and working up to the present. I would like to know how you got each job, what you did, your likes, dislikes, earnings, and so forth. Where do we start? Did you have any jobs while attending high school?*" In talking about various jobs, applicants will normally provide spontaneous information concerning many of the factors listed under work history on the Interview Guide. When they fail to provide such information—or if they do not discuss important factors in sufficient detail—interviewers should prompt them by adroitly worded follow-up questions and comments.

Remember, too, that the work history should be kept pure, in the sense that the interviewer encourages applicants to concentrate on *jobs*, without supplying much information about other interview areas. When applicants begin to ramble or to provide too much descriptive information, the interviewer controls the situation by adroitly interrupting them with a carefully timed compliment and bringing them back to the subject under discussion.

Military service should be discussed at the point at which it occurs chronologically in the individual's work history and should be treated just like any other important job. Thus, in the case of a man who went into the army after completing high school, we would discuss the jobs he had while in high school and then launch into a thorough discussion of his army experience. This would be followed by a discussion of jobs he may have had after getting out of the army. In order to avoid spending too much time on the military experience, take individuals quickly through their various assignments. Then ask about their overall likes and dislikes about the military experience as a whole, rather than getting reactions to every assignment. Look for relationships with superiors and associates, any leadership experience, and specific skills (and/or training) which may be relevant to the job for which they are being considered. Since the military experience often represents a period of appreciable individual growth and development, it is usually beneficial to ask a question such as, "In what ways do you think your military experience changed you? What specific traits or abilities do you think you developed during that time?"

A discussion of each of the factors listed under work history on the Interview Guide follows in this chapter. Each factor is treated in some detail, in terms of both how to get the information and how to interpret the resulting data.

Relevance of Prior Jobs

Other things being equal, job relevance plays an important part in deciding the extent to which applicants may be qualified for a given job. The fewer *adjustments and adaptations* individuals have to make in moving from previous jobs to a new job, the more likely they are to find the new job satisfying, and the more quickly they should be able to make a meaningful contribution. If, in undertaking a new assignment, individuals are asked to perform operations under environmental conditions they have grown used to on previous jobs, they usually find it possible to adapt to the new job quite comfortably and quickly. On the other hand, if everything is completely new to them, they often suffer a certain amount of "culture shock," in the sense that they find so many new things to learn and to get used to that they initially have great difficulty getting organized and concentrating on what is expected of them.

As an applicant relates her or his job history, the interviewer mentally checks this experience against job description and behavior specifications of the job under consideration. If the applicant has no specific job in mind the interviewer makes a mental comparison of the general similarity of the individual's work experience to the job description which that experience most closely approximates. Before the interview is terminated, both interviewer and interviewee must have agreed on the specific job for which the applicant seems best qualified.

Duties

As indicated previously, applicants should not be permitted to devote too much time to a description of job duties, particularly in the case of the initial jobs. When they get to their more important experiences, however, they should be encouraged to talk in some detail about what they actually did on these jobs. For the most part, interviewers do not expect applicants to have performed duties that are exactly the same as those they will be responsible for in a new job. Rather, they evaluate the general nature of candidates' experience, assuming that they should be able to carry out new duties that are generally similar to what they have done in the past. In hiring an engineer for the design of automatic-control systems for jet engines, it may not be absolutely necessary to find someone whose previous experience has been devoted to jet engines. If the candidate has successfully designed automatic-control systems for other highly technical power plants, such as those concerned with guided missiles or torpedoes, he or she should be able to assume design responsibilities on jet-engine control systems without too much orientation.

Information concerning the duties of the candidate's more important jobs also tells the interviewer about the degree of responsibility the candidate has assumed. Such responsibility may have been highly technical or it may have involved the supervision of other people. In either case, the interviewer needs to know the degree of responsibility assumed—the exact nature of the technical duties or the number of persons supervised. To get this information, the interviewer may have to interrupt the applicant's story from time to time, to get more specific information. As the candidate goes from one job to another, the interviewer has an opportunity to note the progress in assuming responsibility. Such progress—or the lack of it—may provide clues to the individual's general ability. Where considerable progress has been made, the interviewer will probe for the *why*—those specific traits and abilities that have been responsible for the individual's success. Where lack of progress is evident, the interviewer will be equally interested in trying to find the underlying reasons. In the latter case, particular note will be taken of any attempt on an applicant's part to rationalize failures, as a possible clue to immaturity.

In evaluating the degree of responsibility assumed in the course of military experience, the interviewer will be guided by the understanding that promotions frequently take place because the particular individual happened to be at the right place at the right time. In other military situations, the individual may have had little opportunity for promotion because she happened to find herself in a group where many of her associates had more experience and training in the particular specialty. At the same time, rapid promotion in the military establishment is normally based on ability and leadership qualifications. In such instances, the interviewer will naturally attempt to identify the particular factors responsible for the individual's success.

When interviewers encounter people who have made unusual progress, they should use the following question: "What traits do you think you demonstrated that caused your supervisors to move you ahead so rapidly?" This usually results in responses such as, "I worked very hard" or "I was very reliable; I never missed a day" or "I got along very well with people." It is a good idea to probe further here: "What other traits were responsible for your progress?"

Likes

Since attitudes and reactions to a particular job experience normally tell us much more about people than a recitation of job duties, a great deal of attention should be devoted to likes and dislikes. If candidates omit this from their discussion, they should be reminded by such a follow-up question as, "What were some of the things you liked best on that job?" Moreover, interviewers should not be satisfied with a single response. They should probe for additional likes.

Ideally, the most favorable situation develops when the applicants' likes on previous jobs correspond with important elements of the job for which they are being considered. If they have previously shown a liking for report writing, for example, they should find little difficulty adjusting to the report writing function on the job for which they are being evaluated. Or if they have shown a decided preference for jobs involving a considerable amount of contact with people, they should be able to adjust to the contact aspect of the new job with no great difficulty.

Likes on previous jobs can of course supply many clues to abilities, personality traits, and motivation. Someone who has shown a liking for responsibility—particularly where people are concerned—*may* have a certain degree of initiative and leadership ability. Someone who derives particular satisfaction from contacts with workers in the shop may possess a considerable amount of common touch. Since likes and abilities tend to be fairly highly correlated—in the sense that we tend to do best on those tasks we enjoy most—a liking for mathematics may indicate that the individual has a fair amount of aptitude for mathematically oriented work.

But likes are equally valuable in providing clues to possible shortcomings. The woman who liked a job because of its regular hours, frequent vacations, and lack of overtime work, may be the kind of person who does not like to extend herself by putting in extra effort on a job. If this can be supported by subsequent clues pointing in the same direction, the interviewer will have come up with an important finding concerning the woman's lack of motivation.

As indicated above, likes may provide clues to both assets and shortcomings. Someone who enjoyed a given job because she had a good deal of freedom may be saying that she is the kind of person who, on the one hand, likes responsibility but, on the other hand, tends to be overly independent. In response to such a finding, then, the interviewer would do some two-step probing in an effort to find out what there was about having a completely free hand that gave the individual so much satisfaction.

Things Found Less Satisfying

Having had a chance to discuss likes in considerable detail, the candidate is normally quite willing to talk about dislikes, particularly if good rapport has been established. At the same time, the interviewer should approach this subject adroitly by softening the follow-up question. Instead of asking about a person's dislikes, he should pose such a question as, *"What were some of the things you found less satisfying on that job?"* It is possible that an applicant may not have any actual job dislikes in a particular situation, but considered relatively there are always some aspects of a job that are less satisfying than others. In the event that the candidate is able to come up with very little in the way of things that were less appealing to her, the interviewer should stimulate the discussion by means of a laundry-list question. He can say, "What were some of the other things that were less appealing on that job—were they concerned with the earnings, the type of supervision you received, the amount of detail involved, or perhaps the lack of opportunity to use your own initiative?"

If the interviewer has previously formed an initial hypothesis about certain possible shortcomings, he will include pertinent items in the laundry-list question. Thus if he suspects laziness, he might include such an item as "and an overly demanding supervisor" in the laundry-list question as one of the possible job factors the individual may have found less satisfying. Remember, too, that probing for job dislikes often results in spontaneous information as to why the person eventually left the job. If such information can be obtained indirectly and spontaneously, the real truth of the matter is more likely to be elicited. The candidate may say, for example, "I just couldn't see eye to eye with my supervisor, and quite frankly that was why I left." In such a situation, the interviewer would naturally play this down and probe deeper by saying, "Some bosses are certainly very hard to get along with. What was your boss's particular problem?"

Information concerning job dissatisfactions can provide a wide variety of clues to the individual's possible shortcomings. He may admit, for example, that the mathematical-calculations aspect of his job represented a factor of dissatisfaction, and he may further disclose the fact that he does not consider himself particularly qualified in this area. The interviewer would then have a strong clue to lack of mathematical aptitude. If test scores are available and if they show below-average numerical ability, the interview finding in this case would confirm the results of the test. Another applicant may volunteer the information that she disliked being left on her own so much of the time without much direction from above. This might provide a clue to lack of confidence and a tendency to be dependent upon others. In another job situation, the candidate may reveal that the assignment was not sufficiently well structured. This may indicate a clue to the inability to plan and organize, as well as a possible lack of initiative. Still another may complain about the fact that he was required to juggle too many balls in the air at one time. Such a comment might point to the possible lack of flexibility and adaptability. Lack of general mental ability might be another possible interpretation. In any event, the interviewer carefully catalogues such clues and looks subsequently for supporting data.

Discussion of job dislikes can also reveal clues to assets. In fact, the very willingness to talk about dislikes frequently provides clues to honesty, sincerity, and self-confidence. In supplying negative information, the individual in a sense says, "This is the way I am constituted; if you don't have a place for me here, I am confident of my ability to locate something somewhere else." When an applicant discusses negative information candidly and objectively, the interviewer soon comes to the conclusion that she is getting the complete story, and she gives the person credit for being honest and sincere.

Conditioned to Work?

People who have become conditioned to hard work and long hours in the past can be expected to apply themselves with like diligence in the future. Particularly when they have found it necessary to extend themselves by working 60 or 70 hours a week or by going to school at night while carrying on a full-time job during the day, they normally develop a greater capacity for constructive effort than might otherwise have been the case. In contrast, when they are subsequently confronted with an 8-hour day, they find it quite possible to apply themselves vigorously throughout the 8-hour period without feeling unduly weary. A boy brought up on a farm often gets up at five o'clock, milks the cows before school, and does the chores at night after having studied all day. Having become accustomed to long hours, he normally finds it very easy to work hard in the shop for a normal 8-hour period, provided he can adjust to the confinement of indoor work. A young woman who works after school and during summers while going to high school and college normally develops work habits that stand her in good stead later on. On the other hand, the college graduate who has never worked at all may be expected to find adjustment to the first postcollege job somewhat difficult. Of course, such individuals should not be excluded from further consideration because of lack of any kind of work experience, but this should nevertheless be included in the overall evaluation as a possibly unfavorable factor.

As the applicant talks about working conditions on previous jobs, the interviewer should mentally compare such conditions with specifications of the job for which he is being evaluated. If the job requires working under pressure, for example, the interviewer will look specifically for any previous jobs carried out by the applicant where pressure was an important factor. In addition, she will try to get the subject's reaction to such pressure. If an individual found it hard to work under pressure and even includes this as a reason for leaving a particular job, his qualifications for the new job would be viewed with some question. Or, if the new job is fast-moving and requires quick changes of reference, the interviewer would look specifically for previous exposure of the applicant to situations of this kind. If he has enjoyed and been stimulated by such working conditions in the past, this would obviously represent a definite asset. Today, it becomes an increasingly important asset as companies restructure and assign employees to new responsibilities.

In an earlier chapter of this book, we discussed the value of not tipping one's hand—getting the information from the applicant before giving information about the job. This is especially true with respect to working conditions. If the individual really wants the proposed assignment, she will hardly be inclined to express dissatisfaction about certain job factors that she knows exist in the position for which she is applying.

Working conditions also include the degree of supervision to which individuals have become accustomed. Here again, using the job specifications as a base, the interviewer should try to determine the extent to which the type of supervision may be expected to represent an adjustment factor, in terms of the contrast between the degree of supervision to which applicants have become accustomed and the supervision they would encounter on the proposed assignment. People who have grown accustomed to relatively little supervision on past jobs—where they have ordered their own lives, laid out their own work, and made many of their own decisions—will ordinarily chafe under close supervision in a subsequent job situation. Obviously, they are not excluded from further consideration on this basis alone, but it nevertheless represents a negative factor. The type of supervision under which people worked in the past may provide clues to possible abilities and personality characteristics. If they have operated successfully without close supervision, for example, they may be the type of people who have a good bit of initiative and who have so much ability that their supervisors trust them to carry out day-to-day tasks without checking up on them very frequently. Moreover, natural leaders are normally people who like to work without close supervision. They enjoy the degree of responsibility that such a situation permits. And they derive satisfaction from an opportunity to exercise their own initiative.

Level of Earnings

Since information about earnings may represent a somewhat delicate subject in the case of some applicants, this question should be approached with considerable adroitness. In the first place, as noted earlier, interviewers should get candidates in the habit of talking about earnings by asking them to give this information on early jobs. Since few people object to talking about the salary they made on jobs some years ago, they willingly supply these facts. If, moreover, they are encouraged to give salary information on each job, they provide salary figures on their most recent experience pretty much as a matter of course. On the other hand, if interviewers wait for the most recent job experience before asking about earnings, applicants may try to fence with them. A question such as, "What happened to your earnings on that job in terms of starting and ending compensation?" usually proves quite efficient.

Pattern of earnings over the years represents one important criterion of the individual's job progress to date. In cases where the applicant's earnings have gone up rather quickly, it can usually be assumed that she is a person of some ability. In cases like this, the interviewer will want to probe for the reasons why the individual has done so well, since such probing may provide clues to her major assets. Again, the question, "What traits were you able to demonstrate that caused your supervisor to raise your salary so handsomely?" will often result in valuable information. On the other hand, earnings are not always a true reflection of ability. A man may have been in the right place at the right time, may have been given special treatment because his father was a partial owner of the company, or may have been successful in impressing his superiors on the basis of his persuasive personality rather than because of his real ability.

Just as a rapid rise in earnings normally points to the existence of assets, so does lack of salary progress frequently reflect a series of significant shortcomings. A woman in her middle thirties who has shown relatively little salary progress in the last 10 years is usually lacking in either ability, effectiveness of personality, or motivation. In probing for the reasons, however, the interviewer may find that the applicant has been confronted with circumstances somewhat beyond her control. He may find that the individual has been working in a relatively low-paying industry such as the utilities industry or that she has been reluctant to give up the security of that particular job because of the serious illness of a family member. In probing for the real reasons, the interviewer should obviously avoid such a direct question as, "How do you account for your failure to earn more money over the years?" Rather, he should approach this situation more indirectly, bringing up the question under the discussion of job dislikes. If the applicant does not mention salary as a factor of dissatisfaction, the interviewer can say, "How do you feel about your salary? Are you relatively satisfied with what you are making or do you think that your job merits somewhat more?" The subsequent response may indicate a number of interesting clues to behavior, including lack of salary aspirations, bitterness over lack of salary progress, rationalization of the situation, or general recognition of shortcomings and willingness to accept her lot in life.

In evaluating salary progress, one should keep the level of the individual's basic abilities in mind. If a person is bright mentally and has good general abilities, lack of salary aspirations may point to inadequate motivation. In the case of an individual who is somewhat limited intellectually but has nevertheless been moved along rapidly, subsequent frustration will almost certainly occur if and when such progress comes to a halt. Such a person has become accustomed to rapid promotion and hence expects this pattern to be maintained. In the case of the overachiever, the time will undoubtedly come when mental limitations will preclude further promotion, at which time the person will probably become a most unhappy individual. On the other hand, a mentally limited individual who has learned to accept such limitations and not to expect too much has usually attained an admirable degree of emotional maturity.

Performance Appraisal

As indicated in Chapter 1, many managers do an inadequate job of rating the performance of those reporting to them and an even poorer job of feeding back the results to the individuals involved. Even so, it is often fruitful to ask applicants about their performance appraisals on important jobs. After discussing duties, likes, dislikes and earnings, then, probe for appraisal results, first getting the over-all rating (excellent, above average, average or below average) and subsequently asking about strengths and indicated development needs.

Always ask about strengths first: "What were the traits or abilities your supervisor said that she liked about you?" Then: "What other traits did she like?" After you have been able to develop information about several strengths, switch to the discussion of development needs: "What traits or abilities did she think needed a little more development?" If, as in so many cases, the supervisor did not discuss any shortcomings say: "Well, what traits do *you* think you could have improved?"

Do not ask about performance appraisals on every single job or this will become redundant and will detract from the importance of the discussion of the overall strengths and development needs which takes place at the end of the work history. When a candidate has had a series of co-op experiences while attending college, for example, say: "What showed up on your performance appraisals as the traits that your various supervisors liked about you?" Then: "What traits did they think you needed to work on in order to develop yourself further?"

In most cases, the information gleaned from the discussion of performance appraisals tends to be quite consistent and provides interviewers with important findings concerning applicants' motivation, mental ability, and maturity. And this information also gives them a storehouse of data from which they can "prime the pump" in helping applicants subsequently to discuss their over-all strengths and shortcomings.

Reasons for Changing Jobs

This is one of the most delicate aspects of the interview, since many applicants are sensitive about their reasons for having left certain jobs. Therefore, we try to get this information spontaneously and indirectly by probing for job dislikes. If this fails, however, we have to approach the situation more directly with a softened follow-up question such as, "How did you happen to leave that job?" In posing this question, the interviewer should of course give particular attention to her facial expressions and vocal intonations, in order to give the appearance of seeming as disarming and permissive as possible. Even so, some applicants may not give the real reason why they left a certain job. Hence the interviewer must be alert for any indication of rationalization, since this type of response usually means that the individual is trying to hide the real reason by attempting to explain away the situation. If an interviewer is not convinced that a person is telling the truth, she certainly should not challenge him at this point. To do so would be to risk loss of rapport and subsequent lack of spontaneous discussion throughout the remainder of the interview. Rather, she should wait until the interview is nearly concluded—when there is little or nothing to lose. If she is still interested in the candidate's qualifications, she can reintroduce the subject by asking him more directly to elaborate upon his reasons for the job change in question.

When a candidate leaves a number of jobs to make a little more money on subsequent ones, she may represent the kind of person who has too strong an economic drive. Now strong desire to make money is a definite asset on some jobs—particularly those involving selling on a commission basis. The salesperson who wants to make a lot of money is usually one who will work harder to get it. At the same time, when the economic drive becomes too strong, the individual often develops into something of an opportunist. In other words, she will immediately jump into any new situation that pays her a little more. Such a person seldom develops strong loyalties. The interviewer has a right to say to himself, "Since this person has a habit of leaving each job whenever she gets a chance to make a little more money, I wonder how long we would be able to keep her happy here?"

When an applicant leaves a series of jobs because of dissatisfaction with job duties or working conditions, he may be the type of person who lacks perseverance and follow-through. Perhaps unable to take the bitter with the sweet, he "pulls up stakes" whenever he is confronted with anything really difficult or not to his liking. If such proves to be the case, a clear indication of immaturity will be apparent. When dissatisfaction appears to be chronic from job to job, the individual concerned may be poorly adjusted emotionally, in the sense that he may be somewhat bitter toward life and may take a negative attitude toward things in general.

If reactions to a series of jobs indicate friction with supervisors or coworkers, interviewers should look specifically for indications of quick temper, inflexibility, intolerance, oversensitivity, and immaturity. When they suspect the possible existence of some of these traits, they should use such a question as, "How did you feel about your relationships with your superiors and associates on that job? Were you completely satisfied with these relationships or, in retrospect, do you think that they could have been improved to some extent?"

Discussion of reasons for leaving jobs may provide clues to assets as well as liabilities. In talking about a previous job from which he had been fired, for example, an applicant may assume some of the blame, indicating that he was "just off base" in that situation. Such candor often reflects objectivity, honesty, and maturity.

In leaving certain job situations, moreover, the individual may demonstrate such positive factors as initiative and desire for further growth and development. If she has been in a dead-end situation with little opportunity for promotion, she certainly cannot be blamed for leaving it. If she is a person of considerable ability and leaves a given job to obtain broader experience and responsibility, this is again something that one should expect in any competent individual.

In discussing job changes, it is often helpful to explore how such changes came about. Did the candidate take the initiative herself? Did the suggestion come from her superiors? Or was she recruited for a better job by another company? The latter, incidentally, may tell something about her general reputation in her field.

Leadership Experience

Throughout the discussion of the work experience, interviewers should carefully note the frequency with which applicants have been promoted to supervisory responsibility, together with their reactions to such responsibility. If individuals have derived considerable satisfaction from this kind of experience, and if they have been asked frequently to take over the direction of others, they are quite probably people of some leadership ability. Certainly, a number of their previous superiors have thought so. Moreover, people who have led successfully in any situation have acquired skills in handling others that nothing but experience of this sort will provide.

In evaluating the possible effectiveness of an individual as a supervisor, look specifically for demonstrated ability to communicate, to plan and organize, to delegate important responsibilities to others, to be contagiously enthusiastic, to be fair, and to be sensitive to the feelings of others. It is equally important to find out whether the individual has shown a tendency to be autocratic or whether the candidate has been able to motivate other people to work because they like and respect him or her.

Number of Previous Jobs

In evaluating the applicant's work experience, interviewers should note among other things the frequency of job changes. Since many students in school do not get very much in the way of vocational guidance, it sometimes takes them a little while to find the right type of job once they have graduated. Hence, frequency of job change is not particularly unusual during late adolescence or in the early twenties. But if this pattern extends through the late twenties and thereafter, it can be assumed that such individuals may have some rather deep-seated problems. If they fail to stay with any of their jobs at least 3 years, they may very well be the kind of person who has not yet found him or herself, thus demonstrating immaturity. Many "job jumpers" lack self-discipline, perseverance, and follow-through. Some of them are opportunists and still others are not very stable emotionally.

A certain number of job changes over a period of some years is of course to be expected. Many people have good reasons for leaving one job to go to another—to increase their earnings, enhance their opportunities for promotion, and broaden their experience. In some occupations, such as advertising, moreover, rather frequent job change is considered something of a matter of course. An advertising agency may obtain a large account and hire as many as 30 or 40 additional people to handle this additional business. At the end of the year, the agency may lose the account and be forced to terminate a considerable number of its employees. Even so, such an organization can usually find a place for a new employee who has turned in an outstanding job performance.

Structuring Work History with Older Candidates

Candidates 35 or older have such a body of work experience that very early experience becomes less meaningful and too time-consuming to explore. Instead of asking such candidates to discuss every single job they had while attending high school and college, interviewers should say: "Did you have any jobs during high school or college that you believe appreciably stimulated your early growth and development?" If the response is affirmative, take the time to discover how that experience influenced development. Then proceed immediately to the first post-college position with the question: "How did you go about getting your first job after college?"

Since the last 10 years of an older person's work history are normally the most likely to yield clues to current behavior, pass rather quickly over the early post-college jobs concentrating primarily on *how the person got the job, how long he stayed, the beginning and ending earnings, and why he left.*

In the subsequent, more important positions, of course, take the time to explore duties, likes, dislikes, performance appraisals, and levels of responsibility. Since many older candidates will have had management experience, probe here for *management style*: "How would you describe your management style?" Then: "Do you think of yourself as a tough manager, an easy one or somewhere in between?" Such questions often supply clues to mental toughness, an extremely important requisite for effective management.

With older candidates, it is very important to check the more recent experience with the job description in order to determine the possible "fit." As pointed out earlier, some high-level candidates even negotiate the job description in order to bring the charter more in line with their own desires and expertise.

Achievements

Once interviewers have discussed the applicants' complete job history— from the first position to the most recent assignment—they should try to help individuals summarize *achievements*, in terms of abilities and personality traits, that have been brought to light as a result of their experience on various jobs. This is done by formally introducing the technique of *self-evaluation* for the first time in the interview. In order to accomplish this, use the question which appears on the Interview Guide. *"What did you learn about your strengths as a result of working on all of those jobs? Did you find, for example, that you worked harder than the average person, got along better with people, organized things better, gave more attention to detail—just what?"* It will be noted that the technique of self-evaluation is introduced by means of a laundry-list question. This is because most individuals will not have taken the time to analyze their strengths in terms of the abilities and personality traits interviewers are seeking to identify.

Helping Candidates Discuss Their Assets

Interviewers should ask individuals to discuss assets candidly, pointing out that they should do this objectively without any feeling that they are bragging. Immediately after each asset has been presented, moreover, interviewers should *lubricate the situation* by giving candidates a verbal pat on the back. If an individual indicates that he is a hard worker, for example, and if the interviewer has already seen abundant evidence of this trait, she might say, "I'm sure you are a very hard worker, and that's a wonderful asset to have!" On the other hand, if she has a question about the individual's motivation, she will simply nod her head, ask the applicant to indicate some of his other assets, and resolve to reintroduce the subject of hard work later on when talking about the individual's shortcomings.

Some candidates may find it difficult to list their real assets. In this case, interviewers should stimulate the discussion by pointing out one or two strengths he has already observed. Thus, he might say, "Well, I have observed that you seem to get along unusually well with people, and this of course is a tremendous asset in any job situation." After "priming the pump" with one or two such observations, the interviewer should pass the conversational ball back to the candidate, asking her to tell about some of her other strong points. If she seems to be unable to come up with any additional assets on her own, make use of the *calculated pause*, in this way giving her an opportunity to organize her thoughts. If, after 10 or 12 seconds, she is still unable to come up with anything, the interviewer should "take her off the hook" by introducing another asset which he has observed during the interview or which has come to light as a result of discussing performance appraisals on various jobs. In some cases, a considerable amount of "pump priming" may be necessary before the candidate begins to talk about some of her own strengths, but the interviewer should wait her out, using as much patience as he can muster.

The interviewer should not leave this important subject until he has developed a significant list of genuine assets, even if he has to interject a number of these himself. Once the applicant has been encouraged to think critically about her own strengths, she frequently warms to the task and generates a considerable amount of very useful information here. She may reveal, for example, that she gets along particularly well with people. And she may be able to document this by telling about the closeness of her relationships with certain individuals, pointing to correspondence and other contacts that she has had with those individuals since leaving the company, or by the fact that her friends surprised her with a dinner in her honor at the time she left. Or, she may list creative ability as an asset. In probing more deeply for evidence of such ability, the interviewer may find that the applicant has several patents to her credit and has published a series of articles in the technical journals. When such evidence is presented, the interviewer will of course want to know whether these patents and articles came as a result of the individual's single-handed achievement or whether other people were also involved. Since applicants are naturally interested in selling themselves, their stated achievements cannot always be taken at face value. This is why they should be encouraged to supply documentary evidence.

It is extremely important that the interviewer help the applicant develop a sizable list of assets, since this paves the way for a subsequent discussion of shortcomings. In other words, one cannot expect a person to discuss shortcomings at length if the applicant is not certain that the interviewer is well-acquainted with his or her strengths. When the list of strengths becomes sizable, many applicants become quite anxious to reveal some shortcomings in order to give the appearance of objectivity. More important still, in successfully developing a list of the candidate's achievements, the interviewer will have planted the seed of self-evaluation at this relatively early stage of the interview. And, as a consequence, the applicant may spontaneously volunteer further self-evaluative material during discussion of subsequent areas of the interview—education, and present social adjustment. It is for this reason that the technique of self-evaluation is introduced at this point of the interview.

Development Needs

Having had an opportunity to discuss his or her strengths at some length, an applicant normally finds it relatively easy to talk about some of the areas that need further development. However, since this represents the first real confrontation in terms of asking specifically about shortcomings, appropriate rationale must be provided. This subject can be introduced by the question that appears in the Interview Guide: *"Did you get any clues to your development needs as a result of working on those jobs? You know, we all have some shortcomings and, the person who can recognize them, can do something about them. Was there a need to acquire more self-confidence, more tact, more self-discipline—to become firmer with people—just what?"* This question and the one pertaining to achievement appearing on the Interview Guide should be committed to memory verbatim, in that way helping interviewers develop more facility during the interview.

Helping Applicants Discuss Their Shortcomings

In discussing an applicant's developmental needs, always use the word "shortcomings" rather than "weaknesses," "faults," or "liabilities." The latter three words carry the connotation that the trait may be so serious that very little can be done about it. The word "shortcomings," on the other hand, implies that the trait is just a little short of what it might desirably be and that hence the person may be able to improve upon it or eliminate it. In talking about shortcomings, moreover, refer frequently to the phrase "ways in which you can improve yourself." Thus, instead of saying, "What are some other shortcomings?" it is better to say, "What are some other ways in which you might improve yourself?"

Immediately after each shortcoming has been presented, the interviewer should "play it down," in much the same way that any other piece of unfavorable information is played down throughout the interview. When an individual admits, for example, the need to develop more self-confidence, the interviewer might say, "Well, confidence is a trait that a lot of people need to develop further. I'm sure your self-confidence will improve with more experience." When a person admits a shortcoming, such as lack of mental toughness, the interviewer should play this down by complimenting the individual for having recognized it and for facing up to it. Thus, the interviewer may say, "You deserve credit for being able to recognize this. And, because you have recognized it, you probably have already taken certain steps toward eliminating it."

When the applicant finds it difficult or seems reluctant to present any shortcomings, the interviewer may stimulate the discussion by the use of *double-edged questions*. If an interviewer has already noted that the applicant is quite lacking in self-discipline, for example, she may say, "What about self-discipline? Do you think you have as much of this as you would like to have, or does this represent an area in which you could improve to some extent?" Such a question makes it easy for a person to admit shortcomings. Again, if the interviewer has noticed a general tendency to be lazy, she might say, "What about work habits? Do you think that you usually work as hard as you should, or is this something that you could improve a little bit?"

For the most part, indicated shortcomings can be taken pretty much at face value. Seldom will one draw attention to shortcomings that do not really exist. At the same time, there is the occasional individual—one who is exceedingly insecure and tends to underestimate his or her abilities—who will bring up something as a shortcoming that is not a deficiency.

The interviewer's role in the self-evaluation discussion is a pivotal one. If he tries to stimulate the discussion by introducing assets or shortcomings that are not part of the applicant's makeup, the latter quickly loses respect for him. On the other hand, if he is able to introduce traits that go to the very heart of the individual's personality and motivational pattern, the latter gains appreciable respect for him.

The Value of the Self-evaluation Technique

As noted above, this technique can be of considerable value to both applicants and the interviewers. Applicants gain by getting a clearer picture of their strengths and developmental needs, thus acquiring greater insight. And interviewers gain because they are frequently able to get more documentary evidence concerning a given candidate's overall qualifications. The extent to which candidates benefit from insight resulting from self-evaluation will be discussed in Part 4 of this book in the chapter on feedback.

When interviewers are able to get applicants to agree with them on the presence or absence of certain traits, this obviously provides strong support for the original diagnosis. When, for example, an interviewer has seen several clues to insecurity throughout the interview, she waits expectantly for some indication of this in the candidate's self-evaluation. If lack of self-confidence is spontaneously admitted, or admitted as a result of probing with a double-edged question, the interviewer has of course developed further confirmation of her original hypothesis. And since the person is aware of this developmental need, he may be able to do something about improving himself in this respect.

Occasionally the applicant will mention a trait that may not have consciously crystallized in the interviewer's mind but for which he sees abundant evidence as soon as it is verbalized. In other words, he may have been only vaguely aware of the trait but, when the applicant mentions it specifically, he can immediately think of a number of clues that actually pointed in that direction. If the applicant had not mentioned this trait, the interviewer might not have factored it into his overall decision.

When the candidate mentions an asset or shortcoming for which the interviewer has seen no support, it is well to ask the individual to elaborate. Subsequent remarks may convince the interviewer that the applicant actually possesses the trait in question, thus bringing to light valuable information that might otherwise have been missed. To illustrate this point, let us assume that the individual mentions mental toughness as an asset. If the interviewer has seen little or no evidence of this, she might say, "What are some of the things you have done in the past that helped you reach this conclusion?" In the ensuing discussion, the candidate may point to a series of confrontations that had not previously come up in the conversation. After getting this additional information, the interviewer may be quite convinced that the individual really is tough-minded. In this instance, the self-evaluation technique operated as insurance against leaving out something that was really important. In trying to justify tough-mindedness as an asset, on the other hand, the individual's supporting reasons may be altogether superficial. In that case, of course, the interviewer would simply nod her head and ask for additional strong points, still not convinced that the person is in fact tough-minded.

In dealing with young applicants who have had limited work experience, do not confine the discussion of strengths and shortcomings to the work situation alone. Broaden the laundry-list question as follows: *"What did you learn about your strengths as a result of working on those jobs or as a result of any of your other life experiences?"*

Factors of Job Satisfaction

At this point, the interviewer has not only discussed the applicant's jobs but has tried to plant the seed of self-evaluation by asking for a summary of strengths and development needs of which the applicant has become aware while working on these various jobs. Hence, we can now give our attention to another very fruitful area—factors of job satisfaction. This subject can be introduced with the laundry-list question on the Interview Guide: *"What does a job have to have to give you satisfaction? Some people look for money, some look for security, some want to manage, some want to create—what is important to you?"* Again, the applicant's response to such a depth question may provide clues to analytical ability and intellectual depth. One individual may say, "Oh, I just want a job where I can be happy and make an honest living." Another person may reflect a great deal more discernment and intellectual depth by such a remark as: "In looking for a new job, I have given this subject a great deal of thought. I am looking primarily for an opportunity to grow and develop—to find the type of job that will provide the greatest challenge and do the most to bring out the best that is in me. Money is of course important, but I consider that secondary. Security probably ranks at the bottom of my list, since I feel that I can always make a living somewhere." A response such as this tells the interviewer a good bit about the individual's drives and aspirations, as well as about the quality of his or her thinking. The applicant's lack of emphasis on security, moreover, may provide a clue to his or her self-confidence.

If a candidate "blocks" at this point, give him a chance to organize his thinking by making use of the *calculated pause*. If he still seems to have a problem, repeat part of your laundry-list question or select one of the items and ask him rather directly how he feels about it. The interviewer may say, "Well, how do you feel about security, for example? Is this important to you or perhaps not so much so?"

Actually, discussion of job-satisfaction factors presents the interviewer with an excellent opportunity to obtain further confirmation of clues that have come to her attention earlier in the work discussion. For example, if she has noted some dislike for detail, she can include the phrase, "Some like detail while others do not," in her laundry-list question. If the applicant seizes upon this with the statement, "Well, for one thing, I certainly do not want to be involved with such detail; I prefer to delegate this to others," the interviewer is presented with additional confirmation of her original hypothesis. If the interviewer has a suspicion that the candidate may be lazy, she can include in her laundry-list question the phrase, "Some people want regular hours while others do not mind spending extra time on a job—time that may interfere with family life." Again, the applicant might say, "I believe that 7 or 8 hours a day on a job is enough for anybody. My family certainly comes first and I don't intend to let my job interfere." Such a statement may indicate that an individual is unwilling to make present sacrifices for future gains, and this also may provide an additional clue to lack of motivation.

When applicants appear to have answered the question on job satisfaction to the best of their ability, probe further, using some of the items in parenthesis at the end of this question on the Interview Guide. Say, for example: "What else should a job have to give you satisfaction? Should it be structured or unstructured?" Once that has been answered, say: "Should it be more theoretical or more practical?" After that response, say: "If you had a choice, would you prefer a job that had a fair amount of detail or one that did not have so much?" Responses to these questions can throw further light on factors that may enhance optimal placement.

Factors of job satisfaction represent a very fruitful area for discussion: hence, at least 4 or 5 minutes should be devoted to this subject. The interviewer should then mentally compare the applicant's expressed desires with the specifications of the position in question. If a woman is looking for a job that provides a great deal of mental challenge, for example, it would be a mistake to assign her to a job situation that made few mental demands. Or, if a man seems to be greatly interested in money, this factor should be considered in terms of the salary opportunities in the position for which he is being considered. Of course, many young people just out of school may not be able to come up with very much in the way of job-satisfaction factors. This obviously should not be held against them, since they have not been exposed to enough job situations to enable them to form any real conclusions as to the factors that give them greatest satisfaction.

Type of Job Desired

The work-history discussions should be concluded with a question concerning the kind of job for which the candidate is looking. In the case of older people with some years of specific experience in a given area, this question may be unnecessary, since they may be applying for a definite type of work. This may also be true in the case of people who were referred to the company as a result of a newspaper advertisement. On the other hand, many younger people have no specific job situation in mind. In fact, many such individuals are looking for some kind of guidance in this respect. If they do mention the kind of a job they think they would like to have, it is good to say, "What is there about that type of job that you think might interest you?" The ensuing discussion may reveal that the individual has some good and valid reasons for his or her choice and, in the case of a younger person, this would provide a definite clue to emotional maturity.

When a candidate says she really does not know what she wants, however, the interviewer should attempt to narrow the field for her to some extent. In the case of a recently graduated engineer, for example, he could say, "Well, do you think you might prefer basic research, development work, production, or technical service work?" The interviewer would then try to get the individual's reaction to these fields of work and compare these reactions with what he has already learned about the person as a result of the previous discussion. The individual frequently does a little self-evaluation at this point. She may say, for example: "Well, I certainly know that I don't want research or development work. I learned in school that I am no whiz on a purely technical assignment." If, on the basis of available test results and previous work-history discussion, the interviewer concurs with the candidate, he may then explore the individual's possible interest in production or technical service. Or, he may decide to postpone this particular discussion until the end of the interview—until he has learned more about the individual and thus has a better basis for helping her with her placement decision.

As the work-history discussion draws to a close, the interviewer mentally reflects on the candidate's total job accomplishment. Has the individual made normal progress in terms of salary? Has he acquired a solid background of experience in his specialty? Has he shown an ability to assume gradually increased responsibility? If the answer to any of these important questions is negative, the interviewer may begin to have a real reservation concerning the candidate's overall qualifications. In some cases, in fact, the situation may be so clear-cut that the interviewer can decide then and there not to hire the applicant. In such a situation, she would talk very briefly about the individual's educational background and then terminate the discussion. Not only is it unfair to waste the applicant's time but the interviewer also has to be economical with her own time.

EEO Considerations

1. Many members of minority groups need no special consideration with regard to the interpretation of work history. Their achievement speaks for itself.
2. There are other minority men and women whose work history does not appear very impressive because they have not yet been given an opportunity to demonstrate what they really can do. Since interviewers must try to *screen in* as many minorities as possible, it becomes their job to identify those individuals who have *potential* for greater achievement than their work history would seem to indicate. Some of the following areas may give evidence of such potential:
   a. Probe especially for how each job was obtained, as a possible indication of initiative.
   b. Look for any increased responsibility within a job, even though the job may have been rather routine. For example, the individual may have been promoted to lower levels of supervision such as crew leader, straw boss, or chief clerk.
   c. Give special attention to indications of hard work, such as extremely long hours or physically demanding job duties. A good question here: "To what extent was that job demanding physically?"
   d. Be quick to note significant progress from job to job in terms of more responsibility or higher pay, even though many of the jobs have been routine.
3. Do not be critical of job changes when the new jobs represent increasingly better situations. We cannot expect a person to stay with a low-level, uninteresting job for any great length of time if advancement is possible elsewhere. In probing for reasons for changing jobs, then, try to determine whether or not the new job really did represent a measurable improvement over the previous one or whether the hopping from job to job is because the person finds it difficult to stay put.
4. In discussing *factors of job satisfaction*, give favorable consideration to the man or woman who seems to have a genuine desire to make something better of himself or herself, even though the individual may not yet have been given much of an opportunity. People who have not given up hope deserve more consideration than those who have become cynical or pessimistic.

5. With all applicants, the discussion of *strengths* and *shortcomings* at the end of the work history will be difficult. Interviewers must therefore exercise great patience in developing this information. They will have to do more "pump priming" in terms of introducing strengths and shortcomings that they have observed during the interview. But, once applicants have acquired a definite understanding of what they are expected to do, they can often come up with very valuable information about themselves.

6. In thinking back over the entire work experience, try to determine whether the person was consistently overqualified for many of the jobs held, in the sense that the person could have handled more responsibility if given an opportunity. This situation would seem to indicate that, with special training, the applicant could take over the job under consideration even though his or her work experience may not have been relevant to the job in question.

10
Interpreting Education and Present Social Adjustment

Applicants for most higher-level jobs will usually be college graduates, and many will have gone to graduate school. These years represent a large segment of the individual's life, during which time he or she has had ample opportunity to develop a considerable number of assets or shortcomings. Interpretation of the educational history, then, is not only concerned with whether or not the individual has acquired sufficient training to carry out the job in question; it is also concerned with the evaluation of abilities, personality traits, and motivation.

In the case of younger applicants, in particular, the educational experience may represent the most important period of the individual's life and, as such, may provide the greatest source of clues to behavior. Although education does not represent quite such a dominant factor in the case of older applicants, it is nevertheless exceedingly important. The traits that individuals develop while in school often remain with them throughout life. Moreover, the discussion of educational history frequently provides additional confirming evidence of traits that had been tentatively identified during the discussion of work experience. Thus, applicants who tend to be lazy on the job can be better understood if it can also be determined that they did not apply themselves in school.

In this chapter, we shall discuss the items appearing under education and training in chronological order as they are listed in the Interview Guide. Each item will be discussed not only in terms of its contribution to the individual's educational attainment, but also in terms of possible reflection of clues to abilities and personality.

Structuring the Discussion of Education

Having completed the discussion of work history, the interviewer uses a comprehensive introductory question to launch the subject of education. In so doing, she tries to make the transition from the first interview area to the second in such a way that the discussion appears to be a *continuing conversation*, rather than a segmented one. Thus, the interviewer may preface her comprehensive introductory question by saying, "That gives me a very good picture of your work experience; now tell me something about your education and training." In the comprehensive introductory question the interviewer should point out that she would like to have the applicant talk about such factors as subject preferences, grades, and extracurricular activities. She should also indicate that she would like to have the individual start with a discussion of high school experience and go on from there to college. A comprehensive question such as the following should suffice: *"I would be interested in the subjects you liked best, those you did not like so well, the level of your grades, and your extracurricular activities. Start with high school and go on to college. What were your favorite subjects in high school?"*

Chronology is just as important here as it is in work history. The interviewer should get the full story of the candidate's high school experience before permitting her to talk very much about college. If the candidate jumps ahead by beginning to talk about college before she has given a complete picture of her activities in high school, the interviewer should control the situation by making a positive comment and redirecting her to the high school area. He might say, for example, "Being able to play on the college basketball team must have given you a great deal of satisfaction. By the way, were there any other extracurricular activities in high school?" In getting the high school story first, the interviewer can trace the candidate's progress through school. He may note, for example, that an individual did quite well with high school studies but experienced more difficulty as the subject matter became more difficult in college. Or he may observe that the candidate was a "big frog in a little puddle," while in high school but, up against sterner competition in college, was not able to compete successfully. Findings such as these represent probable indications of some limitations and help the interviewer to establish the level of the candidate's vocational ceiling.

In response to an adroitly worded comprehensive introductory question, the candidate will normally discuss much of her school experiences spontaneously. If she leaves out important items or does not discuss certain topics in sufficient detail, the interviewer will use appropriate follow-up questions in an effort to get the complete story. He will also use such questions to probe more deeply for the underlying implication of certain of the applicant's remarks. After the individual completes the discussion of her high school experience, the interviewer may wish to repeat part of his comprehensive introductory question by saying, "Suppose you tell me a little about college now—your subject preferences, grades, extracurricular activities, and the like."

Best and Poorest Subjects

If the candidate forgets to include subject preferences in his discussion, the interviewer should approach this by asking about his subject interests, particularly since interests tend to correlate with abilities. She can say very simply, "What were some of the subjects you enjoyed most in high school?" Preference for such highly verbal subjects as English, history, and languages normally reflects a certain amount of *verbal ability*, particularly when grades in such subjects have been relatively high. If verbal ability represents one of the job requirements, the interviewer will have identified strong clues to an important asset. Another applicant may reflect strong scientific interests through preferences for chemistry, biology, and physics. When such preferences are combined with interest and ability in mathematics, considerable aptitude for work of a technical nature would normally be indicated.

In discussing subject preferences in college, it is good to ask the individual whether she most enjoyed the more practical subjects or the more highly theoretical courses. In the case of an engineer, for example, the interviewer might say, "Did you enjoy the more practical courses such as unit operations and your laboratory work, or did you derive more satisfaction from the more highly theoretical courses such as thermodynamics?" Lack of interest and ability in the more theoretical courses may sometimes indicate certain mental limitations—inability to deal with things in the abstract. This interpretation of course becomes all the more valid if test results reflect mediocre mental equipment. Other things being equal, the more practically oriented engineers usually derive greatest satisfaction from assignments in production, applications engineering, or technical service. The more theoretically inclined technical people usually get more satisfaction from research and development.

Subject dislikes, introduced by such a question as, "What were some of the subjects you found less satisfying?" can provide important clues to shortcomings. When an applicant dislikes a subject, it may mean that he had either little aptitude for that subject or failed to study hard enough to awaken an interest in it. When a person does poorly in a subject that represents an important factor in the specifications of the job for which he is being considered, an important shortcoming will have been identified. And this is particularly true when poor performance in school is supported by low aptitude-test scores. Some knowledge of course content in various fields is also helpful to the interviewer. If a given individual has relatively poor mathematical ability, the interviewer can understand the candidate's difficulty with physical chemistry, since this course has a high mathematical content.

It is not enough to know that an applicant liked or disliked a certain subject. The interviewer should be interested in finding out *why*. She does this by using a typical "why" question, "What was there about physics that seemed to trouble you?" In response the applicant might say, "Oh, I was completely over my head in that subject. Even though I studied hard, I never could quite seem to understand the theoretical aspects." Or in response to a question as to why he did not like quantitative chemistry, an applicant might say, "That subject requires a good memory, and memory has never been one of my attributes." As indicated in an earlier chapter, probing for the *why* of subject preferences often provides clues to analytical ability and intellectual depth. Some people may be unable to give other than superficial reasons whereas others can provide detailed, analytical statements.

Grades

If the candidate does not specifically mention grades, the interviewer may say, "What about grades? Were they average, above average, or perhaps a little below average?" Note that such a question makes it relatively easier for the individual to admit grades that were below average. Where grades are indicated as above average, an attempt should be made to determine the applicant's actual ranking in the class. Was it upper half, upper third, upper quarter, or upper tenth? When a person provides a ranking, such as ninth in the class, he or she should be asked about the number in the class. It is conceivable that the entire class may have had no more than eleven or twelve students. On the other hand, a standing of ninth in a class of four hundred would represent a real achievement.

School achievement as reflected in grades may provide clues to *ability* and *motivation*. They also may reflect the academic standards of the school. In any case, the interviewer should make a real effort to identify the major factors responsible for grade level, whether such level is high or low.

If test scores are available, the interviewer's interpretation of grade level is greatly facilitated. A high score on a mental test means, among other things, that the individual has the ability to learn rapidly, absorbing new information quickly. Hence, such a person is expected to get good grades in school. When an individual with a high mental-test score indicates having made poor grades in school, the interviewer should be alerted to the possibility that the applicant did not work very hard. Further probing may indicate lack of perseverance, procrastination, or disorganized study habits. Moreover, many gifted people find it possible to get along in school without "cracking a book." Such people not only fail to make the best use of their abilities but may develop habits of superficiality, never learning to dig down to the bottom of things. If this habit persists through life, these individuals are seldom able to realize their full potential.

In the case of an applicant whose mental ability has been evaluated by the interviewer as "no better than average," high grades in school suggest at least three interpretive possibilities. First, there is the possibility that the person may not be telling the truth. Secondly, the academic standards of the school may have been relatively low. Or in the third place, the individual may have studied so hard that high grades were obtained despite somewhat limited mentality. If the latter proves to be the case, the individual is almost certainly hard-working, persevering, and highly motivated to succeed.

High grades in a school of established high academic standards normally provide clues to both intellect and motivation. This is particularly true, of course, where the applicant has selected a difficult major course of study. In the best schools, a student has to have a reasonable degree of mental ability and has to study reasonably hard in order to achieve a good academic record.

The Overachiever

People whose grades are better than might have been expected of them in the light of the level of their mental ability are known as overachievers. Many such people make high grades on the basis of sheer hard work rather than high native ability. Many naive interviewers assume that high grades reflect high intelligence but such an assumption cannot be made without knowing something about the academic standards of the schools attended and the effort involved in getting the grades.

Many overachievers end up with emotional problems. Some become victims of "burn-out." Others do very well so long as the demands of their jobs are such that they are able to compensate by means of hard work for what they lack in mental capacity. But, as they progress through various levels of management, the time will come when hard work alone will not be enough. Since they have never encountered this situation before, some of them become very frustrated and even "fall apart" emotionally. Hence, companies should make every effort to identify their overachievers and be very careful not to promote them beyond the level of their abilities.

College Boards

The majority of people today under the age of 25 or 26 will have taken SATs (Scholastic Aptitude Tests) during their senior year of high school, and most of these people will have been told their specific scores on these tests. Scores on these tests give us a good "fix" on the applicant's mental ability, verbal ability, and quantitative or numerical ability. High school seniors take two specific tests prepared by Educational Testing Service in Princeton, New Jersey—one test on verbal ability and another test on quantitative or numerical ability. A perfect score on each of these two tests is 800. The table below represents the distribution of scores on each of the two tests made by the high school senior population.

Test Score	Interpretation
700–800	Excellent
575–700	Above average
425–575	Average
300–425	Below average
Below 300	Poor

However, the above distribution includes a great many people who never made it to college. Hence, the distribution for college graduates—the population we are dealing with here as candidates for high-level jobs—is appreciably higher than that shown above.

In fact, today the colleges with the highest academic standards look for a combined score on these two tests of 1300 to 1350. This means that a boy might be taken into a good engineering school with a verbal score of 575 and a numerical score of 725, since the engineering course content places greater demand on mathematical aptitude. Or, a girl with a score of 750 on verbal ability might be accepted into a top school of journalism even though her math score was no more than 550.

Even the less-prestigious schools look for a minimum combined score on the SATs of at least 1000. Hence, a score of less than 500 on either the verbal or the math test reflects a relatively low aptitude for a person who has graduated from college. And, of course, the higher the score, the better the aptitude.

As noted above, most young people will have been told their college board scores and will remember them because of their importance in getting into the college of their choice. Yet, some of them may be reluctant to disclose their scores, particularly if they are not especially good. As a result, they may simply say they have forgotten the scores. Failure to reveal SAT scores should not be regarded as a clue to dishonesty. An individual has a right to withhold this information if he or she so desires.

In approaching this question, the interviewer *assumes consent* with such a direct question as, "What were your college board scores?" Note that she does not say, "Do you remember your college board scores?" or "Did you take the college board examinations?" Applicants are much more likely to respond to a direct, definitive question here since the interviewer does not make it easy for them to "get off the hook." If they profess not to remember their scores, the interviewer can say, "Well, were they in the 500s, 600s, or 700s?" Or she may say, "Did you do better on the verbal or the mathematical test?"

It has been the author's experience that most younger people will respond to the question on college board scores, particularly if good rapport has been established and maintained. The resulting information—providing you feel that you can believe the individual—can be unusually helpful, particularly if it is consistent with clues to intelligence and aptitudes which have come to light previously. Of course, some applicants may not remember their SAT scores correctly or may even lie about them. Hence, if the reported scores do not seem consistent with other clues to aptitudes, they should be disregarded.

The tests are normally taken in the junior year of high school for practice and taken again in the senior year. The latter represents the official score and is often appreciably better than the score achieved during the junior year. Hence, the interviewer must make certain that the scores the person provides resulted from tests taken during the senior year.

Since these tests are taken during the high school experience, the subject of college boards should be introduced during the discussion of high school, immediately after getting the individual's high school grades and class standing, as indicated on the Interview Guide.

Extracurricular Activities

The degree to which individuals have participated in extracurricular affairs may provide many important clues to personality traits. If little or no participation has taken place, individuals may have a tendency to be shy, self-conscious, inhibited, and introverted. In fact, they may freely admit that they tended to be "backward" and retiring at that stage of their lives. Of course, such people may have changed materially over the years, but the chances are very good that certain vestiges of these shortcomings may remain today. On the other hand, people may say that they did not participate in student activities because they did not care very much for the type of classmates with whom they were associated. Such a remark should prompt the interviewer to get further elaboration as a possible indication of snobbishness, intolerance, or a "sour grapes" attitude. The latter in particular may indicate some lack of emotional adjustment. Obviously, still other people fail to participate in student activities because of lack of motivation. They are content with the social relationships they develop on the outside. Finally, there is the "bookworm" or "grind." People of this type devote all their energy to getting top grades. As a result, they often graduate with honors but fail to achieve the social development acquired by the average college graduate. People who fall into this category are often the first to admit later in life how they failed to get much out of college. Since many jobs require a fair amount of social facility, such people often find themselves inadequately equipped to deal with others.

Those who do participate in extracurricular activities, however, often develop appreciably on the social side during their four years of school. In dealing with others of their own age, they frequently become more sociable, develop more tact, become more aggressive, and acquire traits of leadership. A girl elected president of her sorority, for example, is confronted with responsibilities that are entirely new to her. She is naturally anxious to show up well in the eyes of other members of the group and therefore takes particular pains to do the best job she can. In the course of shouldering these responsibilities, she often matures perceptibly, acquiring new poise, learning how to handle the more difficult people, and developing the kind of infectious enthusiasm that sparks an organization.

Participation in athletics—contact sports in particular—often fosters the development of competitive spirit, cooperation, and ability to serve as an effective member of a team. One who has a tendency to "hog the show" is frequently batted down rather quickly by teammates.

People who reach college at a younger age than their classmates often experience problems of adjustment. Such people often have difficulty gaining acceptance on the part of their older associates. Older students frequently have a tendency to "write them off," taking the view that they are not old enough to appreciate their thinking or to engage in their activities. Inability to compete successfully with one's contemporaries in college—either academically or socially—can have a marked effect on the individual's behavior. Some may develop feelings of inferiority that remain throughout life. If this turns out to be the case, they may have a tendency to underestimate their real abilities and may lack the confidence necessary to achieve up to their potential.

Effort

This subject should be introduced after the discussion of extracurricular activities (see Interview Guide), so that applicants will be not quite so likely to relate effort to grades. In other words, first talk about all the academic factors such as subject preferences, grades, and college boards before the discussion of extracurricular activities. Only after the latter have been thoroughly explored is the question of effort brought up. This should be introduced with the question that appears on the Interview Guide: "*How conscientious a student were you? Did you work about as hard as the average person, a little harder, or perhaps not quite so hard?*" If an individual seems to have difficulty with this question, help him or her to become more definitive: "Well, how many hours a day did you study on the average and what time did you normally get to bed at night?"

The amount of effort expended in order to get grades—a topic almost completely disregarded by most untrained interviewers—can often provide one of the most important keys to the assessment of intellect and motivation. If a candidate obtained good grades in a school with high academic standards without working unduly hard, possession of good mental ability can be assumed. On the other hand, if no better-than-average grades were obtained in a school with questionable academic standards despite unusual effort, there would seem to be some question about the level of mental ability. The latter individual, however, can be given credit for strong motivation. It is not unusual for such a person to say, "I really had to work for everything I got. I certainly burned a lot of midnight oil. In fact, I used to be envious of my roommate who was always able to get things twice as easily as I could."

When interpreting grades in terms of the amount of effort expended, it is also necessary to factor in the amount of time spent on extracurricular activities as well as time spent on part-time jobs. People with average grades in a good school who have devoted a great deal of time to student activities or to financing their own education of course deserve credit for their over-all accomplishments. Such people often develop social skills and work habits that stand them in good stead later in life. Moreover, people who crowd in a great many activities, do a considerable amount of part-time work, and also manage to make good grades are usually the kind of people who have learned to organize their time effectively. Normally, they work on a specific schedule and do a considerable amount of planning.

Special Achievements

Interviewers should be alert to the possibility that certain individuals may have attained achievements beyond those of most of their classmates, and such achievements may provide additional clues to mental ability, specific aptitudes, and leadership strength. Some individuals are basically modest and may not reveal this type of information unless they are specifically asked to do so. Hence, when a liberal arts student indicates that she made top grades in college, the interviewer should ask her if she made Phi Beta Kappa. A top technical student should similarly be asked if he achieved any academic honors, such as Tau Beta Pi or Sigma Xi. People achieving such honors are normally those who possess both high mental ability and strong motivation.

If asked about special achievements in high school, an applicant may say that she won the mathematics prize, the physics prize, or the oratorical contest, thus revealing the possible existence of special aptitudes. Likewise, it is good to ask an athlete if he was ever elected captain of a team. Again, responsibility of this kind fosters the development of leadership traits. In the case of persons elected to the student government or to the presidency of the student body, the interviewer has a right to assume that such individuals were popular with their contemporaries and probably possessed some degree of leadership ability. Of course, school politics are responsible for the fact that some people are elected to class offices, but the people involved usually display some traits that set them apart from the crowd. At the very least, they are ordinarily liked by others, have a genuine interest in people, and have developed an ability to get along amicably with people on all levels.

In the development of education information, interviewers should make certain that they get all the information about high school (subject preferences, grades, extracurricular activities, and effort) before permitting applicants to discuss their college experiences. The questions on the Interview Guide should be repeated for the college experience in the same indicated chronological order.

Training Beyond the Undergraduate Level

Where the application blank indicates graduate training, interviewers explore this area immediately after getting the complete description of the college experience. Even in the case of those who do not have graduate training it is good to ask, "Did you ever give any thought to going to graduate school?" A question such as this frequently provides clues to the strength of the individual's theoretical drive. A person may say, for example, "I had enough of studying in college; I'm not the academic type, you know. As soon as I finished college I wanted to do something practical where I could earn some money."

Except for the fact that they usually do not ask about extracurricular activities, interviewers explore graduate training in much the same way that they carried out the college discussion, concentrating on subject preferences, grades, amount of effort involved, and any special achievements. In some graduate schools, grades are either satisfactory or unsatisfactory, but other schools give letter grades, insisting that courses counted for graduate credit must be at a B level or better. In such a case, it is interesting to learn whether the graduate student obtained mostly B's and a few A's or made practically a straight A record.

Special attention should be devoted to the individual's thesis or dissertation. Even though the applicant's field may not be very familiar to the interviewer, the latter can still ask the individual about the problems she encountered and how she went about solving such problems. Evidences of creative ability may be revealed here, particularly in cases where the candidate solved most of her own problems rather than relying upon her sponsors. It is also good to ask about the extent to which the research findings may be expected to make a contribution to the field. In some cases, individuals publish articles in technical journals even before they are awarded their degree. In evaluating graduate training, again consider the academic standards of the school. A Ph.D. from some schools means a great deal more than it does from others.

Consideration of postgraduate training should not be confined to formal courses taken with a view to getting a master's or doctoral degree.

Many people take special courses of one kind or another, including extension work, correspondence courses, and company-sponsored courses. Moreover, many such courses are taken at night, after putting in a full day on the job. Such attempts to improve oneself frequently provide clues to perseverance, aspiration, and energy level. In going to school at night individuals often extend their capacity for constructive effort. Many courses taken in the evening also equip people to turn in a better performance on their jobs.

After-hours courses may also reflect an individual's attempt to broaden his horizons. Sensing a lack of cultural background, he may take courses in history, art appreciation, or government. In a sense then, the selection of evening courses may tell as much about a person as the kind of elective courses selected in college.

How Was Education Financed?

The interviewer will have acquired much of this information as a result of having discussed the applicant's early jobs under work history. But it is good to reconsider such information mentally while discussing the applicant's educational background. As indicated above, awareness of the fact that applicants worked their way through school may cast a different light on the kind of grades they received or on the extent of their participation in extracurricular activities. Individuals who have to work their way through school by carrying out part-time jobs frequently develop greater maturity and motivation than people who did not have to earn any of their college expenses. When individuals help finance their own education, they usually appreciate it all the more and try to get the most out of it. In the course of this experience, they frequently develop sound work habits, perseverance, and resourcefulness. On the other hand, people whose parents pay for their entire education may become accustomed to having things too easy. In fact, they may suffer a rude shock when they do finally get out into the world and find it necessary to earn their own living. Certainly in those cases adjustment to industry will be more difficult than for people who have already learned to earn their own way.

Many people will say that if they had it to do over again they would borrow money rather than work so hard while going to college. They seem to feel that they missed a great deal by not being able to participate in extracurricular activities, for example. All things considered, the greatest overall development probably comes to the student who tries to maintain some kind of balance with respect to academic work, extracurricular activities, and part-time jobs. Too much concentration on any one of the three at the expense of the others usually has some retarding effect on the overall growth of the individual.

When the interviewer concludes the discussion of education, the entire experience is mentally evaluated in terms of the extent to which it has equipped the person to handle the job under consideration. In making this evaluation, formal courses in high school and college, training acquired while in military service, special company-sponsored courses, extension work, and correspondence courses are of course all included. Then the interviewer considers whether or not the applicant has the specialized training that the job requires, whether the applicant has developed the necessary skills, and, equally important, whether or not the applicant has developed the kind of thinking demanded for the job in question. Many job descriptions indicate simply that the incumbent should be a college graduate. This usually implies a certain degree of cultural background, the ability to think logically and to reason from cause to effect, and the ability to get along successfully with other people on the college level.

In evaluating the factors mentioned above, the interviewer naturally takes into consideration all major achievements such as grades, participation in sports, membership in clubs, offices held, and any special effort involved in financing education. How much the individual benefited from the educational experience is also considered. Did the applicant look for the easiest way out by selecting the easiest possible major course of study and by taking snap courses as electives? Or was a reasonably difficult major course of study and electives undertaken, designed to develop a broad cultural background? Is there any indication that the individual became so interested that additional unrequired reading was done? Was any really significant research work accomplished in connection with graduate studies? Answers to questions such as these help to cast the educational experience in its true perspective.

Obviously, too, the interviewer will evaluate the educational history in terms of resulting clues to abilities, personality traits, and motivation. Particular interest should be paid to those clues that supply further confirming evidence to support interpretive hypotheses which were established in the discussion of the applicant's work experience. It is to be expected, in addition, that the interviewer will have picked up some new clues to behavior that did not come to light during the earlier discussion. For the most part, these new clues will have added to the understanding of the candidate. At the same time, some of the newer clues again provide only tentative hypotheses. For example, the interviewer may have noted that the individual's extracurricular activities in school were confined to such "loner" activities as chess, hiking, and coin collecting. Suspecting that the individual may possibly be introverted, the interviewer will look for further confirming evidence in subsequent areas of the interview and will probe specifically for the possible existence of such traits as oversensitivity, lack of confidence, lack of tough-mindedness, and the like.

Finally, the interviewer must take the long view with respect to traits that the candidate developed while in school. In the case of older people it is probable that they have grown and developed considerably since school days. For example, they may have been quite immature as students but may have caught up with their chronological age group in this respect long since. The simple fact of not working hard while in high school and college need not mean that such candidates do not work hard today. Experience has nevertheless shown that people are seldom able to "change their spots" entirely as they grow older. In other words, if their performance in school reflected serious, deep-seated shortcomings, there is a good chance that vestiges of these shortcomings still remain with them as part of their makeup today.

Structuring Education with Older Candidates

In working with the Manager of Human Resources of a multi-billion dollar organization, the author was told that the individual needed particular help with the assessment of mental ability in higher-level candidates. The manager was told that many valid clues to intellect naturally flow from the discussion of education. He responded: "I never talk about education with highly placed managers in their forties or fifties; I never thought that they would be willing or interested in talking about school." But, after observing a demonstration interview that included education with a top ranked candidate, the Human Resource Manager began to change his mind. And, when he, himself, included education with a similar candidate, he became completely convinced that he had been omitting a valuable part of the interview, one that actually did indeed provide many good clues to intellect.

Now many people in their forties or fifties may feel initially that their high school experience has had little relevance in terms of their current job qualifications. Hence, we do not use the same *education lead question* with people of that age. Rather, as we complete the discussion of work experience, we say: "Let's talk briefly about your educational background. *Did you have any experiences in high school that contributed materially to your development?*" Interviewers will discover that this is a great question since it stimulates most older candidates to launch into a meaningful discussion of the high school experience, a discussion that often includes grades, subject preferences, and extracurricular activities. However, the high school experience should be passed over rather quickly, reserving most of the time allocated to education for talking about college.

After spending a few minutes highlighting the high spots of high school, most older applicants are quite prepared to discuss college. Use the question: "Let's talk about college now—your subject preferences, grades, extracurricular activities, and your achievements." At this point, interviewers should refer to the Interview Guide and explore each item in the indicated chronological order, in much the same way they carry out this discussion with younger applicants.

Present Social Adjustment

After completing the discussion of applicants' education, interviewers begin to explore current social adjustment. As will be noted below, outside interests and hobbies often help to determine the extent to which applicants are reasonably well-adjusted socially. As in the case of all the other interview areas, this discussion can also provide many clues to other traits and abilities. In particular, the resulting information often brings into focus such factors as sociability, intellectual breadth, and intellectual depth. Obviously, discussion in this area is usually less significant in the case of young men and women just out of college than with somewhat older people. In talking with young people about their extracurricular activities in college, interviewers will already have learned a great deal about their social adjustment.

Interviewers lead applicants into this area by means of a simple question concerning interests and hobbies. Such a question as, *"Well, now, what are some of the things that you like to do for fun and recreation outside of work?"* will usually launch this discussion very effectively. And much of the information developed in this area may provide confirming evidence of clues to behavior developed earlier in the interview.

Sports

Since the United States is very sports-conscious, many applicants will be found to participate in such sports as golf, tennis, handball, racquetball, and softball. Many others will jog several miles every day. Participation in sports obviously represents an asset, since most sports participants try to keep in good shape physically. A healthy person may have fewer absences from work and may be able to devote more energy to the job. Sports activity also provides clues to energy level. People who are able to engage in sports that are physically demanding, after working a full day on their jobs, certainly have a high level of energy.

A discussion of sports may also provide an indication of an individual's competitive spirit. A finding of this sort is meaningful because a competitive spirit represents an important aspect of leadership.

It is important to note whether sports tend to be carried out alone or at best with one other person, such as backpacking, jogging, weight lifting, and the like. Individuals who tend to devote themselves exclusively to these kinds of "loner" activities, often have an inclination to be shy and somewhat introverted. Because such activities, moreover, do not give them much *practice* relating to others, individuals whose interests are limited to such pursuits are often lacking in poise and social facility. At the other end of the spectrum, individuals who participate frequently in team sports get a greater opportunity to sharpen their social skills and to learn what adjustments have to be made in performing as a member of a team.

It should be pointed out here, though, that introversion is not necessarily a shortcoming. In fact, introversion represents an asset in such detail-oriented jobs as accounting, computer programming, or laboratory research, where the confining nature of the work would make adjustment very difficult for a relatively extroverted person.

Community Involvement

As in the case of sports, community involvement also offers an opportunity for practice in social situations. Activities associated with a church, local government, or various community clubs, not only provide practice in getting along with people, but may very well offer opportunities for leadership. Such activities, moreover, often reflect the type of person who takes their community responsibilities seriously and cares enough to get involved. More often than not, such people reflect the attributes of a solid citizen and tend to be people of good character.

Interviewers should give particular attention to the extent to which women returning to the work force have participated in community activities. Because such women have often spent several years at home raising their children, they often have relatively little relevant work experience. Many such women are extremely talented and these talents often show up in their participation in community affairs. Some women acquire valuable experience heading fund drives or serving as an important officer in various clubs. Many such responsibilities require a good level of intelligence, judgment, the ability to plan and organize, and the ability to persuade others to their point of view.

Reading

Here, as in all other areas of the interview, every effort should be made not to put words in an applicant's mouth. Such a leading question as, "Do you enjoy reading?" or "Do you read much?" pushes the applicant to say "Yes." On the other hand, an open-ended question such as, *"What about reading? Do you have any opportunity at all to read or do other activities leave little time for this?"* sets the stage for an objective response. In response to such a question, applicants do not feel embarrassed to admit that they do not read very much.

The extent to which people read provides excellent clues to intellectual depth and breadth, particularly if the reading ranges over a number of areas and includes some books of a more serious nature, such as biographies and philosophy. As soon as an applicant professes an interest in reading, then, interviewers should ask about the kind of books he or she likes to read as well as the number of books the individual reads per month. Remember, we make every possible attempt to *quantify* information. Some people may profess to be avid readers but when asked to tell how many books they read per month they may reply "Oh, at least one book every month." Such a person would not qualify as an avid reader in the minds of most interviewers.

In asking about kinds of books read, it is also interesting to note whether or not an individual's reading habits reflect unusual intellectual curiosity. This may represent an important clue, since people with a high degree of intellectual curiosity are more likely to be creative.

Experience has shown that brighter people tend to read more than people with no more than average intellect. Thus, if interviewers have picked up a number of earlier clues to high-level mental equipment, they will find additional confirming evidence of this ability in people who do a considerable amount of reading. This is not to say that all bright people read. In particular, engineers and other technically oriented people often concentrate so much on technical subjects in college that they have little time for the humanities. As a consequence, many such technical people have not had a real opportunity to develop good reading habits. At the same time, it should be a matter of interest to the interviewer as to whether or not technical people try to keep abreast of new developments in their fields by reading the various journals.

Interest In the Arts

An appreciation of music, painting, dance, the theater, etc. may reflect breadth as well as a good cultural background. And people with a good cultural background bring another dimension to the decision-making process. In sharp contrast to those who have difficulty "seeing the forest through the trees," people with good cultural backgrounds often find it possible to put things in proper perspective. In view of the long hours that many top-level managers spend on the job, it is often surprising to find how many of them *do* have an appreciation of the arts.

In discussing interest in the arts, interviewers should not be satisfied with such a comment as: "Oh, I like music very much." Rather, they should probe for the type of music enjoyed as well as the individual's favorite composer. Such probing often reveals whether artistic interest are superficial or quite deep-seated.

Energy Level

High energy level, vigor, and stamina, obviously represent extremely important assets. In fact, few people attain genuinely high vocational achievement unless they possess these important qualities in some abundance. Given a reasonable degree of intellect, educational training, and personality effectiveness, the degree of energy and stamina a person possesses may account in large part for his or her ability to win promotions over associates.

By the time interviewers have reached this stage of the discussion, they will, of course, have acquired numerous clues to individuals' energy level and stamina. If interviewers are not certain of an applicant's amount of energy at this stage of an interview, they may ask specifically about this by saying, *"How would you describe your energy level—as average, somewhat above average, or perhaps a little below average?"* Most younger people like to think that they have an above average energy level. Hence, if they admit that they have no more than an average degree of this important quality, they may have even less than that amount. Other clues to lack of energy may be reflected in an applicant's tendency to take the easy way out, to procrastinate, to be unwilling to make present sacrifices for future gains, and to reflect a rather phlegmatic general manner.

Mental Review of Present Social Adjustment

Just as interviewers mentally review other areas of the interview upon completing them, so should they try to determine what the discussion of outside interests has told them about a given individual's social adjustment. Do interests reflect a "loner" who seems to have no friends and is not an altogether cheerful or happy individual? Such findings *may* provide clues to lack of emotional adjustment. The latter shortcoming may also be reflected in people who "bite off more than they can chew" and who spread themselves so thin that they find it difficult to marshal all of their energies and focus them appropriately on a given task.

People with good social adjustment are normally those who enjoy the companionship of others, who participate in enough activities so their lives are relatively full, who are capable of deriving genuine satisfaction from achievements, and who do not take things so seriously that they worry unduly.

EEO Considerations

1. Make sure that educational standards (high school graduation, for example) established for selection of new employees are consistent with the educational attainment of employees already working on those jobs in the plant or office. An artificially established educational standard may screen out a disproportionate number of minorities, and this is unfair (and cannot be defended) if some of the workers already on the job do not meet the new standard. (New educational requirements can only be established if the technology changes.)

2. Hard and fast grade requirements, such as a B average, are difficult to defend. Many factors affect grades, such as an outside job, an inordinate number of extracurricular activities, or the academic standards of schools attended. Do not be overly critical of low grades before giving an applicant a chance to explain.

3. Even if educational requirements can be defended, an organization must consider the extent to which additional recruitment may be necessary to provide a sufficient number of qualified minorities and women to meet its EEO commitments.

4. The effect of educational requirements on the handicapped must also be considered. Many handicapped people have not been able to obtain a formal education because of their inability to attend classes due to architectural barriers. In such cases, try to determine if the individual has obtained an informal education that is in any way comparable through self-study or other means.

5. Do not ask questions about marital status, children, arrangements for taking care of children while working, or health.

11
Mental Ability, Motivation, and Maturity— A First Consideration

The interviewer is required to search for so many traits and abilities that it seems justified here—at the risk of some redundancy—to point out that three factors take precedence over all others. These factors may be referred to as the 3 M's—mental ability, motivation, and maturity—the level of importance in that order.

If an applicant is bright mentally, highly motivated to succeed, and mature emotionally, he or she undoubtedly represents a good candidate for some kind of job in any given organization. The specific job for which such a person is qualified, of course, depends upon such secondary factors as relevance of work experience, educational background, specific aptitudes, and temperament.

In this chapter, then, we shall point out the reasons why mental ability, motivation, and maturity loom so importantly in the evaluation of any candidate. And we shall review the major clues which help to identify these three factors, bringing together material from a number of the previous chapters.

Just as mental ability, motivation, and maturity represent the three most important factors to be identified in selecting an employee for industry, so do they also represent the three most important requisites to be considered in selecting students for college. This will be discussed in some detail at the end of this chapter.

Mental Ability

As implied above, mental ability probably represents the single most important factor to be considered in any evaluation of a candidate for a higher-level position. Despite this seemingly obvious fact, many highly placed managers in industry have been observed evaluating candidates for important positions without making any real effort to determine the individual's intellectual level or to give appropriate weight to that important factor. The reason for this omission may lie in the fact that most managers have not been trained in interviewing techniques and therefore do not know how to judge a candidate's mental capacity.

Yet, mental ability represents the *power* factor, in the sense that it means the individual's ability to acquire new information, to generate new ideas, and to solve complex problems. And in determining the *potential* for ever-increasing responsibilities, we must again give major consideration to the level of the individual's mental capacity. This is particularly true today since, as companies restructure, they need more people with potential and versatility.

Keep in mind, too, that there are some jobs which cannot competently be performed by a person who is not really bright—such jobs as demanding research positions, engineering design, and high-level management.

It is equally important to identify the intellectual factor in candidates for less intellectually demanding jobs—jobs that have a fair amount of routine detail, such as laboratory control work, some types of engineering testing, and door-to-door sales. Most really bright people, placed in a job that is routine and not at all intellectually challenging, become quickly "fed up" and leave. Obviously, therefore, it is necessary to staff such jobs with people whose intelligence is no better than average or perhaps even slightly below average.

Although aptitude tests represent the best means of establishing the individual's intelligence, most companies are still not equipped to give these tests, and many organizations shy away from them because they are afraid of being accused of unfair employment practices. Consequently, it becomes all the more important *to be able to identify mental ability without giving additional tests.* Actually, an applicant's mental ability can be quite accurately assessed by means of a comprehensive interview, *provided the interviewer is well-trained and has developed a broad frame of reference, in the sense that he or she has evaluated many people and can thus compare a given applicant's qualifications against those of many others seen for that same type of job.* Although clues to mental ability have been brought to light in several of the preceding chapters, it will perhaps best serve our purposes if these clues are pulled together and presented again here.

High School and College Grades in Relation to Effort Required to Make Such Grades

Although grades per se are not a reliable indication of mental ability, they become significantly more reliable when considered in the light of the amount of effort the individual expended in order to get these grades, particularly if the academic standard of the school attended is factored into this equation. Thus, if people attained relatively high grades in schools with acknowledged high academic standards without having to expend a great deal of effort, it can be assumed that they are reasonably bright individuals. In sharp contrast, if students are not able to obtain better-than-average grades in schools of questionable academic standards, despite a great amount of effort and long hours of study, they are quite probably somewhat limited intellectually.

College Board Scores

Most individuals 25 or younger will have taken SATs (Scholastic Aptitude Test) during their senior year of high school, will have been informed of their scores, and will undoubtedly remember them still. Actually, Scholastic Aptitude Tests are made up of two separate tests— *verbal* and *quantitative*, or numerical. A perfect score on each of these tests is 800. In our attempts to identify a given individual's mental ability, we must consider the *combined score* resulting from both of these tests. Thus, if a person obtained a score of 575 on the verbal test and 625 on the numerical test, the combined score is 1200.

Most colleges today look for a certain minimum combination score on the SATs to qualify for college entrance. And the level of this minimum required score tells us a good bit about a given college's academic standards. Many of our most prestigious colleges and universities require a minimum combined score of at least 1300, although some other colleges require no more than a combined minimum score of 1000.

Since most mental ability tests are made up of verbal and numerical items, the combined score on an individual's SATs represents quite a good indication of intellectual level. The table below represents a distribution of the combined scores on two SAT's for the high school senior populations.

Combined Test Score	Interpretation
1400–1600	Excellent
1150–1400	Above average
850–1150	Average
600–850	Below average
Below 600	Poor

However, the above distribution includes many people who did not make it to college. Therefore, the distribution on the college population is much higher. In fact, a combined score of 1000 represents a rather marginal score for a college graduate. Scores ranging higher than this, of course, reflect higher mental ability—the higher the combined score, the brighter the individual.

Graduate Record Examination Scores

A person applying for graduate study leading to a master's or a doctoral degree in most of the better colleges and universities will be required to take the Graduate Record Examination. A perfect score on this examination is 800 but, since the test is appreciably more difficult than the Scholastic Aptitude Test, relatively few people make scores in the 700s on this test. A minimum score of at least 500 represents a requirement for entrance at most of the better schools. Scores ranging above 500, of course, reflect higher-level mental ability—the higher the score, the brighter the individual.

In talking with people who have done graduate work—or have even applied for graduate study—it is often helpful to ask them about their score on the Graduate Record Examination. Practically everyone who has taken this examination will remember the score because it is pivotal in gaining admittance to the university of his or her choice.

Quality of Response to Depth Questions

Although interviewers should be alert to the quality of the applicant's responses throughout the discussion, they should give extra attention to certain items appearing on the Interview Guide, particularly to achievements, development needs, and factors of job satisfaction (under Work History). Interviewers should be equally alert in examining the quality of applicants' responses to why they liked or disliked academic subjects in high school and college.

The areas identified above—perhaps more than any of the others—require concentration, analysis, and in-depth thinking on the part of the applicant. Hence, responses in these areas should be carefully evaluated in terms of the extent to which they reveal analytical power, perception, self-insight, and intellectual breadth and depth. Obviously, analytical power, perceptiveness, and perspective are directly related to a favorable degree of mental ability.

Achievements Reflecting Mental Ability

High academic achievement such as election to Phi Beta Kappa (liberal arts student) or Tau Beta Pi (engineering student) normally reflects high-level mental ability. Of course, there is the occasional student who attains these high honors by dint of inordinate effort rather than because he or she is particularly bright, but such persons are few and far between. Hence, it can usually be assumed that a person who has attained either of these two scholastic honors has very good mental capacity.

Because certain academic courses require a rather high degree of abstract thinking, people who like and do well in such courses as philosophy, logic, thermodynamics, and differential equations are usually relatively bright. It is equally true that demonstrated ability to handle intellectually demanding jobs represents a further clue to good intelligence.

Motivation

As important as intellect is, it cannot do the job alone. Unless individuals are motivated to utilize what they have, their overall achievement may not be particularly great and will most certainly be less than that of which they are capable. Moreover, many people with average intelligence coupled with high motivation attain a greater success than some other more intellectually gifted people who fail to make maximum use of what they possess. This is another way of saying that many people find it possible to compensate for something less than a brilliant mind by means of unusually strong motivation. As a matter of fact, high-level vocational achievement in certain areas may stem more from strong motivation than from any other single factor.

In view of the relationship of motivation to achievement, therefore, no evaluation of a candidate's qualifications is complete unless the degree of motivation has been identified and its relationship to overall achievement spelled out. In fact, motivation ranks almost as important as intellect as far as the candidate's qualifications are concerned.

As we did in the case of mental ability above, therefore, we have pulled together clues to motivation from various parts of the interview in order that we may treat this important factor here as an entity.

High Energy Level

There is a direct relationship between the amount of energy people possess and the achievement they are likely to attain. One needs only to look around in almost any business situation to understand the truth of this statement. The people at the top—those in important management jobs—will almost invariably be equipped with a great amount of energy. In fact, a highly placed person who does not have great energy will certainly represent a rather rare exception.

Well-trained interviewers—those with a broad frame of reference—can do quite an accurate job in assessing the candidate's energy level. They normally pick up clues to this important factor in all the interview areas. By means of adroit questioning, they can usually tell whether an applicant was able to handle certain enervating jobs without undue difficulty or whether such jobs actually seemed to have taken all the applicant's energy and stamina out of them.

Interviewers should be equally alert to the degree of energy demonstrated during an applicant's educational experience. If a student was able to take a heavy academic load and still participate in many extracurricular activities or carry on an outside job, the evidence speaks for itself.

It is furthermore helpful to note the kind of activities a person is able to carry out after completing a hard day on the job. Some people have enough energy left to participate in all types of physically demanding sports or to "moonlight" on another job. Other people appear to become completely "bushed" at the end of a normal work day.

Vocational and Educational Achievement in Terms of Mental Level

In an applicant whose mental ability has been assessed by the interviewer as not much better than average, there must be some other factor responsible for unusual vocational or educational achievement. That factor is almost invariably strong motivation. Many people have attained rather unusual success in industry on the basis of strong motivation as the primary factor. In fact, *in cases where other qualifications are reasonably good*, strong motivation is often the single most important factor in vocational success.

Some people make such maximum utilization of their rather modest abilities that they manage to do very well in high school and college. Such people are often referred to as "overachievers"—people who have attained a higher level of achievement in school and on the job than might have been expected of them in the light of their level of intelligence.

Conditioned to Work

People who have developed successful work-habit patterns have become accustomed to working hard and expect to extend this type of behavior throughout the rest of their lives. In interviewing such people, it is easy to tell the extent to which they have become conditioned to work by probing for likes and dislikes on their various jobs, by noting the amount of overtime hours they regularly put in on many of their assignments, and by making observations about the kind of things which give them satisfaction.

Strong Drive for Achievement

People with strong motivation are normally those who "set their sights high." In the words of Ralph Waldo Emerson, they have a strong drive to "become." Motivated by a drive to "make something of themselves," they are usually willing to pay whatever price may be required as far as hard work is concerned.

Clues to high aspirations are most often brought to light during the discussion of *factors of job satisfaction* at the close of the discussion of work history. There it is frequently fruitful to ask candidates what level of job they expect to attain at the end of 5 years and then at the end of 10 years.

Maturity

Some bright, highly motivated people fail because they lack *emotional maturity*. As discussed in previous chapters, the development of this important trait stems largely from environmental factors—the major influences which have been brought to bear on individuals from the time of their birth until the time of their appearance at the employment office. Just as in the case of mental ability and motivation, however, individuals have little actual control over the extent to which they mature emotionally. They are not able to select their parents; they have nothing to do with the early environment in which they were raised; for the most part, they have no choice of their teachers; and even their playmates during the early years have to be chosen on the basis of the immediate neighborhood in which they live.

Although most immature people have had very little to do with this lack of development, they nevertheless possess a shortcoming which very frequently stands in the way of success. This becomes immediately apparent when we go back to our earlier definition of emotional maturity: the ability to take the bitter with the sweet without rationalizing, the ability to acquire self-insight, the ability to exercise good judgment, the ability to establish reasonable vocational goals, and the ability to exercise self-control.

People who lack judgment, often make the wrong choice when confronted with important alternatives at critical stages of their lives. They may take the wrong kind of job, may leave a job for the wrong reasons, may select the wrong college major, or may do a poor job of planning their personal and financial affairs.

People who lack self-insight, do not know who they are or where they are going. This often means that the factors they tend to emphasize in their lives may not be appropriately related to success or achievement. They may not even realize the fact that they tend to rationalize their failures because they do not face up to their own shortcomings and hence are inclined to blame others for their difficulties. Furthermore, immature people are often self-centered, expect too much from others, and are too open in their criticism when things do not suit them.

Again, clues to emotional maturity should be brought to light in all the interview areas and have therefore been discussed in previous chapters. However, the factor of emotional maturity is so important that a certain amount of repetition seems justified and we are therefore summarizing some of these clues below.

Good Judgment

Lack of good judgment in leaving a given job, in selecting a major field of study, or in handling finances usually represents a sign of immaturity. Judgment is also a pivotal factor in deciding the type of job individuals desire, in terms of the extent to which that job realistically draws upon their ability and personality assets. Reasons for undertaking graduate study provide further clues to judgment, particularly in the sense that those reasons are consistent with goals and "make sense" in terms of previous educational background and work experience.

That judgment is directly related to maturity and that maturity is directly related to age will be found in the fact that insurance companies assess higher premiums for automobile insurance for males under the age of 25. (It is widely held that boys mature less rapidly than girls.) Many studies have demonstrated that young men often use poor judgment while driving a car, are sometimes inclined to be reckless, and pay too little attention to the consequences of their actions.

Demonstrated Ability to Put First Things First

Mature individuals have enough self-discipline that they are able to make themselves do the things that have to be done even if these things may not be particularly pleasant. Such people resist the temptation to do too much socializing in college, making certain that they get their homework done first. The ability to resist the temptation to buy a new car every other year in favor of saving for a down payment on a home also shows indications of maturity.

Reasonable Vocational Goals

When, in the discussion of factors of job satisfaction, it becomes apparent that people with very modest abilities aspire to positions which are way beyond their reach, it becomes clear that they have not recognized their limitations and learned to live with them.

In assessing the degree of candidates' emotional maturity, they must be compared with their chronological age group. Since maturity is a dynamic rather than a static factor, we normally develop more of this trait as we grow older. Hence, we do not expect a 19-year-old to be as mature as a 25-year-old, despite the fact that some 19-year-olds are far more mature at that age than some other young men and women of 25.

Implications for Selection of College Students

Many colleges still do a relatively poor job of selection, as reflected in the attrition at the end of the first semester or at the end of the first year. In these times of rising costs when many institutions are struggling to remain solvent, inefficient selection creates an unnecessary demand for more classroom space, more laboratory facilities, and more dormitory space and puts an additional burden on the teaching staff. Moreover, students who fail to make the grade often lose confidence and never try again. This is something of a tragedy since many of those students are capable of doing college work but simply *were not ready at the time they applied for admission.*

Now, if we think of the college-admission situation in terms of the 3 M's discussed in this chapter, we find that the colleges have no problem dealing with the factor of mental ability. This is because most applicants today take the college boards, an examination which clearly determines whether or not a boy or girl is bright enough to do college work. But some institutions are modifying their ideas of fixed-minimum-score requirements, now realizing that certain individuals are capable of *compensating* for something less than a brilliant mind. As a matter of fact, even the prestigious colleges are discovering that a student does not need a combined score of 1300 or better on the SATs in order to handle the academic work competently. Accordingly, they are experimenting, taking in some applicants with lower scores, providing they have *something else* in abundance, usually athletic prowess, demonstrated leadership in extracurricular affairs, or perhaps unusual talent in music.

However, the colleges would be well-advised to look for that *something else* in the direction of unusually strong motivation and emotional maturity beyond the student's chronological years. Most students with good SAT scores who fail do so because they are not sufficiently motivated to study or are so immature that they cannot adjust to the college situation.

It seems quite clear that much of the attrition that takes place during the first year of college could be largely eliminated if the colleges would staff their admission offices with trained interviewers. These interviewers should not be so young, incidentally, that they have not yet had an opportunity to do a good deal of interviewing and hence to have acquired a broad frame of reference. The latter is important in enabling the interviewer to compare one applicant with many others that have been interviewed over the years.

Once the colleges were staffed with trained interviewers, they would be in a position to consider the all-important factors of motivation and emotional maturity, in addition to their current concentration on mental capacity. At that point, it would be perfectly logical to take some young people with lower SATs, provided these individuals possessed strong motivation and a high degree of emotional maturity.

12
Terminating the Interview and Writing the Interview Report

With the completion of the third section of the Interview Guide, Present Social Adjustment, interviewers are ready to terminate the interview and subsequently to write the interview report. Under optimal conditions, the report of interview findings should be written immediately after completion of the interview. With interview data fresh in mind, interviewers should be able to write the report in a fraction of the time it would take should they wait several hours after finishing the interview. In this chapter, then, we will discuss the last two functions of the interview—terminating the interview and writing the report.

Terminating the Interview

As noted earlier, it is occasionally permissible to terminate an interview before all the suggested background areas have been discussed. This is only done in cases where a predominance of negative information results from the early discussion. If after a discussion of the work history, for example, it becomes clearly evident that the candidate is not at all suited for the job in question, the interview may be terminated at that point. However, the interviewer should guard against snap judgments, making certain that the decision not to carry the interview any further is based upon adequate factual evidence rather than upon an emotional reaction to the individual concerned. There are occasions, too, when interviewer's impressions of a candidate may change materially after the first half hour of discussion, swinging from a rather negative impression to an entirely positive one. Hence, the accumulation of negative findings must be substantial in the case of an early interview termination.

In a well-designed selection program, applicants scheduled for the evaluation interview will already have been screened by preliminary interviews, application forms, aptitude tests, and reference checkups. For the most part, such applicants will represent likely prospects and will merit the complete interview. And the more likely a prospect the candidate seems to be, the more the interviewer needs to know, in terms of possible shortcomings as well as assets.

Since the vast majority of surviving applicants will get the full interview, termination will normally take place at the end of the discussion of present social adjustment. Termination, in the sense that we are using it here, involves more than the windup of the information-gathering aspects of the interview. It also includes the information-giving aspects. As noted below, every applicant should be given some information about the company and, in particular, about the job for which he or she is being considered.

Terminating the Unqualified Applicant

Even in the case where the applicant is to be rejected, a certain amount of information-giving should take place at the end of the interview. Directed toward the objective of public relations, this should be kept general. In other words, the applicant should be told about general factors, such as company organization, company policy, products manufactured, and the like—rather than about specific factors such as wages, hours of work, and employee benefits. The latter are important only in the case of an applicant who is to be offered a position. Five minutes will ordinarily prove sufficient to tell the unqualified applicant about the company. However, courteous and informative answers should always be given to any questions raised.

An attempt should always be made to terminate the interview on a positive tone. Such a statement as the following will often accomplish this objective, "Well, you certainly have a long list of impressive assets—assets that will stand you in good stead throughout your working life. And, at the same time, you seem to have some insight into the areas to which you should give your attention in terms of further development. I will discuss your qualifications with other interested persons within the company and will let you know the outcome within a day or two. Thank you very much for coming in; I certainly enjoyed talking with you."

Once the interviewer has decided to terminate the discussion, this should be done with dispatch. Otherwise, the conversation will deteriorate into meaningless chitchat. Hence, after a concluding statement such as the one noted in the paragraph above, the interviewer should stand up, shake hands, and escort the candidate to the door.

Rejection of applicants is always a difficult task at best and, as such, must be handled with care and finesse. First and foremost, applicants must be rejected in such a way that their feelings are not unduly hurt and their self-confidence is not undermined. In the second place, the company's public relations are at stake. In other words, rejected applicants should be permitted to "save face," so that they do not bear ill will toward the company. Because this task requires so much skill and finesse, many companies prefer to inform applicants of an unfavorable employment decision by letter. Actually, the latter means is almost uniformly used in the case of applicants for high-level jobs. A carefully worded letter not only represents an expression of courtesy but carries the implication of more thorough consideration. At the same time, the letter should be sent within a day or two after the interview, thus freeing the unsuccessful candidate to concentrate on other job possibilities.

Whether the applicant is informed of the unfavorable decision by letter or at the end of the interview, *the reason for the rejection should be phrased in terms of the job demands rather than in terms of the individual's personal qualifications.* The candidate should be given credit for his or her real assets but, at the same time, should be told that, in the interviewer's opinion, the job will not make the best use of the candidate's abilities. Instead of deprecating the individual's personal qualifications, this approach simply implies that he or she will probably be better suited in some other job with another company.

Another way to help a person "save face" involves a comparison with other candidates for the job in question, on the basis of experience and education. The person can be told, for example, "Although you possess many fine assets, there are one or two other candidates being considered for this job whose specific experience and training are somewhat more appropriate." Note that this statement makes no mention of personal characteristics such as ability to get along with people, willingness to work hard, or leadership traits. In general, it is far easier for an individual to face up to the fact that his or her experience or training does not quite fit the job than to admit that he or she does not qualify because of personal characteristics.

Once in a while an individual will ask for vocational guidance. The applicant may say, "If your jobs will not make best use of my abilities, what kind of a job do you think I should look for elsewhere?" In answer to such a question, the interviewer should refer the individual to a professional vocational guidance counselor. Guidance requires a great deal more academic preparation than does interviewing. Moreover, interviewers are normally familiar only with the requirements of the jobs in their company. To do an adequate guidance job, the counselor must have knowledge of job requirements in a great many different fields. Hence, an applicant who expresses a desire for vocational guidance should be referred to a competent psychologist specializing in this field.

Terminating the Interview of the Qualified Applicant

Although the interviewer ordinarily has the authority to reject unqualified applicants, final responsibility for placing qualified candidates on the payroll usually rests with the head of the department to which the applicant is being referred. Even when the interviewer's decision is entirely favorable, this should not be communicated to the applicant. Rather, the interviewer should express real interest in the individual's qualifications, assuring the applicant that the department head will schedule a later meeting.

The information-giving aspect of the interview takes on even greater importance when the interviewer's decision is favorable. In these situations, everything possible is done to sell the candidate on the job. And the interviewer is in a unique position to do this. With the full knowledge of the applicant's abilities and qualifications in mind, the extent to which these qualifications apply to the job can be specifically pointed out. Where the decision is favorable, moreover, the interviewer should talk in terms of job specifics—earnings, employee benefits, and subsequent opportunities for promotion. In addition, company policies, products, and the organization's position in the industry can be explained. At the same time, the interviewer will be careful not to oversell the job, knowing that this might lead to eventual disappointment and poor morale.

Completing the Interview Rating Form

This chapter provides instructions for recording interview findings on the Interview Rating Form found in Appendix 2 at the back of the book. To help interviewers summarize their thinking, moreover, the chapter also includes a cross-reference section, showing how possible clues from each of the major interview areas can be used to form judgments of the candidate's rating on traits of personality, motivation, and character appearing on page 3 of the Interview Rating Form.

The write-up of the case represents an important, integral part of the interviewing process. As the results are recorded, the interviewer's thinking crystallizes with respect to the applicant's qualifications. By the time the applicant leaves the room, the interviewer will normally have decided whether the man or woman is qualified for the job in question. But the write-up of the case represents an extension of this decision-making. In the process of recording the findings, the interviewer isolates out value judgments and hence is normally able to assign a more precise rating to the candidate's qualifications. The case report forces interviewers to weigh all the relevant factors, and as a consequence they are usually in a much better position to decide whether the applicant's qualifications merit a slightly above-average rating, a well-above-average rating, or perhaps an excellent rating.

Because the recording of interview findings represents such an essential aspect of the entire process, the Interview Rating Form should be completed immediately after the candidate leaves the room. With all the essential facts still fresh in mind, the interviewer usually finds it possible to complete the form within 45 minutes. If this task is postponed, twice the amount of time may be required, and subsequently all the salient information may not be recalled.

In writing the Interview Rating Form, use the space provided under each interview area for recording major findings pertinent to that area. Since the space is obviously limited, the interviewer will have to decide which findings in each area contribute most to understanding the applicant's behavior and overall qualifications for the job in question.

The recording of interview results should not be confined to facts alone, since many of these facts will already have appeared on the application blank. Rather, the interviewers should try to indicate their interpretation of these facts, in terms of the extent to which they may provide clues to the individual's personality, motivation, or character.

Personality and Ability Configurations

We have noted throughout the chapters on interpretation that inter-viewers—with proper training and practice—will normally know whether or not they wish to hire an applicant by the time that individual leaves the room. This is because they have been picking up clues to be-havior throughout the discussion of work history, education, and out-side interests and, by the end of the interview, have acquired sufficient hard, factual documentation to support an objective employment deci-sion. Even so, reference to the personality and ability configurations de-tailed in Figure 12-1 should enable an interviewer to become more de-finitive with respect to the individual's make-up.

Reference to the personality and ability configurations also helps in-terviewers make a relatively quick assessment of an applicant's strengths and shortcomings. Some interviewers find it helpful, moreover, to use these configurations to complete the summary of assets and shortcom-ings of the Interview Rating Form immediately following the comple-tion of the interview. Once having completed this summary, they work backwards in a sense, making certain that their write-up of work expe-rience, education, and present social adjustment contains abundant doc-umentation of the assets and shortcomings they have already summa-rized.

Writing the Work History

Data should be recorded chronologically, in much the same way as it is obtained during the interview. Thus, there should be a brief treatment of early jobs, followed by a discussion of postcollege jobs in chronolog-ical order. Because of space limitations, early jobs may be treated as a group rather than discussed singly.

The discussion should be primarily *interpretive*, drawing upon fac-tual information to highlight clues to personality, motivation, and character. Obviously, it is impossible to draw off meaningful inter-pretations from every single fact presented, but clues to behavior should nevertheless be sprinkled frequently throughout the discus-sion of work history.

At the end of the work history discussion, the interviewer should be sure to indicate an evaluation of the applicant's work experience and its relevance in terms of the job under consideration. The following rep-

Personality and Ability Conformations

PRIMARY

MENTAL ABILITY
- verbal aptitude
- math aptitude
- analytical power
- perceptive
- critical thinker
- intellectual breadth and depth

MOTIVATION
- energy
- willingness to work
- conscientious
- initiative
- self discipline
- perseverance
- aspirations
- personal standards

MATURITY
- judgment
- knowledge of self
- reasonable vocational goals
- does not rationalize
- aware of limitations
- can "take the bitter with the sweet"

SECONDARY

PEOPLE SKILLS
- tact
- empathy
- sensitivity to the needs of others
- friendly
- cooperative

TECHNICAL ABILITY
- math aptitude
- academic preparation
- analytical ability
- critical thinker
- creative
- attention to detail

LEADERSHIP
- assertive
- self-confident
- tough minded
- good communicator
- enthusiastic
- well organized
- bold in thinking
- "take charge person"

CHARACTER
- honest
- reliable
- value system

EMOTIONAL ADJUSTMENT
- able to take pressure
- reasonably cheerful outlook on life
- not a worrier
- not subject to wide swings in mood

APTITUDE FOR MANUFACTURING
- sense of urgency
- production minded— motivated to "get the pieces out of the door"
- flexible
- strong leadership
- able to keep several balls in the air simultaneously
- tough-minded

APTITUDE FOR SALES
- assertive
- self-confident
- tough-minded
- gift of gab
- infectious enthusiasm
- sense of humor
- perseverance
- color
- charisma
- extroverted

APTITUDE FOR FINANCE
- math aptitude
- academic preparation
- attention to detail
- somewhat introverted
- able to take a certain amount of "number crunching"
- able to see the big picture

Figure 12-1.

resents an example of how work experience should be recorded on the Interview Rating Form:

> Early jobs (lifeguard, pressing apples, part-time farming) provided an introduction to work but did not seem to extend him to any great degree or to do a great deal for his development.
>
> Worked two summers (forklift operator, testing carburetors) but did not find either job very interesting.
>
> Enlisted in the Navy in 1963 just prior to taking exams that would have graduated him from college—apparently in a fit of anger because the college failed to extend a loan. This obviously reflected poor judgment, immaturity, quick temper, and impulsiveness. Did radar and missile electronics maintenance in the Navy and thus acquired relevant experience with electrical hardware. Elected to stay on 2 more years after 4-year enlistment "because I could earn $75 more a month and go overseas." This seems to reflect some lack of initiative in the sense that he took the path of least resistance. Did not have any significant leadership experience. Says he "does not like to offend people" and admits to a lack of confidence and mental toughness.
>
> Now earning $11,500 at Crocker Electronics, doing testing work in the manufacturing section. Has enjoyed his work over the past year but now wants something "more professional" such as design or field engineering.
>
> Although he does have some good electrical hardware experience, job history is not impressive for a man of 31, reflecting some lack of drive as well as some failure to make maximum utilization of his abilities.

After completing the write-up of the work-history area, the interviewer should assign a rating to this area by placing a check mark on the horizontal line that extends across the top of this area. Note that the horizontal line represents a continuum, in the sense that the check mark can be placed at any point on the line—directly over any of the descriptive adjectives or, for example, between "average" and "above average." The rating should be made in terms of the job that appears at the top of the form—the job for which the applicant is being considered. In cases where most of the interpretive comments are favorable, an "above average" rating would normally be expected. If the majority of comments are unfavorable, a "below average" rating would normally be indicated. Where favorable and unfavorable comments are about equally weighted in terms of their importance, an "average" rating would usually be made.

Writing Education and Training

As in the case of the treatment of the work history, educational data should also be recorded in chronological order. This means that initially there should be a discussion of high school followed by a treatment of the college experience. Any graduate experience should of course be recorded last.

Again, the recorded information should be largely interpretive, with a liberal use of factual data for documentation. Thus, actual grades and class standings should be noted here. Be sure to record extracurricular activities as well as the extent to which the individual seems to have applied himself or herself.

Here, as in the previous area, be sure to indicate names of schools, employers, and the like. This report should be sufficiently complete so that the reader does not have to refer to the application blank for additional information. An example of the manner in which the educational information should be recorded appears below:

> Did exceptionally well in high school, graduating third in a class of 458 and doing her best work in math and science. College Boards were 630 verbal (good) and 745 math (exceptional). Because she was very shy, Mary did not take part in extracurricular activities and did not date.
>
> Studied very hard at Swarthmore—a top school—and made outstanding grades (3.7 out of a possible 4.0), winning election to Tau Beta Pi during her junior year and graduating magna cum laude. Mary majored in electrical engineering and enjoyed all of the more theoretically oriented courses such as thermodynamics, circuitry, and higher math—a strong clue to her ability to think in the abstract. Also enjoyed and did well in her design courses. Began to "blossom out a bit" in college, becoming more social and beginning to date more frequently. But she almost left college one semester because she was "upset over a relationship with a boy," again raising some question concerning her emotional adjustment.
>
> Mary made an exceptional record at a top school and hence is unusually well trained academically. Obviously, too, she has superior intelligence both with respect to quantity and quality (analytical, perceptive, critical).

Once the interpretive comments have been recorded in this area, the interviewer should assign a rating on the line at the top, in accordance with suggestions discussed above in connection with the rating of work history.

Writing Present Social Adjustment

Interpretive comments in this area should be concerned primarily with value judgments as to the man's or woman's interests and overall social adjustment. Illustration of such comments appears below:

> Interests fairly broad and somewhat intellectual—reads five or six books a month, likes to make her own clothes, has student license as a pilot, and enjoys listening to classical music.
>
> Energy level is admittedly no better than average and, in truth may be somewhat less than average.
>
> Pursues many of her activities by herself or, at best, with one or two other people. Admits that she does not have as much social facility as she would like. Overweight problem probably somewhat of a social handicap.
>
> Seems something of a "loner" and not altogether happy, raising a question concerning her emotional adjustment.

Again, after recording the appropriate information in this area, the interviewer should assign a rating to the area by placing a check mark at the appropriate point on the horizontal line at the top.

Rating Personality, Character, and Motivation

Each of the fourteen traits listed under this area is preceded by a set of parentheses. This permits the interviewer to assign a rating to each trait. As in the case of ratings made in all the other interview areas, value judgments should be formulated in terms of the demands of the job for which a person is being considered. Using a five-point scale, the interviewer places a + in the parentheses to indicate the belief that the applicant has a high degree of the trait in question, an A + if the individual is judged to have an above-average amount of the trait, an A in the parentheses if the applicant is judged to have an "average" or adequate amount of the trait, an A − if the applicant is thought to have a below-average degree of the trait, and a − if the individual is evaluated to be seriously lacking in that characteristic. If the interviewer is unable to decide about a given trait or, if the particular trait has no relevance in terms of the job under consideration, the parentheses is left blank.

In devising forms such as the Interview Rating Form, it is of course impossible to include all the traits of personality, motivation, and character that should be considered in evaluating applicant characteristics for a wide range of jobs. The fourteen characteristics listed on this particular form simply represent some of the traits which experience has shown to be most relevant in assessing applicants for high-level jobs in general. Other characteristics deemed of particular importance in a given case can be listed as representing either a strength or a shortcoming on Section V of the Interview Rating Form, summary of assets and of shortcomings.

In rating an applicant on traits of personality, motivation, and character, the interviewers are called upon to summarize their thinking, in terms of the variety of clues to these traits that have come to light as a result of the discussion of the candidate's work history, education and training, and present social adjustment.

The material presented below is designed to aid the interviewer in thinking through the various kinds of information that might be used to support a rating on each of the fourteen traits listed on the back of the Interview Guide. It is of course impossible to produce an exhaustive list of items that could conceivably merit consideration in rating an applicant for a given job on each of these traits. Hence, the questions appearing below under each trait are designed simply to stimulate the interviewer's thinking, in terms of the kind of positive and negative information that would ordinarily be factored into the rating of that trait. Items preceded by a minus sign represent examples of unfavorable findings with respect to a given trait; those preceded by a plus sign represent examples of favorable or positive findings.

Maturity

− Any tendency to rationalize failures?

+ Has she learned to accept her limitations and live with them?

− Chronic dissatisfaction with job duties and working conditions, reflecting an inability to take the bitter with the sweet?

+ Well-formulated vocational goals?

+ Worked during college summers to help pay tuition, even though parents could have afforded to pay total amount.

+ Responsible attitude toward her family?

− Effort in school confined only to those studies which he liked?

− Rationalizes academic failures by blaming the school or the teachers?

Emotional Adjustment

+ Has she shown an ability to maintain composure in the face of frustration?

+ Has he been able to maintain his emotional balance and mental health in the face of trying personal circumstances, such as a protracted period of unemployment?

− Have there been problems with supervisors, teachers, or parents, which reflected a decided tendency to "fly off the handle"?

+ Is she able to deal with the shortcomings of subordinates calmly and patiently?

− Is he admittedly moody and inclined to experience more than the normal degree of ups and downs?

− Is she inclined to sulk in the face of criticism?

− Do current difficulties with peers seem to stem in part from his tendency to be sarcastic or hotheaded?

+ Is there considerable evidence that she does not allow her emotions to color her judgment?

Teamworker

+ Does he seem to have operated successfully as a member of a team, in connection with sports activities in school, community activities in the neighborhood, or group activities on the job?

− Is she strongly motivated to be the "star" of the team, taking more than her share of credit for accomplishments?

+ Does he seem to place the accomplishments of the group ahead of his personal feelings and ambitions?

− Did she have difficulty getting along with her associates while in the army or navy?

+ Does he have the degree of tact and social sensitivity necessary for the establishment and maintenance of good interpersonal relations with other members of a team?

− Does she show any pronounced tendency to be inflexible, intolerant, or opinionated?

Tact

+ Does the manner in which he phrased his remarks during the interview reflect tact and consideration for the interviewer?

− Has she talked disparagingly about minority groups?

− Has he made a number of remarks during the interview that have been unduly blunt and direct?

+ In discussing her relationships with subordinates, does she seem to have reflected genuine consideration for their feelings?

+ Is he sensitive to the reactions of others to the extent that he is able to structure his approach without antagonizing them?

+ Does she show any evidence of being a good listener?

Adaptability

+ Did he adjust easily to army or navy life?

+ Has she shown a liking for jobs involving contact with many types of people and diverse situations?

+ Has he shown an ability to handle a number of job assignments simultaneously?

+ Has she demonstrated the ability to move from one job to a completely different kind of job without undue difficulty?

− Was he unable to do well in certain subjects "because of the teacher"?

− Was she raised in a provincial small town atmosphere where there was relatively limited exposure to diverse situations and different types of people?

− Does his approach to a job reflect such a tendency to be a perfectionist that he has to do everything "just so"?

Tough-Mindedness

− Does she have a strong dislike for disciplining subordinates?

+ Is he willing to take a stand for what he thinks is right?

+ Has she demonstrated an ability to make decisions involving people that, of necessity, work to the disadvantage of the few but have to be made for the good of the many?

− Is he insufficiently demanding of subordinates, in the sense that he is reluctant to ask them to work overtime or to "push" them to some extent when there is a job to be done within a certain deadline?

− Is she a product of a soft, sheltered, early work experience where there was little opportunity to become conditioned to the seamier side of existence?

− Does he give the impression of being too sympathetic or overly concerned about the feelings of others?

+ Is she willing to delegate responsibilities even though inadequate performance on the tasks delegated may reflect directly upon her?

Self-Discipline

− Has he shown a tendency to procrastinate unduly in carrying out the less-pleasant jobs assigned him?

+ In connection with her academic career, has she shown a willingness to apply herself diligently to those courses which she disliked?

− Did he fail to take full advantage of academic opportunities because he was not able to make himself "dig deeply enough" really to understand the subject?

+ Does she assume her share of civic responsibility, even though community activities in general do not appeal to her?

− Has he been so conditioned by a soft, easy life that there has been relatively little need to cope with difficult problems or situations?

+ Has she demonstrated a willingness to give first attention to those important aspects of a job which are perhaps of less interest to her?

Initiative

+ Has he demonstrated an ability to operate successfully without close supervision?

− Does she show a dislike for situations that have not been structured for her?

+ Does he reach out for ever-increasing responsibility?

+ Is there any evidence to indicate that she is a self-starter, in the sense that she does not have to wait to be told what to do?

− Does he seem to have fallen into a job rut, in the sense that he has been unwilling to extricate himself from a dead-end situation?

+ Has she demonstrated a willingness to depart from the status quo in order to accomplish a given task in a new and perhaps more efficient manner?

Perseverance

+ Did he show perseverance in college by completing his undergraduate work despite a lack of good scholastic aptitude?

− Has she changed jobs too frequently?

+ Once he starts a job, does he continue with it until it has been completed, resisting any tendency to become distracted?

+ Has she completed an appreciable portion of her college education by going to school at night?

− Does he find it inordinately difficult to complete tasks on his own, such as correspondence courses where he does not have the stimulation of group effort?

– Is there evidence to support the view that she starts more things than she can finish?

Self-Confidence

– Was confidence undermined by an overly demanding supervisor who tended to be a perfectionist?

+ Does he reflect a realistic appraisal of his abilities and a willingness to take action?

– During the early years was she unable to compete successfully with those of her own age in athletics or in academic affairs?

+ Does his general manner reflect poise and presence?

+ Does she have sufficient confidence in her assets so that she is willing to discuss her shortcomings objectively?

– Has he been reluctant to take on additional job responsibility because of fear of failure?

– Did she limit her extracurricular activities in school because of a fear of lack of acceptance on the part of her classmates?

Assertiveness

+ Does his personality have considerable impact?

+ Has she done a considerable amount of participation in contact sports where aggressiveness represented an important requisite?

– Has he shown a tendency to let others take advantage of him because of lack of self-assertiveness?

+ Has she operated successfully in sales, expediting, or production supervision—types of jobs conducive to the development of personal forcefulness?

+ Is his history replete with evidences of leadership in school, on the job, or in connection with activities in the community?

– Does she tend to be introverted in the sense that she shies away from group activity?

Conscientiousness

+ Did he show conscientiousness in school by doing more than was actually required by the teachers, in order to satisfy his own standards?

− Does her record on the job reflect a tendency to let things slide?

+ Is he inclined upon occasion to work evenings and weekends, even though this is not actually required by his supervisor?

− Does she tend to be a clock-watcher?

+ Does he have high personal standards for his work?

Hard Worker

+ Has her history been such that she has become conditioned to hard work and long hours?

+ Did he get good grades in school despite limited mental ability?

+ Did she earn a relatively high percentage of her college expenses?

− Does his general manner seem phlegmatic, reflecting a possible below-average energy level?

− Has she shown a strong dislike of overtime work?

+ Has he had any experiences that may have extended his capacity for constructive effort, such as going to school at night while carrying on a full-time job during the day?

− Does she seem always to look for the easy way out?

+ Does he seem to be in excellent health, reflecting a considerable amount of vigor and stamina?

Honesty and Sincerity

+ Has she "come clean" during the interview discussion, in the sense that she has shown a willingness to talk about the unfavorable aspects of her background as well as the favorable aspects?

− Is there any evidence to support the view that he is exclusively oriented in the direction of personal gain, to the point that he does not develop strong loyalties to any organization or perhaps even to his own family?

+ Is she willing to give credit where credit is due?

− Does he seem to derive satisfaction from the discussion of situations where he has been able to get the better of the other fellow or to "pull a fast one"?

− Does she have any appreciable tendency to exaggerate her own accomplishments?

− Does his story seem to be inconsistent in terms of other selection findings, such as information developed from the application form, the preliminary interview, the aptitude tests, or the reference check-ups?

After completing the ratings on the fourteen traits of personality, motivation, and character, assign an overall rating to this area by placing a check mark at the appropriate point on the horizontal line at the top. In making this rating, the interviewer will of course be guided by the preponderance of pluses or minuses, as the case may be. At the same time, the pluses and minuses should not be added algebraically, since certain traits obviously merit a greater weighting than others. For example, a minus rating on "honesty and sincerity" would undoubtedly be sufficient to outweigh plus ratings on all the other traits. Moreover, certain traits such as maturity, emotional adjustment, and willingness to work hard are more important to job success than traits such as tact, tough-mindedness, or personal forcefulness. In assigning an overall rating on this area, the interviewer must also be guided by the demands of the job for which the candidate is being considered. The trait of assertiveness, for example, would be given more weight in the case of a candidate being considered for production supervision than in the case of a person being evaluated for a job as office manager.

Writing the Summary of Assets and Shortcomings

Items listed under assets and shortcomings in this section of the Interview Rating Form should be concerned with the most important findings, in terms of the applicant's overall qualifications. And these items, for the most part, should in themselves represent a summation of a number of individual factors. For example, the interviewer would list as an asset an item such as "effective sales personality," rather than trying to list all the factors of which the so-called "sales personality" is composed—factors like aggressiveness, sense of humor, poise, presence, social sensitivity, and persuasiveness.

The summary of assets and shortcomings should include major findings from all the selection steps, with special emphasis of course on aptitude tests and interview results. Thus, in addition to principal interview findings, this section should include any available test results such as mental ability, verbal ability, numerical ability, mechanical comprehension, or clerical aptitude. Interviews should also combine test and interview findings in such a way that they summarize the *quality* of the applicant's thinking. Items concerned with quality of thinking would of course be expressed in such terms as: analytical ability, ability to plan and organize, criticalness of thinking, and intellectual breadth and depth.

In writing the summary of assets and shortcomings, interviewers should select items of particular importance in terms of the job for which the candidate is being considered. Thus, in addition to listing appropriate items of ability, personality, motivation, and character, they should always note the relevance of the candidate's work history and educational preparation.

Writing the Overall Summary

In completing the overall summary on page 4 of the Interview Rating Form, the interviewer should write a brief description of the candidate's qualifications for the job in question. This takes the form of three paragraphs—the first paragraph devoted to a summation of the applicant's principal assets, a second paragraph which describes the most serious shortcomings, and a third paragraph in which interviewers seek to *resolve* the major assets and shortcomings in such a way that they show whether the assets outweigh the shortcomings or vice versa. And, in this third and final paragraph, interviewers show how they arrived at their overall rating. The three paragraphs of the overall summary will of course draw upon the summary of assets and the summary of shortcomings which appear above. Hence, there will be some obvious redundancy but every effort should be made to word the summary in such a way that the individual seems to "come to life" as a unique person. An example of an appropriately worded overall summary appears below.

> Harry Ritter deserves great credit for what he has been able to make of himself in view of what he has had to work with. Without much in the way of early financial, educational or cultural advantages, he has managed to attain a very good record of achievement both in the army and at Elmer Electric. He has done this primarily as a result of his tremendous energy, his willingness to work hard and to put in long hours, and his ability to make maximum utilization of his abilities. In addition, Harry has some natural leadership ability as a result of his personal forcefulness, self-confidence and toughmindedness. Finally, his experience with Elmer Electric represents a strong plus in terms of his ability to fit in here.
>
> Negatively, Harry is not especially gifted intellectually, although his intelligence probably falls within the average range of the college population. Nor does he have a great amount of intellectual depth or breadth. Hence, he is more of a "doer" than he is a "thinker." The kind of a person who tends to push people a bit too hard, Harry needs to develop more tact and social sensitivity.
>
> Harry Ritter's assets clearly outweigh his shortcomings—to the point that he represents a very good candidate for the first level of supervision in the manufacturing function. Actually, he has a rather ideal personality for production supervision in the sense that he is at

his best when he can "put out the day-to-day fires" and move the "pieces out the door." Harry should be able to progress to the middle management level without much difficulty but it is somewhat doubtful that his intellectual capacity will carry him much beyond that point.

Making the Overall Rating

By placing a check mark on the line at the bottom of page 4 of the Interview Rating Form, the interviewer makes the final selection decision. In so doing, the interviewer weighs the evidence that has been accumulated from all the selection steps. Thus, not only the ratings made in each of the six major interview areas on the Interview Rating Form being considered but also all pertinent information that has been derived from the preliminary interview, the application blank, the aptitude tests, and the reference checkups is kept in mind.

In making the final rating, the interviewer will of course be guided by the extent to which the applicant's assets outweigh liabilities, or vice versa. Remember, no applicant is expected to possess all the qualifications listed in the worker specifications for a given job. The interviewer's task is to weigh the strength of the applicant's assets against the severity of his or her shortcomings. The interviewer must evaluate how much the candidate's shortcomings are likely to be a handicap in the job under consideration. And, at the same time, the interviewer estimates the extent to which the individual's assets should lead to a successful job performance.

The interviewer must remember, too, that assets of considerable strength may compensate for certain shortcomings. For example, in some cases strong motivation, relevant work experience, and good intellectual qualifications may compensate for below-average educational preparation. In such instances, an "above average" overall rating might be justified, despite the "below average" rating on education and training.

As pointed out earlier in this chapter, however, certain liabilities may be so damaging to the candidate's cause that they disqualify the individual regardless of the number of favorable ratings in other categories. An applicant decidedly lacking in honesty and sincerity, for example, or one exceedingly immature would undoubtedly merit a low overall rating despite the number of high ratings that may have been given in other important areas.

In assigning a final, overall rating, the interviewer thinks in broad terms. Does the person have the appropriate skills to handle the job? Is he or she willing to work hard and apply these skills? Has the candidate demonstrated ability to get along with people? Is he or she basically a person of good character? Has the candidate been sufficiently prepared academically?

Overall ratings are of course made in terms of the job demands. In other words, an overall rating of "average" means that the candidate should be able to turn in an average job performance, not much better and not much worse. Applicants rated "above average" should be able to turn in a good performance, while those rated "excellent" should, in the interviewer's opinion, be able to do a top-notch job.

The overall rating of "excellent" is normally reserved for applicants who have a great many assets and whose shortcomings are not at all serious. People rated "above average" are well-qualified individuals whose shortcomings, while a little more serious than the excellently rated person, are not serious enough to handicap them unduly. Candidates rated "average" are those whose assets and liabilities are about equally weighted. However, none of their shortcomings should be serious enough to keep them from turning in an adequate or average job performance.

Ideally, only those individuals with excellent or above-average ratings should be hired. In a tight labor market, however, it may be necessary to employ a number of applicants with only "average" qualifications. Candidates rated "below average" or "poor" should not be hired under any circumstances, both in terms of the good of the organization and in terms of the long-range benefits to the individuals themselves.

In making the final decision, the interviewer should be guided by one further consideration—the applicant's potential for further growth and development. Thus, although the candidate's qualifications for a given job may be only "average" at the present time, he or she may be a person of such potential that the candidate could one day become a most productive employee. The age of the individual of course represents an important factor in this connection.

Further Uses of the Completed Interview Rating Form

In the case of those individuals who are employed, the completed Interview Rating Form becomes an important part of the employee's permanent file. And since shortcomings have been carefully recorded, this information can become the basis for the employee's further development. Apprised of the new employee's developmental needs, supervisors can take immediate steps to help the employee beginning the first day of the job.

The completed Interview Rating Form also can provide the basis for follow-up studies designed to improve the selection procedures. The overall interviewer rating can be subsequently compared with performance on the job. Such follow-up information helps interviewers to identify their own interviewing weaknesses and makes it possible for them to make an effort to eliminate these weaknesses in their future discussions with other applicants. Moreover, follow-up studies of this kind enable the employment manager to evaluate the interviewing staff, in terms of both additional training needs and possible reassignment to other employment functions.

PART 4

Additional Applications of Interview Techniques

13

The Campus Interview

As discussed in Chapter 1, the Campus Interview deserves increased attention since this represents a given company's greatest opportunity to recruit truly outstanding young people. And, because campus recruiters are usually forced to crowd some 12 to 15 interviews into a single day, the task is both difficult and enervating. Accordingly, today, the more sophisticated companies send some of their best people to the colleges and train them thoroughly in intensive interviewing.

Normally, recruiters discover that they can devote no more than 30 minutes to each student—20 minutes to the interview itself, 5 minutes to the interview report, and 5 minutes to prepare for the next student. This means that recruiters have only a scant 20 minutes to decide whether a given student merits further consideration. Continuation of the interview process involves travel expense to company headquarters and subsequent interviews by several important and highly paid people in the organization. This costs a company more money than most people realize. Hence, a great deal is riding on each decision a recruiter makes.

Preparation

Careful examination of each student's résumé prior to the interview can pay big dividends. Such study, for example, can reveal the extent to which the individual has any concentration of courses or work experi-

173

ence that fits the recruiter's job description. A student's extracurricular activities might suggest qualities of leadership. In those résumés where grades are not included, recruiters naturally wonder whether the grades may not be very good. And, where high grades appear, recruiters must determine if such grades are a true reflection of high intellect or perhaps an indication of an overachiever. In short, examination of the personal history résumé can help recruiters decide where they might spend the most time and where they should probe for more information.

Reference to the Campus Interview Guide shown in Figure 13-1 reveals that these interviews should begin with Small Talk, usually based on some special award or achievement. Recruiters should therefore search for such a topic in the résumé and prepare a three-part question, as discussed in Part 3 of this book. If they discover, for example, that a student has won a prize for mathematics, they might formulate such a question as:

> I am impressed that you won the Hogue Mathematics Prize. Tell me what the competition was like, what preparation you made, and what the award has meant to you.

Or, if no special awards appear on the résumé, it is often helpful to ask the student to compare life in his or her home town with life in the college area:

> I noticed that you grew up in Peoria. How would you contrast life there with living in Boston—with respect to attitudes of the people, cost of living, climate, educational opportunities?

Beginning questions like these—introduced casually and with appropriate facial expressions—tend to put the interviewee at ease and encourage the person to talk at some length.

The Twenty-Minute Interview

As in the case of the longer evaluation interview, it is equally important in this short discussion to encourage the interviewee to do most of the talking. This is accomplished by employment of rapport-inducing techniques discussed earlier in the book—Small Talk, Lead Questions, Facial and Vocal Expressions, the Calculated Pause, Reinforcement and Play Down of Negative Information.

Since the educational experience is the most important experience people in their early twenties have had, it is wise to spend the major

Campus Interview Guide

Begin the Interview with Small Talk—a three part question. "I am impressed that you won the Hillard award. Tell what you had to do to win that award, what the competition was like and what it meant to you."

Then: "Let me tell you about our discussion today."

"In our company we believe that the more I can learn about you the better able I will be to place you in a job that makes the best use of your abilities. So, today, I would like to have you tell me everything you can about your education and a little about your work experience. Let's start with your education.

EDUCATION

SUBJECT PREFERENCES. "What subjects did you like best in high school? What was there about that subject that appealed to you?" (*Probing for an indication of analytical thinking*)

GRADES. "What about grades in high school? Were they average, above average or perhaps a little below average?" "What was your class rank?"

COLLEGE BOARDS. "What were your SAT scores—verbal and math?"

EXTRACURRICULAR ACTIVITIES. (Sports, offices, music, clubs) "Beyond your classwork, what activities did you participate in during your high school years?"

EFFORT. "How conscientious a student were you? Did you work about as hard as the average student, a little harder or perhaps not quite as hard?"

COLLEGES APPLIED TO. "What colleges did you apply to? Which ones accepted you?"

(Repeat these questions for the college experience)

WORK HISTORY

LEAD QUESTION. "Did you have any jobs during high school or college that you think added materially to your growth and development?"

LIKES AND DISLIKES. "Did you get a performance appraisal on that job? What traits or abilities did your supervisor like about you? What traits did your supervisor think needed further development?"

IF NO PERFORMANCE APPRAISAL SAY: "If there had been an appraisal, what traits or abilities do you think your supervisor would have liked about you? What traits do you think your supervisor would have said needed further development?"

TERMINATE THE INTERVIEW: "You have given me a fine picture of your background and it is clear that you have many important strengths—strengths that will help you in the future. Thank you very much for talking with me today."

Figure 13-1.

NOTES TO INTERVIEWER

AT THE BEGINNING OF THE INTERVIEW. By means of frequent lubrication, facial expressions, and "play down" of negative information, try to get the student to do most of the talking. Place a small clock on the table immediately in front of you and refer to it frequently in order to keep the interview to 20 minutes. Look at this Guide constantly and use all of the questions verbatim and in the indicated order.

AT THE END OF THE INTERVIEW. Take the time to sell your company only to those students you wish to recommend for a plant visit. Drawing upon information on the sheet titled: PERSONALITY CONFORMATIONS, dictate a few paragraphs on each student.

(Continued)

portion of the 20 minutes on high school and college background—perhaps as much as 15 minutes. This gives interviewers an ample opportunity to discuss the educational background in depth. When time is limited, experience has shown that it is better to discuss one important area of the interview in genuine depth than to spread one's self too thin by trying to cover all of the areas.

If one covers all of the questions found on the Campus Interview Guide verbatim and in the indicated order, abundant clues to mental ability, motivation, and maturity will normally come to light. Clues to mental ability, for example, should emerge from discussion of grades, effort required to get the grades, SAT scores, response to depth questions, and academic standards of schools attended.

Clues to motivation can often be found in such factors as decision to embark on a difficult college major, effort expended on studies (late evening study and study on weekends), and participation in extracurricular activities such as a grueling sport. The latter activities provide valid clues to energy and stamina.

Clues to maturity can be found in the kind of judgment exercised in such major decisions as choice of college, choice of college major, and how the student expected to utilize the major after college graduation. The level of maturity can also be assessed by noting the extent to which the student was able to "put first things first" by concentrating on studies first rather than becoming too distracted by time-demanding extracurricular affairs.

Probing for Clues to Behavior

Utilization of the Two-Step Probing Question should result in appreciable evidence of analytical and critical thinking. This technique, of course, is designed to probe for the "Why" of the various decisions the student has made during high school and college careers. In discussing the high school experience, for example, interviewers should ask students what course they most enjoyed. (The first step of the Two-Step Question.) Should the response be mathematics, the interviewers would then ask: "Why mathematics?" If the reply should be: "Oh, I guess it was because I liked the teacher and it was easy for me," this reply would not show any high degree of analytical power. If, on the other hand, a student should reply:

> I like math because it always results in a clear answer; it's either right or wrong. Mathematical equations, moreover, represent a wonderful means of problem solving. And there is no theoretical top to mathematics. The more you learn about the subject, the more you realize how much there is still to explore.

A reply such as this obviously shows far more evidence of analytical and critical thinking.

In probing for the reason behind the choice of the college, one student might say, "Because it had such a beautiful campus and because I was so favorably impressed with the people I met on my first day there." Another student might reply: "It was because I had learned that this college has the best department in aeronautical engineering on the east coast, and that the faculty here is top-notch." The second reply, of course, represents a far more mature reaction.

It is also a good idea ask how students went about choosing their college major. One student might say: "Oh, I guess I just drifted into it. I liked the teachers and found the subject easy." Another student might provide a far more mature and analytical response:

> I chose biology because of it is a very orderly and systematic science, and I guess I am that way. Biology also gave me an opportunity to learn how my own body functions. And in these days of burgeoning bio-genetics, an undergraduate degree in biology represents a great springboard for interesting graduate work.

Exploring Work Experience

Because there will be so little time left to talk about work experience— perhaps as little as 5 minutes—it is obviously impossible to touch upon all a student's summer and after-school jobs. Hence, it is well to encourage students to relate their single most important work experience: "Have you had any jobs in high school or college that you think added materially to your growth and development?" Every student has had at least one such experience and is usually anxious to talk about it. The interviewer then guides the student through a discussion of likes, dislikes, number of hours worked, and how that particular experience stimulated development. This discussion culminates in questions about the results of the performance appraisals found on the campus interview guide. Here, it is important not to be satisfied with one or two strengths or development needs. Say: "What other traits did your supervisor like about you?" And, "What other traits did your supervisor say you needed to improve?"

The All-Important Factor of Control

Interviewers will find that the only way to keep the campus interview within twenty minutes is to place a small clock immediately in front of them and to refer to it every two or three minutes. This requires stiff discipline. That is the only way to process some twelve to fifteen students in a single day. With practice, interviewers will be quick to pick up any tendency to over-elaborate and to move the student along to another topic. And they will do this by interrupting with appropriate timing and lubrication discussed in an earlier chapter. Some interviewers "dig a pit" for themselves by spending so much time on high school that there is inadequate time left for college and work experience. Again, though, frequent glances at the clock will help interviewers to pace themselves and get everything that is possible to obtain in a short 20-minute period.

Interviewers also need to control the discussion in such a way that they get more *evaluative* as opposed to *descriptive* information. And they need to concentrate on getting *hard data*. This means that they should ask for *quantification* wherever that is possible—number of hours worked on a given job, class standing, how late the student studies normally at night, and how many hours are put in in weekend study, and, when a student indicates long hours spend on a part-time job while attending school, how many credit hours were taken simultaneously.

Selling the Company

As discussed in Chapter 1, many campus interviewers make a big mistake by concentrating their major efforts on "selling the company" rather than on evaluating the individual student. This is not to say, however, that selling the company does not represent an important factor. Many companies will vie for what they consider "the best student" and they will offer every possible inducement. Obviously, then, the "sales pitch" represents an important aspect of the campus interview. But, as we shall subsequently see, this should be introduced at the very end of the interview—after the student has been evaluated.

Some companies try to get a "leg up" on their competition by scheduling an evening discussion prior to their subsequent interviews with individual students. This procedure can be highly recommended since it removes some of the sales burden from the individual interviews. Evening discussions provide a great opportunity for explanation of company policies, training programs, wage structure, opportunities for advancement, and the like. And "Question and Answer" periods can result in a great deal more information than the interviewer could possibly have time to discuss in the interview itself.

The Insufficiently Qualified Student

Interviewers who see some 15 students in a given day will probably find only 3 or 4 whom they consider sufficiently qualified for further consideration. This means that in the vast majority of cases there is no real need for a big sales job. In the case of those students who are not to be recommended interviewers can pass out any printed company material, thank students for their interest, and tell them that they will be hearing from the company within the next few weeks. They can also take the time to answer any immediate questions briefly. This brief windup gives the interviewers a few minutes of much needed rest prior to seeing the next student and helps them husband their energies and maintain their sanity in an otherwise impossible day.

The Qualified Student

When it has been determined that a student is qualified for further consideration, interviewers can "pull out all stops" in their effort to kindle interest in their companies. And, because we have placed the sales function at the end of the interview, they are in a position to sell *specifically* rather than *generally*. For example, when they have determined that a given candidate has a compelling interest in computers, they can describe in detail the company's computer facilities and spell out potential for upward mobility in that area. Or, in the case of students with demonstrated leadership ability, they can emphasize the extent to which their companies provide early opportunity for people with genuine leadership ability.

By positioning the sales function at the end of the interview, then, interviewers give themselves more "breathing space" in the case of students in whom they are not interested and, by the same token, find it possible to make a much more positive impact on the students they want to attract.

Recording Interview Results

In general, campus recruiters do a very poor job of recording interview results. Sometimes, they only make a few check marks on a form that has very little meaning in the first place. And some recruiters even wait until they have seen several students before they try to record results on the ones they decide to recommend.

Dictation Equipment Strongly Recommended

Without question, campus interviewers should be provided with portable dictating equipment. Expenditure of only a few hundred dollars, will provide several interviewers with dictating equipment as well as the equipment needed by a secretary to transcribe the results.

Learning to dictate does require practice. But most people pick it up within a few days and subsequently discover that dictation is not only a terrific time saver but extricates the busy campus interviewer from a great deal of boring paperwork.

Most important, however, dictating equipment makes it possible to record results *immediately after the interview.* With all the data freshly in mind, interviewers can dictate a few paragraphs that capsulize an individual's qualifications and they can learn to do this in a surprisingly short time.

The Interview Report

Reference to the sample campus interview report, which is shown in Figure 13-2, embodies the kind of information that is possible to obtain by an experienced interviewer within a 20-minute period. Of course, reports such as this cannot be written without some prior training.

Before beginning their reports, interviewers will find it helpful to refer again to the Personality and Ability Conformations repeated in Figure 13-3 for your convenience. It is suggested that this page be copied and placed under a sheet of clear plastic for ready reference. In addi-

DANIEL

It will be abundantly clear from this short interview that Dan's accomplishments to date have come as a result of truly incredible motivation. And these accomplishments are indeed impressive—Tau Beta Pi, outstanding physics award and high grades in high school and college. But, he studied 40 to 50 hours a week in college—including many all-nighters—and regularly studied on week-ends. Unquestionably, Dan possesses great energy, stamina, and willingness to work.

It also seems apparent that Dan is strong technically. He has a high math aptitude (650 SAT math score), has been keenly interested in mechanical engineering since he was a small boy, and seems to have a high mechanical aptitude (proud of his ability to tear down the engine of his car and put it back together). Over the past four summers, moreover, he has acquired relevant engineering experience as a result of his intern experiences at Northrop. During these summers, he has apparently developed a reputation for reliability, hard work, and "hands-on" expertise.

Dan's principal shortcomings stem from his low verbal aptitude. His SAT verbal score of 415 is very low; he has always had trouble with English; and his current supervisors are critical of his writing skills. It will be noted from the interview, too, that Dan's vocabulary is not very extensive and that he is really not all that articulate.

There is also reason to believe that Dan tends to be a one-dimensional person. He has put so much effort on study and summer work that there has been little time for anything else (no extracurricular activities at all in college). And he does not appear to have developed socially to the extent that many others of his age have. Nor is he very sophisticated intellectually.

In summary, Dan is the classic case of the overachiever, one who attains results primarily on the basis of hard work. He does not have a first class intellect. Nor is there much evidence of leadership. There are further clues to lack of self-confidence (the need to stay close to home, to cite one example.) Dan deserves great credit for what he has managed to accomplish and gives the appearance of being a wonderful human being. He can be recommended for further consideration as a direct hire but does not seem to represent a top candidate for the Carter Training Program, a program that costs the company some $100,000 per person and seeks to recruit only the "cream of the crop."

Figure 13-2. Campus interview guide.

(One might ask: "What are the reservations about hiring an over-achiever—someone who will work so very hard in order to accomplish what is expected of him?" The answer, of course, is that there are no reservations about hiring such a person for a *specialized* assignment where high potential for advancement is not an important requisite. But many overachievers do have a strong drive for upward mobility and the time will surely come when such individuals discover that hard work alone will not be enough to solve the complex problems that confront upper-level management. Nor will they be able to draw upon the *generalized thinking* which represents such an important requirement for success at the top.)

(Continued)

tion to recording the extent to which a given candidate measures up to certain aspects of the job description, therefore, interviewers can also record qualifications in terms of such important factors as maturity, motivation, intelligence, leadership, and people skills.

Personality and Ability Conformations

PRIMARY

MENTAL ABILITY
- verbal aptitude
- math aptitude
- analytical power
- perceptive
- critical thinker
- intellectual breadth and depth

MOTIVATION
- energy
- willingness to work
- conscientious
- initiative
- self discipline
- perseverance
- aspirations
- personal standards

MATURITY
- judgment
- knowledge of self
- reasonable vocational goals
- does not rationalize
- aware of limitations
- can "take the bitter with the sweet"

SECONDARY

PEOPLE SKILLS
- tact
- empathy
- sensitivity to the needs of others
- friendly
- cooperative

TECHNICAL ABILITY
- math aptitude
- academic preparation
- analytical ability
- critical thinker
- creative
- attention to detail

LEADERSHIP
- assertive
- self-confident
- tough minded
- good communicator
- enthusiastic
- well organized
- bold in thinking
- "take charge person"

CHARACTER
- honest
- reliable
- value system

EMOTIONAL ADJUSTMENT
- able to take pressure
- reasonably cheerful outlook on life
- not a worrier
- not subject to wide swings in mood

APTITUDE FOR SALES
- assertive
- self-confident
- tough-minded
- gift of gab
- infectious enthusiasm
- sense of humor
- perseverance
- color
- charisma
- extroverted

APTITUDE FOR FINANCE
- math aptitude
- academic preparation
- attention to detail
- somewhat introverted
- able to take a certain amount of "number crunching"
- able to see the big picture

APTITUDE FOR MANUFACTURING
- sense of urgency
- production minded—motivated to "get the pieces out of the door"
- flexible
- strong leadership
- able to keep several balls in the air simultaneously
- tough-minded

Figure 13-3.

14
Visioning

"Would you tell me, please, which way I ought to go from here?"
"That depends a good deal on where you want to get to."
"Well, I don't really much care."
"Then, it doesn't matter which way you go."

These lines from Lewis Carroll's *Alice In Wonderland* could be applied to many business situations. But Visioning, or creating tomorrow's reality, can help to alleviate such lack of clarity and direction.

The ability to create and implement a vision rests with our ability to probe and question where we are today and what we want to be in the future. Hence, the same kind of probing, open-ended questions we use in the interview can be put into practice here. Many companies, therefore, prefer to obtain the services of a consultant, skilled in the techniques of the Evaluation Interview, to help place the visioning process into operation.

The consultant meets with the head of the business unit involved and that person's immediate staff—usually eight to ten people. Together they address questions such as the following:

- What are the critical dynamics of our organization's environment? How do things really work?

- To what degree are trends changing the nature of our industry, and does this pose opportunities or threats?

- How is our organization distinctive and unique?

- What is our potential as an organization, and where can we be five years from now?
- How would we feel about the vision we want to create? Would we want it if we could have it?

Of course these questions are only part of the analysis an organization needs to complete. But, if the analysis is thorough with respect to strengths and weaknesses as we see ourselves today, we stand a greater likelihood of developing opportunities with which to create tomorrow's reality.

The effectiveness of any organization is based on the following principles:

- A stated purpose as to why the organization exists.
- A vision that inspires people to reach for what they could be and to rise above their fears and preoccupations with current reality. This enables people to clarify and realize what they really want.
- Alignment of people to the vision which, in turn allows them to operate freely and fully as part of the larger whole. Alignment is not agreement; it deals with the more inspirational aspects of purpose and vision. Alignment indicates a common purpose and helps people to transcend their differences.
- Empowerment that allows people and groups to take responsibility for and control of their lives. In such situations, people value personal power because they are committed to the same goal and direction. The increase of individual power increases total power of the organization.
- Results are achieved in truly meaningful ways because employees' goals are consistent with organizational goals.

Drawing on the above criteria to achieve organizational success, it is evident that developing a vision for an organization is fundamental to its business results and people effectiveness. People need some framework to guide their day-to-day decisions and priorities. Visioning can provide an emotional appeal with which people can identify. It can focus on *excellence, continuous improvement, and being better than the best.*

Visionary planning requires us to be insightful in answering the following six basic questions. Here the consultant draws upon two-step probing questions of the evaluation interview to develop more complete and in-depth responses.

Where Are We Today? The importance of answering this question lies in the fact that only from our current knowledge can we build a foundation for the future. Answering this question shows us what we now have and leads to the next question: "What do we want to keep?"

Where Do We Want to Go?   This is a fundamental question if we are to be all that we can be. We can envision what we want to create, but we must question and probe more deeply our assumptions if we are to achieve a vision of the future.

How Are We Going to Get There?   Identifying a vision is only one phase of the visioning process. In order for the vision to be actualized, it must be implemented. Too often, lofty goals such as "excellence, total quality, or commitment to greatness" are set without the first steps toward those goals being identified.

When Will It Be Done?   By placing a time frame on the planning and implementation of the process, we make a commitment to the realization of the vision. Unfortunately, many times visioning gets stuck at the planning stages and is never implemented due to other priorities. But, identification of benchmarks can help secure commitment and involvement.

Who Is Responsible for What?   Commitment flows through involvement. And, giving people a chance to participate in the process gives them a feeling of ownership. Making people responsible and accountable increases the likelihood of success.

How Much Will It Cost and What Are the Benefits?   It is axiomatic that the benefits of any change must outweigh the costs in order for a desired change to take place. This is crucial if the visioning process is to have meaning.

In summary, it is self-evident that when an organization has a clear sense of its purpose, direction, and desired future state, employees can better understand what the organization is trying to accomplish. This helps each person to see what the future holds as an extension of the present. When this vision is widely shared, people are better able to find their own roles in the organization. Everyone then gains a sense of importance because employees are all engaged in a creative, purposeful venture. What follows is enthusiasm, commitment, and pride.

Example

A small high-tech company found itself in the midst of change due to explosive growth over 3 consecutive years. These 3 years had been marked by a 30 percent earnings growth. But the forecast for the next 2 years indicated growth of only 5 to 7 percent. The company was operating without much planning as to what the future might hold or how to achieve better results.

Top management decided that the company needed a much clearer vision of its future and engaged the services of a consultant to initiate the visioning process.

The Current State of the Company

The first step involved an assessment of how the company saw itself today. This analysis revealed that much of the company's success had been due to its service orientation—its provision for fast, dependable, quality service to its customers. But, admittedly, marketing was never very aggressive, nor was there any strategy for the identification of present or future customers. Various functions operated independently and without integration.

Current realities suggested that growth had come about in an "after market" with little proactive marketing or selling. In fact, 75 percent of sales came as a result of adding on to compatible instrumentation of competitors through a low cost distribution system. An important further source of revenue came from the sale of spare parts and accessories from a catalog of low-cost replacement parts that could be shipped within 7 days.

As the company grew, the service department did not keep pace and was no longer the "shining star" of the organization. In fact, a lack of leadership and high turnover plagued this department. Contracts and commitments had not been set and customers were calling with complaints. Equally serious, little proprietary instrumentation had been developed.

Employees felt that the organization lacked direction and, therefore, were not sure of their own roles. And this, understandably, had an adverse effect on morale.

Identification of Issues that Needed to be Addressed

The next step in the organization analysis involved the identification of issues that needed to be addressed. These included: (1) the need to develop a proactive marketing strategy, (2) a complete revamping of the service department, (3) the expansion of the spare parts market, and (4) the establishment of a strategy for long-range planning.

Planning was something relatively new to this company. In past years, the company had been barely able to handle its current business, and as a result, planning took a back seat. There was, therefore, a need to define such common terms as quality, proprietary instrumentation, and alignment. A statement of the company's mission in the future helped define these terms.

Development of a Vision

The third phase involved the development of a vision that examined strategy, structure, systems, style, staff integration, skills, and shared values. In the course of this examination, it became clear that the organization required new leadership in the area of marketing, sales, and service.

The new vision also included a determination to "become a strong number three in market share" through the expansion of product line.

The organization also defined its "corporate personality" by describing the qualities to which it aspired. These included being ethical, consultative, supportive, knowledgeable, efficient and effective, courteous, and "willing to go the extra mile." The company even developed a motto that encompassed both the customer and employee: "Get-em, Keep-em and Develop-em."

Implementation

The fourth phase involved action that needed to be taken to propel the vision forward. The company initiated a search for a new service manager and a new director of marketing and sales, it developed a new training program for the service department that stressed customer service, it hired a marketing consultant to work on promotional literature, and it established a group which was charged with the responsibility for long-range planning.

Results

Over a period of time, this company has gone through a series of changes—all positive. For the first time in its eight-year history, it has a long-range plan and a strategy for accomplishing objectives. The company has developed a culture that fosters innovation and initiative. A new product line has been defined and put into operation. Customer service has been expanded to include customer partnerships as well as exchange and coordination.

The new vision resulted in a decided change in the attitude of employees. In prior years, people tended to be lethargic, uninterested, and often left their jobs early. But the new vision changed all of that through clearer job definition and involvement in new task forces set up to initiate projects. A new set of shared values that stressed risk taking, initiative, and self-determination was identified. Perhaps most satisfying of all, though, was a noticeable increase in productivity and employee involvement.

Although financial results of the visioning process are not yet available, there is a general feeling around the company that "nothing can stop us now." Thus, commitment to the vision has been gained through employee participation, an indispensable element to the success of this process.

15
Team Building

Although the use of teams and the concept of team building have been around for decades, there is currently a ground swell of interest devoted to using teams more effectively. Leaner organizations demand that people work together because there are fewer resources with more responsibilities placed on employees. Therefore, people need to work smarter together to get the job done.

It has been suggested that, in order to compete more effectively in the global marketplace, we must begin to work toward a team-based style of management where the whole is greater than all of the individual efforts combined. Hence, those companies that compete by integrating the talent and creativity of all of their employees will gain the competitive edge.

Bell South's current self-description proclaims that, "We are not a bunch of individuals out for ourselves, but are all part of a group." An Army spokesperson states that, "Teams are more reliable and take responsibility for the success of the overall operation." Examples of industrial achievements made through the use of teams abound. Companies like Chrysler, Ford, Monsanto, Motorola, and others have used the team concept to propel their enterprises forward, with improved design changes in cars, computers, and plant machinery.

Individuals working together can create something very special. In sports, for example, we can look back at the United States hockey team in the 1980 Olympics. A group of average players, as compared to other national teams, came together and created a miracle by winning the gold medal. Individually, there were no superstars, but they came together with a common goal and with individual roles to support each other.

Trust, Openness, and Honesty—The Indispensable Elements of Team Building

Traditionally, little time was spent on relations and trust building in the initial stages of team development. Groups were so task-oriented that there was a single-minded focus on specific results. As a result, decision making often got caught up in "hidden agendas" and the need for control and power.

It is widely recognized today, however, that early emphasis on rapport building pays big dividends. And this is where the techniques of the evaluation interview can play a big part—techniques such as reinforcement, playing down negative information, the calculated pause, and facial expressions. These techniques help team members to listen to each other more closely and gradually to build relationships based on trust, openness, and honesty.

Risk Taking and Openness to New Ideas

It is easy to fall back on tried and true approaches and to evaluate alternatives on the basis of what we know *as opposed to what can be.* But, if teams are to move forward as a whole, there has to be an element of risk taking and openness to new ideas. There must be a climate where people can fail and not be judged poorly for taking a chance. Actually, if a team is to be creative, people must be willing to generate seemingly crazy ideas, even if they do not seem appropriate at the time. New strategies emerge only in climates where there is a willingness to change and adapt to new situations.

Self-Evaluation and Feedback

Most important of all, team members must share their perceptions of themselves and invite, too, perceptions of others, to see how closely they match. In a sense, people learn to "expose" themselves to other members of the team by sharing information about themselves and responding to probing questions. Understandably, this can be a rather delicate process and normally requires the services of a knowledgeable consultant, skilled in the techniques of the evaluation interview.

The consultant may decide to administer the Myers-Briggs Type Indicator, an instrument that indicates basic preferences. The results produce neither right nor wrong preferences. They simply reflect different kinds of people who are interested in different things, may be drawn to different fields of work, and may even find it hard to understand each other. The Myers-Briggs Type Indicator is primarily concerned with the "valuable differences in people that result from where they like to focus their attention, the way they like to take in information, the way they like to decide, and the kind of life style they adopt." Each type has its own inherent strengths and weaknesses.

The information resulting from the Myers-Briggs Type Indicator is shared with each team member individually, then the group is divided into subgroups. Members of the subgroup take turns leaving the room while those remaining jointly decide what they perceive as that person's style and basic personality traits. The individual then reenters and the subgroup compares the results of the Myers-Briggs Type Indicator with their joint assessment of that person. This exercise continues until each member has been through this experience. Individual reaction is understandably uneasy in the beginning, but people gradually warm to the experience and subsequently report that this is the first time they have ever had candid feedback from their peers and that they find it very constructive.

The second step of the feedback process focuses on having individuals tell some personal experiences about themselves. Experience has shown that this exercise helps people to grow closer together. A questionnaire such as the one shown in Figure 15-1 can be used to stimulate this discussion. Here, again, the two-step probing question—an important element of the evaluation interview—can be used to advantage in developing additional information from each of these questions.

As team members get to know each other through feedback, they develop confidence in each other as well as mutual trust. Such confidence and trust enhances open and free-flowing communications, participative decision making, and increased productivity through collective group effort. Only then can the team focus on creating a common goal to achieve desired results.

The benefits of a successful team building based on interview techniques can be enormous and far reaching. Teams will progress as their members make them progress. Results of high-performing teams can include:

Output—where the team sets high output or high quality standards and regularly achieves them.

Objectives—where the team shares in the understanding of the purpose and the mission. Members learn to cooperate with one another and have a team spirit.

Energy—where there is a strength that members take from one another.

Team Development Questionnaire

DIRECTIONS: The list of questions below is designed to stimulate group discussion around work-related topics. The following ground rules should govern this discussion.

1. Take turns asking questions, either to specific individuals or to the group as a whole.
2. You must be willing to answer any question that is asked.
3. Work with the person who is answering to make certain that effective two-way understanding takes place.
4. All answers remain confidential within the group.

Questions may be asked in any order

1. How do you feel about yourself in your present job?
2. What are you trying to get accomplished in your work?
3. Where do you see yourself 10 years from now?
4. How are you perceiving me?
5. What would you predict to be my assessment of you?
6. What kind of relationship do you want with me?
7. What factors in your job situation impede your goal accomplishment?
8. Where would you locate yourself on a 10-point scale of commitment to the goals of this group (1 is low, 10 is high)?
9. What personal growth efforts are you making?

Figure 15-1.

Structure—where the team develops its own operating style with respect to how it goes about making decisions, develops an understanding of individual roles and role responsibilities, and establishes the mechanics of setting the agenda items and evaluating their performance.

Atmosphere—where there is a spirit that manifests itself in confidence and risk taking, information sharing and open communication.

Autonomy—where the results of team building are reflected in a high degree of control in the team's ability to make decisions.

Example

The Setting

A division of a Fortune 100 manufacturer found itself in a crisis mode of survival due to poor financial performance over the last 3 to 5 years and was told that, if financial returns did not improve over the next 2 years, it would be sold or spun off. Up until this time, the management style of the division was "from the top down," with little responsibility given to teams to achieve results. Accountability and responsibility were focused on individual managers. A one-year-old restructuring that left the division with 15 percent fewer people made it increasingly difficult to accomplish desired results.

The Process

A consultant was brought in to stimulate a change in management philosophy from an individual contributor style to a team-based style of management.

Initially, the managers of the division were skeptical concerning the shift in management philosophy, feeling that they would lose power and control and would gain very little in return. This concern was dissipated in part by an approach that enabled them to experience the collective value of the team-based style coupled with an individual role with which they could identify.

First, the managers worked through the individual process of getting self-insight described above—an insight that resulted in an understanding of how their individual style interacted with the styles of other managers in the group. They then used the individual feedback as part of the process of getting to know each other better. (One of the problems stemmed from the fact that team members did not trust each other and, when confronted with decision making, typically got hung up in petty squabbles and turf issues.)

The opportunity to share personal experiences gradually increased their individual and collective understanding. This resulted in breaking down communication barriers that had existed for many years. For example, one team member revealed that his perceived aggressive and arrogant style was due in part to his belief that the organization expected him to be tough and aggressive and that, in reality, he was a sensitive and caring person. He admitted that he had worn this "facade" for years. Other team members shared similar concerns and reactions—reactions that brought them closer together. Until this point, in fact, they thought they knew each other pretty well. Thus, the feedback session proved to be both beneficial and essential to the team-building process.

The second step focused on creating the value of the team by having team members experience the power of team decision making versus individual decision making. They collectively participated in several exercises that clearly demonstrated the power that a team could generate. A film was subsequently shown that highlighted the point that the creation of a common goal enables a team to rally around a central theme and achieve superior results by aligning people with a common vision.

The team next worked on the creation of its mission and objectives. While this was in progress, there was a noticeable sense of enthusiasm due to the fact that they had created their own vision and were committed to its implementation. They even created a motto with which they could all identify.

The next phase involved the mechanics of team planning and the setting up of agendas. It should be mentioned here that too often teams are given guidelines—and simply follow them—without having participated in the development of the guidelines. As a result, they do not have a sense of ownership. Teams need, for example, to determine how the group will explore in-depth versus surface issues or how it will maximize its resources. These and other questions were given to the team for the purpose of helping them create their own operating style. This resulted in a sense of team ownership of decision making, responsibility for results, and open and free-flowing communications.

Once the team had established its operating style and policy statement, it concentrated on setting up the agenda for team meetings. In the past, the group had experienced "information dissemination" meetings that often lasted as long as 5 or 6 hours and accomplished very little. The team now decided to focus on three or four areas that they would collectively work on such as: (1) developing a strategy to reduce costs, (2) designing and developing a training program, and (3) creating new system technologies through its management information systems. They then set up subcommittees which were assigned to each task force and set target dates for reports back to the team as a whole. They also developed evaluation forms designed to insure and monitor the progress of the group.

The last phase identified role and role responsibilities for each team member. This helped to bring clarity and focus to individual contribution and was used in the overall purpose of maximizing group performance.

Results

The results were remarkable! In less than three months the team developed cost reduction strategies and created business action teams responsible for product areas. Team meetings were met with enthusiasm and issues were both discussed and resolved. A spirit of cooperativeness and support prevailed—support that resulted in positive evaluation of meetings.

Financial results represented still another measure of success. *The division not only met its financial commitments but exceeded all targets.* One person summed up the results by saying: "We achieved the impossible!"

16
Feedback

Because the feedback of appraisal information involves an interview, every single technique of the Evaluation Interview is applicable in this procedure—the rapport inducing techniques, the probing techniques, and even the control of the interview techniques. Hence, the managers who have trained in interviewing have an enormous advantage in terms of utilizing feedback to enhance performance, confront lack of performance, and shape behavior.

In this chapter we will develop the concept of feedback, emphasize those factors that both the manager and the employee can do to *prepare* for the feedback session, and of course, we will spell out the specific techniques involved in disclosing to the individual both the results of the evaluation interview and the data gleaned from job performance. At the end of the chapter we will include two case histories which illustrate the application of feedback techniques and results that grew out of these sessions.

The Concept

Feedback is the process of communication whereby managers share with employees their view of strengths and shortcomings. This sharing should be done in a way that lays the groundwork for behavioral change. Equally important, employees must be able to "hear" and understand the feedback. The well-trained manager must realize that feedback has two distinct parts—first, to reinforce existing positive behavior and, second, to discuss negative behavior as a prelude to future growth and development.

Traditionally, feedback has been a difficult experience for both managers and employees. In a study reported in 1987, 4000 employees in

190 firms were surveyed concerning reactions to the feedback process in their companies (*Working Women,* Psychological Associates of St. Louis, June 1987). A full 70 percent reported that their managers did not give them a clear picture of what was expected of them and only 20 percent said that their performance was reviewed at all! This provides clear evidence that feedback was not used as an effective management tool on a consistent basis. And, when it is not used with sufficient frequency, neither party feels comfortable in the sharing situation.

Some people who do not receive appraisals or feedback may develop negative feelings toward their managers, feeling that they are not fulfilling their management responsibilities. In some cases, too, lack of performance feedback can cause anxiety and frustration. It may even lower efficiency and productivity.

When feedback appraisals are awkwardly given—as is so often the case—the discussion can become emotionally charged. For example, individuals may take a *defensive stance* in reaction to the discussion of shortcomings and this can be uncomfortable for both parties. But, where feedback appraisals are competently handled from the top down, this often produces a "trickle down" effect. Getting effective performance feedback from one's superior makes it easier to conduct this same kind of quality performance with one's subordinates. And, this type of communication can help avoid duplication of work, overlapping authority, unclear performance standards, unclear job assignments and ambiguous goals.

We hope that the techniques discussed in this chapter will allay anxieties, increase proficiency, and generally make it easier and more comfortable for the manager to give and for the employee to receive feedback.

Feedback—A Shared Responsibility

Feedback is usually seen as the responsibility of the manager or appraiser. But, in the most effective feedback, the recipient plays a more active role than simply being the passive receiver. For, in addition to being open to receiving feedback, employees should seek out this kind of information—expressly ask for it.

There is also a need—a need not often discussed—for people to share information about themselves so that the appraiser can place the feedback in proper context, by putting it in a form that has the most meaning for the recipient. Hence, the information concerning short-term and long-term goals, factors of job satisfaction, how much and what kind of supervision they prefer, what talents they feel they have that they are not utilizing, and how they feel about their present job—all these pieces of information can be most helpful to the manager. This is why an evaluation interview prior to the formal feedback session has so much meaning.

Feedback—An Ongoing Process

The feedback review is not an event; rather, it should be viewed as an ongoing process that embodies the concept of continuous development. Only in that way can it expect to influence performance, benefiting both managers and subordinates. From a manager's perspective, it helps to maintain and improve current employee job performance. For employees, it answers the often unspoken question, "How am I doing?" and, hence, provides reassurance and helps to boost morale.

Despite the fact that feedback should be an ongoing process, employees often receive very little of this. As indicated earlier in this chapter, many do not even get an annual review and, when they do, they frequently find the experience unsatisfactory.

Managers shy away from feedback because they have been given so little help in terms of how to carry it out. We will therefore devote the rest of this chapter to the annual review, with the thought that, once managers learn how to do this comfortably, they will subsequently give more attention to the ongoing process.

Preparation—the Employee's Role

There has been much more information published on the process of *giving* feedback than there has been on how to *receive* it. Yet, the latter is of equal importance. Both are necessary conditions for effective utilization of the process. Just as the manager plans for the feedback meeting, so should the employee prepare for this discussion. By assuming a positive attitude, the employee can expect to get a great deal more out of the experience. The following principles should prove helpful for employees at all levels:

- Try to view feedback as a process of continuous development—ongoing and dynamic. It should not be viewed as an isolated experience. Solicit feedback from managers on a regular and relatively frequent basis. Taking the initiative and seeking out feedback creates some measure of control as opposed to the more passive approach of waiting until someone decides to give it. The act of seeking out this information conveys the message that this is important to you.

- Be prepared to share information about yourself—your short-term and long-term goals, the kind of work that provides the most satisfaction, and how you feel about your job.

- Try to be open and nondefensive. Try not to "explain away" negative feedback by merely saying to yourself, "Managers don't understand me." Blaming others is easy. Doing something about one's shortcomings is more difficult. It is important to listen and understand what is being said and to determine how you can benefit from the criticism.

- Maintain an open attitude toward the content of the feedback. This will maximize the chances that it will be constructive. Go into the interview with the idea of giving serious consideration to all suggestions and to taking whatever action may be necessary to make this a positive experience. Develop a "can do" attitude.

- Take an active role in the interview. Discuss the feedback, ask questions, and seek clarification. When a point is made that does not ring true, do not be afraid to ask for additional evidence or documentation. In short, try to get as much information as possible before evaluating the meaning of the comments. Then, if you agree with the comments, acknowledge their value and let the manager know how you feel about what you are hearing. It might be well to say, "That has a lot of meaning for me and I can understand how I might profit from it." This reflects a far more positive attitude than simply sitting there with a blank stare.

- Be aware of possible nonverbal messages you may be transmitting with such factors as eye contact, facial expressions, gestures, and posture. Leaning back in the chair with your arms crossed, for example, may convey the message that feedback will be resisted despite any of your claims of openness. On the other hand, sitting forward conveys the message of interest, and nodding your head shows involvement and participation.

The Feedback Reaction Form shown in Figure 16-1 provides employees with a helpful tool to use after the feedback session. Use of this form can help employees synthesize the feedback information, react to it in an intelligent way, and in effect, gain "ownership" of it. This form also forces the individual to reflect upon what has been shared. By writing reactions, individuals can begin to see those areas that need attention. They may even attempt to validate the manager's perception of strengths and development needs with some of the people who are closest to them and know them the best. In this way, employees become both accountable and responsible for the feedback information.

Feedback Reaction Form

Areas of major strengths: _____

_____

_____

_____

Areas I want to work on: _____

_____

_____

_____

Observations I accept: _____

_____

_____

_____

Observations I do not accept: _____

_____

_____

_____

Things I want to think about: _____

_____

_____

_____

Observations I do not understand: _____

_____

_____

_____

How I feel right now: _____

_____

_____

_____

Figure 16-1.

Preparation—the Manager's Role

Feedback sessions present an opportunity to communicate to employees precisely where the organization is going, its longer-range future, and the potential fit with respect to the employee's skills and the organization's needs. The session tries to create an "interdependency"—an integration of the company's needs, the employee's needs, and a fit of the two.

In approaching the feedback meeting, managers should plan to tell employees to expect three types of information. They can expect to receive information that is familiar in the sense that they have heard it before and understand where it comes from. They can expect to receive information that is new and not readily understandable in terms of where it may fit in. And, finally, they may regard some of the information as irrelevant and without merit. By introducing feedback in this way, managers can reduce the employee's level of anxiety and help them remain open to the process.

The following principles should prove helpful:

- *Be prepared to document from the employee's job performance every single item you plan to convey. If you are not in a position to provide this kind of documentation for a given item—whether it represents a strength or shortcoming—it has no place on your list.* If you plan to discuss a need for better organization, for example, you should be able to provide documentation such as the following: "Do you remember when you began work on the Z project two months ago? We had to interrupt after three days and ask you to start over, utilizing a different action plan. I suggested then that that was a matter of prioritizing and organization. Yesterday I had to ask you to rewrite one of your reports, using a different plan and procedure. Wasn't that also a matter of organization?"

- Keep a record of each employee's performance so that specific examples of both positive and negative performance can be cited. If, for example, you plan to tell a person that she tends to be "overly dominant," you should be able to cite several incidents such as: "In yesterday's meeting you had a tendency to do most of the talking and relatively little listening. As a result, other people did not feel involved or did not feel they had an opportunity to express their own opinions."

- Plan to be specific rather than general. Too often employees leave feedback meetings without a sense of what occurred because the discussion was too general and nonspecific. As a result, they either dismiss what they have heard or do not take ownership for the situation.

A manager may say, for example: "Your speech was O.K., but you left out bits of information that might have strengthened your presentation." An employee may wonder what was effective in the presentation and what specifically he could have done to make it better. A more effective feedback statement might have been: "The aspects of your presentation that were effective included your visual presentation, handouts, and discussion points. On the other hand, you needed to bring in factual data to support your position. I was at a loss because I wasn't sure how you came to your conclusions." Thus, when you are candid and frank, you leave nothing to the imagination.

- Remember that feedback must be limited to those factors within the individual's control. Most people are understandably resistant when criticized for something they are powerless to change or improve, such as mental ability, nervousness, or some aspects of personal appearance. To be told that one is not all that sharp or intelligent, for example, can be a devastating experience.

- You should plan to state the objectives of the performance review— the extent to which the information will be used for salary increases, for training needs, for morale building, or simply to enhance performance. There should also be an agreement between employee and manager on goals, the standards by which performance will be measured, and what constitutes superior performance.

- Remember that the intent of feedback is to help people, not to hurt them. Some managers, unfortunately, like to use feedback as a leverage or power tool—to build themselves up at the expense of others.

- The review should be regarded as an opportunity for you to offer guidance, encouragement, and suggestions for improvement. You should plan to use it as a means of developing a set of constructive plans for strengthening identified weak areas and helping people to grow and develop their full potential.

- Plan to focus the discussion on behavior rather than on the person. Instead of telling an employee that he is rigid or inflexible, it is better to point out situations in which such behavior has occurred: "In our team discussion, you tended to reiterate your point of view over and over again as opposed to adopting a more open attitude."

- The process should be as much counseling and coaching as it is evaluative—as much a listening as a talking activity. Ask questions to clarify what has been said. Keep the focus on the employee. Active listening requires full attention. Make it clear that you consider this meeting to be important. One important objective is to increase motivation and self esteem. Make it a "we", not a "you" discussion.

- As pointed out earlier, you should conduct reviews both formally and informally. There should be continuous feedback about results. However, too much feedback may be viewed as overly close supervision or control. Even so, ongoing feedback is most effective when people have clearly defined job objectives and have a means of measuring their own job performance.

- You should plan to make your feedback candid and frank. If work has been less than satisfactory, you must acknowledge this. You must be prepared to give honest criticism so employees know where they stand. If employees have some concern about your level of honesty, they begin to wonder about possible hidden agendas.

- Probe more deeply for needs and motivations in order to gain additional insight concerning those reporting to you. Ask such questions as: "Where does your drive for achievement come from? Do you feel a need to be competitive or is it a drive for accomplishment? What are some of the satisfiers for you in your job? Some people look for security, financial rewards, or personal recognition. What is important to you?"

- Remember that feedback should be appropriately timed. Immediate feedback is best. Actually, it should be delayed only to avoid embarrassing an employee in front of others or to get more information about a particular situation. Comments should not be saved for a later formal setting. Employees cannot be expected to improve if they do not know that a problem exists. Informal feedback is a powerful tool since it provides a constant reminder that performance matters. An appropriate reminder: "I am pleased that you brought this project to a close under budget. That is quite an accomplishment! Is there something we can learn from your experience?"

The more formal annual review, then, should become a summary of all the pieces of recognition the employee has accumulated throughout the year. In this way, the annual review will hold few surprises and will be less traumatic and more meaningful.

Finally, the proper person from management should be selected to conduct the formal review session, and this person must possess sufficient credibility and power to make the session productive. Credibility comes from the extent to which employees believe that the manager has enough first-hand information to evaluate their performance. Actually, credibility is a function of two factors—expertise and trust. In addition to being considered trustworthy, the manager must be perceived as possessing the expertise to judge behavior accurately, and this, of course, means a familiarity with the task itself and the employee's own performance on that task.

Power represents the means of controlling valued results. In general, the higher the power of the source of feedback, the more likely the recipient will try to respond positively. This influences the extent to which employees accurately perceive the feedback and resolve to try to do something about it.

Types of Feedback

There are several different types of feedback. Each serves a different purpose and is suited for particular situations.

Tell and listen.   In this type of feedback, the manager assumes a more passive role while the employee clarifies, explains, and acknowledges the feedback. Example: "You have told me that my handling of the meeting yesterday was too directive and that I didn't allow other people sufficient opportunity for input. Let me give you some background on why I used more authority than is usual for me." While this approach has merit in some situations, it places full responsibility on the employee and limits the manager's effectiveness as a coach and mentor.

Tell and sell.   After feedback is given, the manager discusses its value and usefulness. In this setting, the manager maintains an active role by talking about how an employee might improve performance. Example: "The reports you write are not condensed enough. It is difficult to find the important facts and figures. You need to become aware of the importance we place on concise, well organized reports. Look at this report and see where you might cut and improve it."

In this type of session, the manager is more active and the employee is more passive. The "selling" by the manager may be a turn off to the employee. The only reason for change may be to please the manager. This may bring short-term change, but not necessarily long-term improvement. In a sense, the manager is mandating or dictating the necessary improvement. Commitment on the part of the employee is therefore minimized.

Problem-solving approach.   This involves a joint relationship with the manager and the employee working together in order to understand the problem and how to solve it. Example: "Our department has had trouble the past two months reaching production figures. Let us go over what we have been doing and try to see where the problem is. In particular, the people in your area seem to be absent more than is usual. What do you believe is going on?"

Generally, the most effective feedback session is one where both manager and employee participate fully. This approach sets the stage for a longer lasting change to occur and for the employee to feel that the manager is vested in the improvement goals and, at the same time, is concerned for his well-being.

Formal Annual Review

We have pointed out the value of interview training as a prelude to feedback. At the same time, we realize that many managers will not have received this training. Even so, they can profit from techniques of the evaluation interview discussed in Parts 2 and 3 of this book. In this section, therefore, we will call attention to some of these techniques and show how they can not only make the manager and employee more comfortable in the feedback session, but can also help to make the review a more positive and constructive experience.

The Importance of Building Rapport

Since the initial purpose of the annual review is to get the employee to feel at ease, open up, and participate extensively in the discussion, the manager should draw upon all of the rapport-inducing techniques described earlier—*small talk, the calculated pause, facial expressions, positive reinforcement (verbal and nonverbal), and partial play down of negative information.* Only when rapport has been established can the employee be expected to "hear" what is being said, as a result of minimizing filters of defensiveness and other "emotional noise."

This interview should begin in much the same way any other interview should begin—with *small talk.* In the course of seating herself and throwing out the question informally and with an appropriate smile, the manager might say: "I know that you participate in our fitness center. I think that's great! Tell me about your routine and what you think the experience is doing for you." By encouraging the subordinate to talk for 2 or 3 minutes about this extraneous topic, the manager not only begins the interview in a pleasant, nonthreatening manner, but subtly conveys the impression that she expects the employee to do a good bit of the talking.

With the small talk concluded, the manager discusses the purpose of the review and encourages the employee to discuss factors of job satisfaction and both short-term and long-term goals: "Let me tell you a little about our discussion today. As you know, we get together once a year to summarize what has happened to you over the past twelve months in terms of your achievements and opportunities for further development. But, I believe I can be more helpful to you if you tell me a little about your short-term and long-term goals and the aspects of any job that give you the most satisfaction. Let's start with the latter. What does a job have to have to give you satisfaction? Some people look for money, some for security, some want to manage, some want to create. What's important to you?"

Once the manager has discussed factors of job satisfaction, the kind of job the employee would like next, and where he sees himself five years hence, she is ready for the solid core of the interview—strengths and development needs.

Strengths

We always begin this section of the review with a discussion of strengths. This permits us to "accent the positive" at the very start and helps the recipient to understand his importance to the organization and how much he is valued.

Few people have done a very good job of evaluating their strengths and some may even feel somewhat self-conscious about reviewing them. This often stems from early upbringing which may have instilled the dictum, "Don't blow your own horn." At any rate, the manager may ease this situation by borrowing the question on strengths from the Interview Guide: "Let's begin by highlighting some of your major accomplishments over the past year. Do you think you have worked harder than the average person, organized things better, gotten along with other people better, given more attention to detail—just what?"

As each asset surfaces, the manager should "build up" or emphasize the importance to the organization of that strength, provided of course, she agrees with it: "Attention to detail is an all important asset to this aircraft engine company where we are all striving for zero errors!" By developing a sizable list of strengths and accenting the importance of each one, the manager begins to build a psychological advantage, in the sense that the employee will subsequently be more willing to disclose shortcomings now that he knows his supervisor is aware of all his good points and values his accomplishments.

The manager should "stay with" the discussion of strengths for a considerable period, "priming the pump" from the list of strengths she has prepared on that particular individual prior to the review session. Some managers tend to rush through this discussion in order to get to areas that need improvement. This is a big mistake since it not only fails to build self esteem and boost morale, but also makes it subsequently more difficult to stage a constructive discussion of shortcomings.

Be sure to tie in strengths to job performance. It is not enough to tell a man that you know he is a hard worker. It is much more meaningful to say, "I appreciate all the hard work and overtime hours you spent in order to complete the Zan project on schedule. I know that involved a lot of self sacrifice and support from your family."

Development Needs

After the discussion of strengths has been completed, the session should focus on areas where performance was below expectations. As indicated earlier, it is crucial for the manager to have prepared thoroughly for this part of the interview prior to the session. She must be able to document each shortcoming with examples and hard data gleaned from job performance during the period of the review. This is important because it is human nature to try to improve only in those areas where the person is convinced of the need to improve.

Here again, we can borrow the question on development needs from the Interview Guide: "You certainly have an impressive array of strengths. Now let's talk a bit about some of the things you could improve. You know none of us is perfect; we all have traits or abilities that can stand improvement. And the person who becomes aware of such traits is in a position to do something about them and, hence, to grow and develop a lot faster than might otherwise have been the case. What are some of the areas you think you could improve?"

In response to this question, the employee may volunteer several of the items on the manager's list. Each item should be completely discussed and the conversation on each point should conclude with an agreed-upon action plan, with milestones for improvement and evaluation. This shows that the manager really wants to help, and it also establishes the fact that she expects the employee to improve. Make certain that you let the person know you have confidence in him even when he may have failed upon occasion to achieve what he has set out to do in the past: "I know that you will find a way to make the necessary changes so that this project will be completed and be as successful as your strong track record in project management indicates."

When the employee can think of no additional areas for improvement, the manager should introduce other items on her list one by one, using the evaluation interview's double-edged question: "What about firmness with people? Do you have as much of this as you would like to have, or is this something you could improve a little bit?"

When the employee says he sees no real need to improve this, the manager must supply documentation from her prepared material: "Well, you have admitted to me from time to time that you have two people under your supervision who perform far less well than the rest of the group. Is it possible that you are giving these people too much of the benefit of the doubt when you really should have separated them? You know you mentioned earlier that you have aspirations for upper level management and all of us around here feel that mental toughness or the ability to make hard decisions about people represents one of the truly critical factors in functioning effectively on that level."

If the employee agrees at last that mental toughness does represent an area in which he could improve, the manager and subordinate must work out an action plan to influence this development. The manager might say as one of her suggestions: "How would you feel about taking the company course in assertiveness training?" Or: "Let's keep tabs on the absenteeism in your group and see if that can be improved over a period of time."

As implied above, there is little point of giving negative feedback unless this is accompanied by specific suggestions as to how the individual might go about making the necessary behavioral change. The manager and employee should work together to create a developmental action plan. Such a plan is crucial since it represents the link between feedback and how the individual can expect to make the appropriate changes. A constructive feedback review might come up with four or five areas for self-growth and improvement together with steps necessary to facilitate the change. To cite another example, let us assume that better presentation skills have been identified as an area for improvement. In this case, the developmental action plan might include such specific steps as taking a course in effective presentation skills, video taping one of the individual's presentations, or observing a presentation of some other person who is considered expert in this area.

End The Feedback on a Positive Note

The manager should always conclude the review on a positive note. A brief summary at the end should list the most important strengths and the fact that these are highly valued by the manager: "You certainly have an impressive array of strengths. I depend on you to provide the creative input we need in this department as well as your unique ability to see that things get done."

The manager should also ask the employee to provide his own summary of what he has heard. If the person is missing something important, ask questions to get at the facts. Listen carefully for evidence that the individual really understands the problem areas and intends to do something constructive about them.

Focus on the future. Feedback should present an opportunity for future successes. The crucial question is: "How can we set things up so that you can do an even better job next time?" Forward-looking questions are positive and reflect promise for continued improvement.

Nonverbal Feedback

Since most psychologists now agree that nonverbal signals represent an important aspect of communication, no discussion of feedback would be complete without some attention to this factor. It has been our experience, in fact, that the nonverbal factor plays a significant, though often unrecognized, role. Nonverbal feedback involves body language and other cues which are used—often unconsciously—to express interest or to convey lack of attention. Some of the more common types of nonverbal communication include the following:

- Appearance—What "message" does your clothing convey? Authority? Informality? Does your appearance fit the occasion?

- Gestures—What are your hands saying? Clenched hands often symbolize tension and nervousness. Curled fist may indicate anger. Hands in pockets may portray resignation.

- Posture—Does your posture fit your verbal message? Are you leaning forward in interest toward the person or pushing back in your chair to keep at a distance? Frequent shifting of positions may be interpreted as impatience or lack of interest.

- Eye Contact and Facial Expression—Is the eye contact you maintain one of interest or a "glare" of intimidation? Does your facial expression betray your real feelings despite the words you are using?

- Voice—Does the intonation, volume and rate of speech reflect the mood you wish to induce? Speaking too loudly, for example, may tend to intimidate the other person, causing that person to "clam up" rather than "speak up."

Awareness of all the factors involved in effective feedback enhances the probability that this important function will be given and received constructively. Creation of a base of open communication and trust stimulates managers and employees to engage in feedback regularly, thereby making continuous improvement a reality. The more formal feedback review, then, becomes a summary discussion of shared perceptions of past performance and results, a vehicle for developmental goals, and a chance to share the vision of the future.

Case History: George

The Setting

George, a middle-level manager with eight years' experience in a large industrial company was considered by management to be a "high potential" employee. In fact, he was seen as an individual with a chance to progress right up to the Vice President or General Manager level. Each year he had come up with ideas that had earned him significant bonuses for his work.

Interestingly enough, the organization had identified this track record for George, but had never consulted him about his own expectations, needs, and career goals. George's situation is not unlike that of many others in American industry where highly valued employees with considerable talent have been given so little feedback over the years that they have relatively little idea of management's plans for them.

In George's case, however, his manager did realize at last that this important employee was at a personal cross-roads. The manager knew that there were several conceivable "next steps" for George, but he himself was not certain which move would make the best "fit" both for George and the company. He did realize, though, that George had been in his present position as product manager long enough and was ready for a more demanding assignment. He, therefore, suggested that the company bring in a management consultant to conduct an evaluation interview with George—an interview that would highlight his strengths and development needs and would provide him with specific feedback. George was told that this feedback would make it possible for him to structure the kind of Development Action Plan that would stimulate his growth as a person and, at the same time, would enable the organization to determine whether its perceptions of his capabilities and future goals were consistent with the career track he may have identified for himself.

George was understandably somewhat skeptical in the beginning, but after further discussion, realized that this process might help him validate his perceptions of himself and might enable him to take considerable control over his own career. Moreover, deep down, George was not all that certain himself as to which career path might be best for him.

Interview Findings

Interview results clearly revealed that there were two distinct paths George could take that might prove beneficial for both him and the company. One path could be focused on line management where he could be expected to use his management skills, interpersonal skills, breadth of technical knowledge, and ability to "vision." But further probing disclosed that, while George had some of the necessary skills to be successful in this area, some of his values did not line up with those of the company. For example, George is a family man who relishes the time he spends with his wife and two young children. He began to realize that future line management assignments would probably require several moves to different parts of the country, extensive travel, and even a possible assignment abroad. He also admitted that a line position would require a higher degree of assertiveness and extroversion than he currently possessed. In the past, George had not confronted the issue of sacrifices he and his family would have to make in order to reach the general manager level. But, now he professed a willingness to grapple with the different value systems and to come to some decision.

The second career path would involve a more staff-oriented position in planning and marketing where he could draw upon his analytical, conceptual, and creative skills. He drew attention to accomplishments over the past several years that stemmed from these abilities. He noted, for example, in his prior sales position he spent a large percentage of his time planning an electronic database information system for his customers, developing a strategic plan for extending the market share in his product area, and assisting in computerizing his office through analysis of the effectiveness of several different systems. As he described these accomplishments, moreover, he unconsciously exuded appreciable pride. Traditionally, people who have been successful in sales spend the majority of their time in front of the customer and not in product planning. Although George is very approachable and easy to get along with, he did not gain as much satisfaction from customer contact as he did from the planning and marketing function.

Feedback

Drawing upon the techniques described earlier in the Formal Annual Review, the consultant discussed the strengths and development needs that emerged from the interview. He noted that George is an individual with extremely high intellectual abilities and very strong analytical skills. He is able to assimilate data, recognize key variables, and analyze complex situations. And he has the relatively rare capacity to look for and evaluate innovative approaches. George presents himself in a professional manner and is able to maintain personal control. He exudes a sense of self-confidence and is respectful of the values and attitudes of others. George is also a true team player.

Areas of improvement centered around the need to develop a more assertive manner in group situations in order to "stand out in a crowd." He could desirably make a stronger impact on people and over a period of time develop a more forceful image. George also needs to acquire a broader business base. He had a solid foundation in financial management, but needs to be tested in the area of business strategy. George took the discussion of short-comings in stride, even offering several of the more important items himself.

Following the feedback session, George took the information that was presented to him and spent some time analyzing it. Then he used the Feedback Reaction Survey to summarize his thoughts and feelings. This resulted in the decision that he wanted to take the career path in planning and marketing. Even so, he realized that there were aspects of leadership in the upper levels of this area, too, for which he was not sufficiently prepared. As a result, he developed an action plan that included the following: attending a marketing warfare seminar, assuming responsibility for a total quality project, attending a leadership skills course, joining an executive managerial seminar, and increasing exposure to management through projects that crossed divisional lines.

Results

After George finalized his Development Action Plan, he had a career conference with his manager to discuss what he had learned about himself and to enlist his manager's help in developing a career framework that would meet both George's and the organization's needs. It became clear to the manager that the career path the organization had identified for George was not consistent with how George saw himself. George and his manager discussed several career options and finally settled on the position of planning and marketing that could eventually lead to the job of Director of Planning for an entire business function. From there, if he proved successful, George might someday become Director of Planning for a whole division.

Had his superiors pushed George into line management, he might have become frustrated and, at some point, may even have left the company. But, as a result of the career discussion with his manager, George has developed a new sense of excitement and enthusiasm and his manager has a heightened awareness of who George really is.

Case History: Mary

The Setting

Primarily on the basis of hard work and willingness to put in long hours, Mary won a promotion from data processing to human resources. In this department her keen insight, conceptual abilities, and systems approach made her something of a natural for organizational planning. Over a period of time, however, lack of follow-through and inattentions to detail began to show up in her work. Drawing upon her conceptual ability, she tended to start a variety of projects, only to be thwarted by politics, getting bored, or general impatience.

Mary decided that she was at a point in her career where she should pursue a more generalist role in the human resources department. However, her manager did not go along with this, feeling that she did not have sufficient penchant for detail or enough interpersonal sensitivity to make a significant contribution in such a role. At the same time, he told her that she was well equipped for her current job in human resource planning.

Mary's manager realized that she was not completely happy in her job, but he did not know what else to do with her. When the company installed a training program for managers in the techniques of feedback, however, the manager knew he had some new resources at his command and resolved to conduct a feedback session with Mary and the others in his department.

Feedback

Mary was initially impressed with her manager's efforts to establish rapport and his apparent interest in helping her to grow and develop. Because she had never before had a complete performance appraisal, she had acquired the feeling that he was not all that concerned with her potential for increased responsibility. But now, for the first time since she had joined the department, Mary had an opportunity to talk about her needs, motivations, and aspirations. The manager discovered that Mary had an intense desire to make a meaningful contribution and to be considered a part of the "team." She also felt that a staff role would not make it possible for her to function in the mainstream of the company.

Together they discussed her strengths at considerable length, with the manager using examples from her day-to-day performance to document each item. He told her among other things that he was impressed with her intelligence, her strong conceptual skills, and her ability to see the big picture. He documented her analytical and organizational skills by calling attention to the exceptional job she had done in organizing and scheduling an executive development

course at Duke University. In the course of this project, she had
analyzed several different courses with respect to their strengths and
weaknesses relative to her company's needs and recommended the
course at Duke as the best for their purposes. Her manager noted that
the hard work and long hours she had expended on this project was
quite typical of her approach to almost everything she did.

When asked to discuss some of her development needs, Mary
readily admitted a need to give more attention to detail and
follow-through. Together they talked about some of the things she
might do to improve this condition. Mary seemed surprised, though,
when her manager brought up the possible need to develop more
tact, social sensitivity, and political savvy. In order to document
these needs, he again referred to the Duke University project which
had not been all that well attended by company executives. He
mentioned that Mary had not involved any of the executives in the
process and implied that, had she consulted and asked for their
input during her analysis, she would not only have gained valuable
exposure to important people in the company, but also might have
encouraged more managers to attend. Mary saw the logic of her
manager's example and thereby understood her need for
improvement in this area.

The manager made a point of concluding the review on a positive
note. He told her that the company valued her organizational and
developmental skills, her critical problem analysis, and her focus on
achieving meaningful results. He suggested that Mary would
eventually find a desirable "fit" within the organization if she
capitalized on her strengths and tried her best to modify her
shortcomings.

Mary wrote a Developmental Action Plan that included the
following: (1) try to increase the degree of tact and social sensitivity
necessary for the establishment and maintenance of better
interpersonal relations; (2) try to become more sensitive to issues of
power and politics and to use consultative skills to promote the
organizational development services, and (3) try to do a better job of
follow-through and prioritizing on all projects and assignments.

In order to stimulate development in the above areas, Mary
committed to the following implementation: (1) schedule regular
weekly meetings with her manager to discuss priorities, set agendas,
and develop timetables, (2) participate in the United Way Campaign
to gain exposure and work with senior management, (3) attend a
one-week course in interpersonal skills and sensitivity training, and
(4) schedule quarterly reviews with middle management to discuss
executive development, succession planning, and management
reviews.

Results

In less than one year, perceptions of Mary's work have changed
significantly—so much so, in fact, that she has earned a promotion

to the position of personnel representative. Mary is more popular with other members of the department and is noticeably better on follow-through. She still has some "rough edges" in the diplomatic area, but she has even shown some improvement there. Mary is extremely pleased with her new job because it gives her access to managers on a day-to-day basis and provides a welcome opportunity to assist them with all of their personnel problems.

Appendix **1**

Interview Guide

INTERVIEW GUIDE

Name_____Date_____Interviewer_____

---

1. WORK HISTORY

a. Duties?

b. Likes?

c. Things found less satisfying?

d. Conditioned to work?

e. Level of earnings?

f. Performance appraisal?

g. Reasons for changing jobs?

h. Any leadership experience?

i. Number of previous jobs?

j. Achievements? "What did you learn about your strengths as a result of working on those jobs? Did you find, for example, that you worked harder than the average person, got along better with people, organized things better, gave more attention to detail—just what?"

k. Development needs? "Did you get any clues to your development needs as a result of working on those jobs? You know, we all have some shortcomings and, the person who can recognize them, can do something about them. Was there a need to acquire more self-confidence, more tact, more self-discipline—to become firmer with people—just what?"

l. Factors of job satisfaction? "What does a job have to have to give you satisfaction? Some people look for money, some look for security, some want to manage, some want to create—what is important to you? (Do you prefer a job that is structured or unstructured? theoretical or practical? with a fair amount of detail or without much detail?)"

m. Type of job desired?

2. EDUCATION AND TRAINING

a. Best and poorest subjects?

b. Grades? "What about grades? Were they average, above average, or perhaps a little below average?"

c. College boards? "What were your college board scores?"

d. Extracurricular activities?

e. Effort? "How conscientious a student were you? Did you work about as hard as the average person, a little harder, or perhaps not quite so hard?"

f. Special achievements?

g. Training beyond the undergraduate level?

h. How was education financed?

3. PRESENT SOCIAL ADJUSTMENT

a. Interests and hobbies
Sports
Community involvement
Reading
Interest in the arts

b. Energy level "How would you describe your energy level—as average, above average, or perhaps a little below average?"

c. Overall social adjustment
"Loner," introspective, seemingly not very happy
or
Meets people easily, considerable group involvement, has many friends, cheerful outlook on life.

4. PERSONALITY, MOTIVATION, AND CHARACTER
   (+, A+, A, A−, −)

( ) a. Maturity	( ) f. Tough-mindedness	( ) k. Assertiveness
( ) b. Emotional adjustment	( ) g. Self-discipline	( ) l. Conscientiousness
( ) c. Team worker	( ) h. Initiative	( ) m. Hard worker
( ) d. Tact	( ) i. Perseverance	( ) n. Honesty and sincerity
( ) e. Adaptability	( ) j. Self-confidence	

Appendix **2**

Interview
Rating Form

INTERVIEW RATING FORM

Name_____

Interviewed for_____

Interviewer_____Date_____

I. WORK HISTORY   Above Avg.   Avg.   Below Avg.

II. EDUCATION AND TRAINING

Above Avg. Avg. Below Avg.

III. PRESENT SOCIAL ADJUSTMENT

Above Avg. Avg. Below Avg.

IV. PERSONALITY, MOTIVATION
    AND CHARACTER
    (+, A+, A, A−, −)   Above Avg.   Avg.   Below Avg.

( ) 1. Maturity   ( ) 6. Tough-   ( ) 10. Self-
( ) 2. Emotional   mindedness   confidence
       adjustment   ( ) 7. Self-discipline   ( ) 11. Assertiveness
( ) 3. Teamworker   ( ) 8. Initiative   ( ) 12. Conscien-
( ) 4. Tact   ( ) 9. Perseverance   tiousness
( ) 5. Adaptability   ( ) 13. Hard worker
                                                   ( ) 14. Honesty and
                                                           sincerity

V. SUMMARY OF ASSETS   SUMMARY OF SHORTCOMINGS

VI. OVERALL SUMMARY

VII. OVERALL RATING   Excellent Above Avg. Avg. Below Avg. Poor

Illustrative Reports of Interview Findings

INTERVIEW RATING FORM

Name____Ruth Horton_____

Interviewed for_Information Systems Analyst_____

Interviewer_Edward Harting_____Date_3/15/83_____

	X		
I. WORK HISTORY	Above Avg.	Avg.	Below Avg.

Ruth had a series of restaurant-related jobs (Sambos, Chili Parlor, Burger King) starting as a dish washer at the age of 15, and gradually acquiring positions of more responsibility. She showed good maturity and self-discipline by saving enough money to buy a car of her own and still have $3500 left at the time she was ready for college.

Worked for Steak and Ale all through college—full-time summers and 30 hrs. a week during the regular school year. This reflects great energy, stamina, and willingness to work hard. She progressed from waitress to hostess. The latter job, in particular, provided an opportunity to develop good people skills as well as a higher degree of sophistication. Wages and tips amounted to about $7 an hour and helped to pay for college expenses.

Selected for the Information Systems Management Program at General Dynamics in June 1982, despite her lack of relevant experience and education. Her willingness to accept this position even though she did not have the technical skills possessed by the other trainees reflects her self-confidence. She evidently adapted very quickly to her first assignment as a programmer, readily picking up the computer languages and adjusting well to the confinement and detail which is so much a part of this job. She also showed good initiative in working on her own to develop a new system, with very little guidance from others. That she was so quick to grasp the new technology would seem to reflect good mental ability. Her job appraisal rating was a 5 out of a possible 6 with special commendation for her hard work, ability to get along with others, and initiative.

Since January 1983, Ruth has been working on her second training assignment in manufacturing systems. Again, she seems to be acquiring the necessary skills for this job quite rapidly. But she recognizes the need to develop better organization and planning skills as well as the need to do a better job of sorting out details as to priority and importance. She has been praised by her supervisor for her analytical skills but also told that she should become more assertive and tough-minded in "standing up" to her customers.

Although Ruth did not have any relevant work experience prior to coming to General Dynamics, she seems to have made good progress on ISMP. Her entire work experience reflects excellent habits of hard work, perseverance, initiative, as well as good mental ability. She would have received a higher rating still in this area if she had made more of any effort to have obtained experience relevant to her field of study during the summers she was in college.

(continued)

	X		
II. EDUCATION AND TRAINING	Above Avg.	Avg.	Below Avg.

Ruth made an excellent record in high school, graduating 22nd in a class of 575. She seemed to do this quite easily, considering that she was working 25 hours in a restaurant. Her college board scores were: math 710 (outstanding) and verbal 630 (very good). Ruth feels that she studied a great deal in H.S., placing her studies ahead of outside activities. Actually, she had little time for the latter because of her part-time job. Her high school experience reflects a degree of maturity beyond her years.

Accepted by Haverford, a college with extremely high academic standards, Ruth majored in economics and did well in all of her subjects. She graduated in the top 20 percent of her class—an excellent record indeed in view of the fact that she worked 30 hours a week on an outside job. She greatly enjoyed her more analytically demanding courses, such as calculus, philosophy, and the more theoretical courses in economics.

Ruth's fine academic record in a top school, her high SAT scores, and the fact that she was able to fit in a 30-hour-a-week outside job provide abundant evidence of high-level intellect. She is exceedingly well-trained in economics but did not take any computer-related courses. Obviously, too, her academic record provides additional evidence of her energy, stamina, and willingness to work hard.

		X	
III. PRESENT SOCIAL ADJUSTMENT	Above Avg.	Avg.	Below Avg.

Ruth has been so busy working and going to school that she has not had much time to develop many outside interests. But the interests she does have reflect her fine intellect and her broad cultural education. She reads 3 or 4 books a month, primarily concerned with biography and history. And she likes to listen to classical music (Bach, Mozart, Brahms).

When time permits Ruth enjoys model building, some such models taking as many as three months to complete. This hobby obviously requires perseverance and great attention to detail.

Despite her busy life, Ruth seems to have many friends and to be well-adjusted socially. But she has never had much in the way of leadership experience, either in school or in the community. She says: "This is still to come and I plan very definitely to seek it out."

(continued)

IV. PERSONALITY, MOTIVATION
   AND CHARACTER
(+, A+, A, A−, −)

	X		
	Above Avg.	Avg.	Below Avg.

(+)   1. Maturity
(+)   2. Emotional
        adjustment
(+)   3. Teamworker
(+)   4. Tact
(+)   5. Adaptability
(A−) 6. Tough-
        mindedness

(+)   7. Self-discipline
(+)   8. Initiative
(+)   9. Perseverance
(A+) 10. Self-
        confidence
(A)   11. Assertiveness

(+) 12. Conscien-
        tiousness
(+) 13. Hard worker
(+) 14. Honesty and
        sincerity

V. SUMMARY OF ASSETS

Superior mental ability
• learns quickly
• articulate
• perceptive
• problem solver
• intellectual breadth and depth

Outstanding motivation
• great energy
• very hard worker
• self-discipline
• sets high standards

Mature
• good judgment
• sets goals
• can make sacrifices
• good self-knowledge

People skills
• tact
• empathy
• sensitive to needs of others
• friendly

Character
• honest
• reliable
• high values

Assets relevant to systems work
• high math aptitude
• attention to detail
• perseverance
• excellent analytical skills

SUMMARY OF SHORTCOMINGS

Needs develoment of leadership
• needs to become more assertive
• needs more mental toughness
• could use more infectious enthusiasm

*Lack of relevant experience and
training*

(continued)

VI. OVERALL SUMMARY

Ruth Horton seems to "have it all together." In fact, she seems to have just about everything that she needs for a successful career in information systems work. She is very bright; she has a high math aptitude; she gives excellent attention to detail; she has high standards; and she possesses strong analytical skills. Conditioned to work at an early age, Ruth has a high degree of energy and is an extremely hard worker. She is also mature beyond her years. Ruth's work as a hostess in a restaurant has enabled her to develop good people skills. In all of her jobs, she seems to have been able to get along well with peers and supervisors alike.

Ruth's shortcomings are not particularly serious. If she wants to become a manager, however, she will need to develop more assertiveness and mental toughness. She is well aware of these development needs and seems determined to do something about them. Ruth's lack of more relevant work experience and education probably represents a further shortcoming. But she is so bright and picks up new information so quickly that lack of relevant experience and training should not handicap her unduly.

In summary, Ruth's assets *far* outweigh her shortcomings in terms of qualification for a career in systems work. She has a large number of important strengths and such shortcomings as she has are well within her control to eliminate. Ruth is capable of eventual promotion to positions of appreciable responsibility in her field. General Dynamics is fortunate to have her.

	X			
VII. OVERALL RATING	Excellent	Above Avg.	Avg.	Below Avg.	Poor

INTERVIEW RATING FORM

Name George Anton

Interviewed for Engineering Training Program

Interviewer Andrew Corning _____ Date___ 3/24/83 _____

		X	
I. WORK HISTORY	Above Avg.	Avg.	Below Avg.

George worked two summers while in high school on a construction crew as a mason's helper, a job secured for him by an uncle. This involved extremely hard work, wheeling wheelbarrows of cement to the bricklayers. That he "stuck it out" all summer and returned to the same job the subsequent summer demonstrates stamina, perseverance, and willingness to work hard.

During the summer following his freshmen year in college, George worked for Bethlehem Steel as a metallurgical observer. This job was secured for him by his father, an employee of the firm. The job was highly relevant to his college major of metallurgical engineering. The indications are that George adapted well to the schedule of swing shifts and got along well with the people. Understandably, he found the repetitive nature of data collection unchallenging.

The following two summers George worked for Alcoa as a metallurgical trainee. Again, his father seems to have played a major role in getting him this job. George was praised by his supervisor for his energy, enthusiasm, and ability to get along with people. But, as his engineering duties became more complex during the second summer, he found it more difficult to understand the projects to which he was assigned. He decided as a result of that experience that the job was too research oriented and that he preferred work involving more practical application. His job appraisal that summer listed "weak technical skills" as a shortcoming. It seems significant, too, that Alcoa did not make him a permanent job offer at the time he graduated from college. This came as a shock and a disappointment but George apparently did not let it get him down, suggesting good emotional adjustment. Even so, the experience at Alcoa raises questions about his mental ability and technical strength. The candid manner in which George discussed this situation during the interview, however, underscores his complete honesty.

Hired by Rocket Engineering in July 1982, George has been assigned to the Engineering Training and has been working on failure analysis. He finds this "too theoretical" and hopes to get a job with more practical orientation for his next program assignment. His manager rated him high on effort and interpersonal skills but has called attention to "certain technical flaws" which the manager believes stem from lack of better academic training.

George's work experience reflects strong motivation, good people skills, and relevant metallurgical experience prior to his employment by Rocket Engineering. But, because all of his jobs have been secured for him by relatives,

(continued)

he has not had much of an opportunity to develop much initiative. And his technical ability appears to be weak. That George hopes one day to become an "engineer-manager" shows that he is not really aware of his limitations and suggests some degree of immaturity.

	X		
II. EDUCATION AND TRAINING	Above Avg.	Avg.	Below Avg.

George made a good record in high school, graduating in the top 25 percent of his class. He candidly admits, though, that he had to work "a lot harder" than the average student in order to make these grades. His college board score was good in math (575) but rather poor in the verbal area (480). George made a letter in football but was not otherwise active in extracurricular affairs. He says: "I was very shy at that stage of my life and didn't have many friends but I have changed a lot since then."

George attended Hopetown College, an institution with questionable academic standards. He showed poor judgment in selecting a very difficult major (metallurgical engineering) and sticking with the major even though he did not really enjoy it and had to study extremely hard in order to make good grades, a further reflection of his immaturity. (George is evidently inordinately influenced by his father who is himself a metallurgical engineer and strongly persuaded his son to follow in his footsteps) George deserves great credit for doing as well as he did in college (3.0 out of a possible 4.0), but he really "took it out of his hide" in so doing. He says: "I regularly studied until 1:00 A.M. or 2:00 A.M. and pulled my share of all-nighters—usually one a week."

George demonstrated terrific motivation in college. But the extent to which he had to work in order to make good grades in college with below average academic standards—together with his low college board scores—suggests lack of good mental ability. It seems quite apparent, too, that he is not really well-trained technically.

	X		
III. PRESENT SOCIAL ADJUSTMENT	Above Avg.	Avg.	Below Avg.

George has devoted so much of his time during the past several years to study that he has not had time to develop many outside interests. Such interests as he has are understandably nonintellectual. George has never been at all interested in reading. He says: "I like to read magazine articles about hunting and fishing, but I almost never read a book. Books have too many pages to get through." George's attitude toward reading is quite typical of his view of music and the other arts. He definitely lacks intellectual breadth and depth.

On the positive side, though, Gorge has developed socially to a very considerable extent since his high school days. He has overcome his shyness to the extent that he meets people a lot easier and now seems to have quite a number of friends.

(continued)

There has never been any question about George's energy. He has not only worked hard all his life but has always made a point of keeping in shape. Even today, he jogs 4 or 5 miles a day and plays basketball at least once a week.

IV. PERSONALITY, MOTIVATION
   AND CHARACTER
(+, A+, A, A−, −)

	X	
Above Avg.	Avg.	Below Avg.

(A−) 1. Maturity   (A+) 5. Adaptability   (A−) 10. Self-
(A+) 2. Emotional   (A−) 6. Tough-   confidence
        adjustment   mindedness (A) 11. Assertiveness
(+) 3. Teamworker (+) 7. Self-discipline (+) 12. Conscien-
(+) 4. Tact   (A−) 8. Initiative   tiousness
                    (+) 9. Perseverance   (+) 13. Hard worker
                                           (+) 14. Honesty and
                                                    sincerity

V. SUMMARY OF ASSETS

Superior Motivation
• boundless energy
• extremely hard worker
• self-discipline
• perseverance
• high work standards

Excellent people skills
• tactful
• empathetic
• cooperative
• social sensitivity

Excellent character
• extremely honest
• very reliable
• genuine

Some prior relevant experience in metallurgy

SUMMARY OF SHORTCOMINGS

Not very strong mentally
• poor verbal aptitude
• can't think in the abstract
• not a critical thinker
• weak analytical skills
• little intellectual breadth or depth

Not very mature for age
• judgment in major decisions has not been good
• unrealistic vocational goals
• somewhat naive
• very dependent on father

Below Average technical ability
• does have good math aptitude, but:
• mediocre academic preparation
• not much analytical power
• does not really enjoy metallurgy
• not at all creative

Little leadership potential
• not self-confident
• lacks mental toughness
• not assertive
• does not communicate well

(continued)

VI. OVERALL SUMMARY

George Anton is in many ways a fine human being. He is extremely honest; he works inordinately hard; and he has learned to make maximum utilization of his modest abilities—to a far greater extent than most of the rest of us do. Once he got over his shyness in high school, George blossomed out socially, acquiring a rather pronounced ability to get along with people. Throughout all of his job and school experiences, he has earned a reputation for tact and sensitivity to the needs of other people. Unlike most other college graduates, moreover, George acquired some relevant experience in his chosen field of metallurgy as a result of his work during the summer months.

In view of the fact that he tries so hard, it seems unfair that George should be somewhat limited intellectually, at least in comparison with engineering graduates. He is not at all perceptive; he lacks analytical power; he is rather poorly prepared academically; and he has little breadth and depth. In short, he is somewhat limited both intellectually and technically. Unfortunately too, George has evidently been so dominated and influenced by his father that he has had relatively little opportunity to make his own decisions. Nor has he had much opportunity to develop self-confidence, assertiveness, or mental toughness. Again, due primarily to his father's domination, George has failed to acquire a normal degree of maturity. As a consequence, he really does not know who he is or where he is going.

In summary, George has many of the assets and shortcomings of the overachiever. He works so hard that he achieves more than might be expected of him in the light of his modest basic abilities. This kind of drive would carry him a long way in some types of work—but not in engineering. He simply does not have enough intellectual and technical strength to compete successfully with the average engineer. George Anton represents a sad case indeed. He has been trained in a field for which he has little potential and now it is almost too late to switch careers. He should never have been hired for the demanding engineering work found in Rocket Engineering. His best bet is to try his luck with a less sophisticated company where the competition would not be so difficult.

				X	

VII. OVERALL RATING   Excellent Above Avg. Avg. Below Avg. Poor

Index

237